Lauer Series in Rhetoric and Composition
Series Editors, Patricia Sullivan and Catherine Hobbs

The Lauer Series in Rhetoric and Composition honors the contributions Janice Lauer Hutton has made to the emergence of Rhetoric and Composition as a disciplinary study. It publishes scholarship that carries on Professor Lauer's varied work in the history of written rhetoric, disciplinarity in composition studies, contemporary pedagogical theory, and written literacy theory and research.

Rhetorics, Poetics, and Cultures

Rhetorics, Poetics, and Cultures

Refiguring College English Studies

James A. Berlin

Afterword by
Janice M. Lauer

Response Essays by
Linda Brodkey, Patricia Harkin, Susan Miller, John Trimbur, and Victor J. Vitanza

Parlor Press
West Lafayette, Indiana
www.parlorpress.com

Originally published in 1996 by the National Council of Teachers of English as part of the Refiguring English Studies series.

Grateful acknowledgment is made to *JAC* for permission to reprint the following works: Linda Brodkey, "Remembering Writing Pedagogy," *JAC* 17 (1997): 489-93; Patricia Harkin, "*Rhetorics, Poetics, and Cultures* as an Articulation Project," *JAC* 17 (1997): 494-97; Susan Miller, "Technologies of Self?-Formation," *JAC* 17 (1997): 497-500; John Trimbur, "Berlin's Citizen and First World Rhetoric," *JAC* 17 (1997): 500-2; Victor J. Vitanza, "Aesthetics, Party Lines," *JAC* 17 (1997): 503-5.

Parlor Press LLC, West Lafayette, Indiana 47906

Printed in the United States of America

S A N: 2 5 4 - 8 8 7 9

Library of Congress Control Number: 2003102885

Berlin, James A., 1942-1994
Rhetorics, poetics, and cultures : refiguring college English studies /
(Lauer Series in Rhetoric and Composition)
Includes bibliographical references and index.

1. English philology-Study and teaching (Higher)-United States. 2. English language-Rhetoric-Study and teaching-United States. 3. Poetics-Study and teaching (Higher)-United States. 4. Language and culture-United States. 5. Pluralism (Social sciences). I. Title. II. Series.

ISBN 0-9724772-8-4 (Paper)
ISBN 0-9724772-9-2 (Cloth)

Parlor Press, LLC is an independent publisher of scholarly and trade titles in print and multimedia formats. This book is also available in cloth, as well as in Acrobat eBook Reader and Night Kitchen (TK3) formats, from Parlor Press on the WWW at http://www.parlorpress.com. For submission information or to find out about Parlor Press publications, write to Parlor Press, 816 Robinson St., West Lafayette, Indiana, 47906, or e-mail editor@parlorpress.com.

Contents

Acknowledgments

I would like to thank the Purdue Center for Humanistic Study for a semester's support and Purdue University for a sabbatical semester, both of which came at crucial times in the work on this manuscript. I would also like to thank the universities that encouraged me in this project by inviting me to share parts of it with them.

The manuscript has profited from a number of critical readings. I would especially thank Patricia Bizzell, James Cruise, Lester Faigley, Geraldine Friedman, Janice Lauer, Vincent Leitch, Alan McKenzie, George Moberg, and James Porter. I also thank the anonymous readers for NCTE, who offered detailed comments on the text, and Steve North, for continued editorial and personal support.

Finally, I want to thank my sons, Dan and Christopher, and my wife, Sam, for sharing with me the best gifts that life has to offer.

Parts of this manuscript have appeared elsewhere in different forms: "Rhetoric, Poetic, and Culture: Contested Boundaries in English Studies," *The Politics of Writing Instruction: Postsecondary,* eds. Richard H. Bullock, John Trimbur, and Charles I. Schuster (Portsmouth, NH: Boynton /Cook-Heinemann, 1991); "Composition Studies and Cultural Studies: Collapsing the Boundaries," *Into the Field: Sites of Composition Studies,* ed. Anne Ruggles Gere (New York: Modern Language Association, 1993); "Freirean Pedagogy in the U.S.: A Response," *(Inter)views: Cross-Disciplinary Perspectives on Rhetoric and Literacy,* eds. Gary A. Olson and Irene Gale (Carbondale: Southern Illinois University Press, 1991); "Composition and Cultural Studies," *Composition and Resistance,* eds. C. Mark Hurlbert and Michael Blitz (Portsmouth, NH: Boynton/Cook-Heinemann, 1991); "Literacy, Pedagogy, and English Studies: Postmodern Connections," *Critical Literacy: Politics, Praxis, and the Postmodern,* eds. Colin Lankshear and Peter L. McLaren (Albany: State University of New York Press, 1993); "Poststructuralism, Cultural Studies, and the Composition Classroom: Postmodern Theory in Practice," *Rhetoric Review* 11.1 (1992): 16-33.

Introduction

English studies is in crisis. Indeed, virtually no feature of the discipline can be considered beyond dispute. At issue are the very elements that constitute the categories of poetic and rhetoric, the activities involved in their production and interpretation, their relationship to each other, and their relative place in graduate and undergraduate work. The turmoil within English studies is of course encouraged by the public attention it now receives. Rarely has the ideological role of English in the political life of the nation been so openly discussed. Within the past few years, for example, both *Time* and *Newsweek* have covered department disagreements over the literary canon in long pieces on "political correctness," while public and commercial television networks have broadcast debates on the condition of literary studies for a national audience. The furor over the political content of a required first-year composition course at the University of Texas at Austin received extensive coverage in the media.

As Paul Berman points out in his introduction to *Debating P.C.: The Controversy over Political Correctness on College Campuses* (1992), considerable agreement exists on all sides about the intellectual and political currents that have nurtured these disputes. (The response of the disputants to these currents is quite another matter.) Their circuit began with the upheaval of French philosophy in the early work of such figures as Michel Foucault, Jacques Lacan, and Pierre Bourdieu. This speculation encouraged new perspectives and new languages for considering the human sciences, developments often collectively labeled the "postmodern." Closer to home, the implications of this thought were manifested more practically in what has come to be called "identity politics." As Berman explains, these were "the movements for women's rights, for gay and lesbian liberation, for various ethnic revivals, and for black nationalism (which had different origins but was related nonetheless)" (11). The result of both impulses has been a general assault on some of the most cherished concepts of liberal humanism, concepts that have guided study in the humanities in the modern university since its formation at the turn of the century.

Berman's account is instructive. He fails to mention, however, that the events he describes have been accompanied by major changes in the work activities and demographic makeup of the society for which college students are preparing. In other words, the intellectual and political disruptions that Berman outlines are closely related to major international economic and social changes that must be considered in understanding the humanities today.

This book is a response to the current crisis in the discipline. It attempts to take into account both the intellectual and political issues at stake in the operations of English studies and the relation of these issues to economic and social transformations. It is, above all, committed to a historical perspective, analyzing the role college English departments have played in the curricula of the past and present and drawing up a set of recommendations for the future. This introduction presents an outline of the path pursued in the study.

First, however, I want to explore in some detail the position from which I enter the debate. I offer my claims about English studies from the point of view of someone situated in the rhetoric division of the department. I am convinced that this perspective offers lessons about the current disciplinary crisis that are difficult, although assuredly not impossible, to obtain elsewhere. My decision to take this stance is inspired by my study of two great moments in the history of rhetoric—Athens in the fifth and fourth centuries B.C.E. and the United States during the last hundred years—as well as by my experience in English departments over the last eighteen years.

For the citizens of ancient Athens, rhetoric was at the center of education because it was at the center of political life, the deepest and most abiding concern of the democratic city-state. The notion that any feature of public activity could be considered above the concerns of politics—above the business of the polis—was unthinkable. The end of democracy, after all, was to enable the open debate of all issues that impinged upon the community. Furthermore, communal engagement was considered essential to attaining virtue, the individual's harmonious integration of knowledge, ethics, and aesthetics in daily activity (Havelock 1964).

For example, for Aristotle the reading and writing of public texts, whether poetic or rhetorical, could never transcend political life. Citizens needed rhetorical education to prepare for public performance when required to speak for themselves before the law and the assembly. Poetic understanding was essential as well, as drama was considered a critical examination of private and political virtue. Indeed, citizens were often paid to attend the theater. For Aristotle, as the *Rhetoric* and the *Poetics* make clear, both rhetorical and poetic discourse played crucial roles in fulfilling the ends of Athenian democracy, including the authentic pursuit of the virtuous life, which could be imagined only within the context of a democratic polity (Nussbaum 1986).

More important to my effort here, however, will be a consideration of the crucial role instruction in text production and interpretation has played in the democratic political life of the United States during the last hundred years. Stated more precisely, I will examine the political purposes, democratic and otherwise, to which English studies has been put, considering both those openly announced and those more tacitly observed. My objective will not be to reject the political involvement of this important area of study, but to offer a critique of it, with a view to locating the best and worst of this political involvement. As I hope to demonstrate, protests against the political involvement of English studies are as futile as protests against death and taxes. Indeed, given the democratic political commitments of the United States, it is as impossible for us to separate literary and rhetorical texts from political life as it was for the citizens of ancient Athens.

The Rhetorical Perspective

As I have already said, my analysis of the past and present of English studies and my proposal for its future are presented from the perspective of one firmly situated in the rhetorical branch of the discipline. While my graduate training was thoroughly literary (a doctorate in nineteenth-century English literature with a dissertation on the relation of Tennyson, Browning, and Arnold to German Idealism), my work in the profession from my first job in 1975 has been in rhetoric, at the start teaching composition to undergraduates and later adding instruction in the history and theory of rhetoric for graduate students. I should note, however, that my position is not meant to stand for all workers in rhetoric and composition. I will instead invoke the rhetorical paradigm that I have been calling the "social-epistemic," referred to here for convenience as simply the "epistemic."

I realize that until just recently to speak about the discipline of English studies from the rhetoric side of the department corridor was, in some circles, immediately considered suspect and radical. So marginalized has rhetoric been in past and present discussions of the discipline that in both Arthur Applebee's history of English as a school subject in the United States (1974) and Gerald Graff's complementary history of English in colleges and universities (1987), the story of rhetoric is conspicuously absent. My own histories of writing instruction in U.S. colleges during the last two centuries are customarily excluded from bibliographies in works on the current state of English studies, including Peter Elbow's *What Is English?* (1990) and the NCTE/MLA-sponsored *The English Coalition Conference: Democracy through Language* (1989), edited by Richard Lloyd-Jones and Andrea Lunsford. But this is not altogether surprising. English studies was founded on a set of hierarchical binary oppositions in which literary texts were given an idealized status approaching the sacred. Against these privileged works, rhetorical texts and their production were portrayed as embodiments of the fallen realms of science and commerce and politics, validating in their corrupt materiality the spiritual beauties of their opposite.

Despite this history of marginalization, the study of the production and interpretation of rhetorical texts has survived in the college English department over its hundred-year history and, indeed, has recently begun a period of growth. Even if so distinguished a literary theorist as Terry Eagleton had not attempted to invoke the 2,500-year Western rhetorical tradition in support of his project for a new kind of literary study, rhetoric in the U.S. English department would have established its claim to serious study. (This is not to disparage Eagleton's project. Workers in epistemic rhetoric are grateful for the support of a fellow traveler.) After all, rhetoric served as the very core of the college curriculum in the United States until the late nineteenth century, as it in fact had in most Western societies up to the end of the eighteenth century (Kennedy 1980; Corbett 1971; Guthrie 1946-49, 1951; and Berlin 1984, 1987).

The central place of rhetoric in the college curriculum in the United States was not challenged until decision making in practical and political matters shifted from the citizenry (restrictively defined, it must be admitted, as primarily white male property holders) to university-trained experts late in the last century. And despite repeated attempts since to banish rhetoric—and with it the concerns of economics and politics—from the college English department (Connors 1991; Miller 1991; and Berlin 1984, 1987, and 1991, "Rhetoric, Poetic, and Culture: Contested Boundaries in English Studies"), it was never completely effaced, returning, as Susan Carlton (1991) has shown, in the form of condensations and displacements in disciplinary discussions of the poetic-rhetoric binary. By the 1970s and 1980s, the willful neglect of the rhetorical had been successfully challenged, as undergraduate writing courses and graduate programs in rhetoric and composition dramatically increased. Part of the effort in this book is to offer an account of this resurgence by relating it to changes in the economy and, within the academy, to the linguistic turn in English studies.

The near century-long suppression of rhetoric has not been easy—although it has been easier for some than for others. In most publicly funded universities as well as many private ones, the first-year English requirement—which the English department itself often supported by making the course (or courses) a prerequisite for literature classes (Ide 1992)—enabled the English department to generate revenue by hiring low-paid teaching adjuncts, usually women, and low-paid graduate teaching assistants, until recently men but now more often women, to teach the majority of these students. Such hirings created an institutionally supported gender hierarchy, with upper division and graduate courses taught by men and lower division courses, especially composition, taught by women (for hard numbers, see Holbrook 1991 and Huber 1990).

The result of all this has been to give workers in rhetoric a unique perspective on English studies, a perspective that includes not only the dominant and privileged but numerically subordinate work of literary studies, but also the minor and disparaged but numerically superior work of rhetoric studies. (I sometimes suspect that the triumph of New Criticism in the 1950s was achieved partly by building a tolerance for such contradictions through the privileging of paradox and the aesthetic resolution of conflicts in the unity of the literary text.) This, of course, is not to argue that the view from the margins is always superior. But there are a number of reasons why the prospect from rhetoric may be useful.

I will immediately dismiss the essentialist contention that rhetoric's prominence in Western education for most of recorded history suggests its "true" status in discourse study. In every case, there were specific historical reasons for its position, not universal supports. At the most obvious level, ruling groups in the West have usually understood, if only tacitly, that maintaining power requires the uses of rhetoric to win the assent of the governed. (Gramsci's argument that willing consent is as important as economic and political constraints in securing power over the long haul is compelling.) These groups accordingly prepared their young in the uses of oral and written discourse—the latter especially when economic arrangements required extensive communication and complex contractual and legal activity. In this way, they prepared the next generation to carry on the work of government and commerce, the sources of their power and privilege. This concern for power meant that the production and interpretation of rhetorical texts did not take a second place to the interpretation of poetic texts. Before, say, a hundred years ago, it simply did not make sense to ruling groups that the ability to interpret works of literature should receive dominant attention in schools, while the ability to construct and interpret economic, political, or legal texts should be relegated to a minor branch of study, to be mastered on the lower rungs of schooling. (Even today this probably represents a minority view outside of English departments.)

Thus, as Eagleton has reminded us, rhetoric in the past took all texts as its province of study. Furthermore, its major concern was with the practices of producing texts and only secondarily with interpreting them. Contrary to what has been commonly argued in English departments, usually unconsciously invoking the specter of Hugh Blair (Berlin 1984), learning to read literary texts is not necessary and sufficient preparation for writing any and all varieties of rhetorical texts—political, legal, economic, or ceremonial. Text interpretation was indeed important to most rhetorics before the late eighteenth century, but it was markedly subordinate to text production. For example, as Marjorie Woods (1990) points out, in medieval Europe, even poetic production was included in rhetorical instruction in the lower schools.

In short, and as a function of all these factors, workers in epistemic rhetoric are less likely to regard the consideration of literary texts as inherently and inevitably superior to the consideration of rhetorical texts. Our historicist perspective on current English studies hierarchies enables us to regard all manners of discourse as worthy of investigation, including film, television, video, and popular music. We are also more inclined to transgress disciplinary boundaries in developing methods of analysis. Our investigation includes the study and teaching of strategies for text production as well as consumption. Workers in rhetoric as a result find themselves aligned with department colleagues in literary theory and cultural studies who are likewise challenging the dominant hierarchies of texts and tasks in the discipline. We also share with these groups a strong commitment to pedagogy, seeing the classroom as central to our professional behavior, not as an evil necessary to support our more important research activity. Finally, we claim alliance with many of our colleagues in cultural studies and literary theory in our preoccupation with the imbrication of English studies in democratic politics.

I would insist, however, that the perspective and projects of rhetorical studies render its members distinct in their observations on the past, present, and future of English studies. While workers in epistemic rhetoric may look on workers in certain varieties of literary theory and cultural studies as fellow travelers, we must, at least at the present moment, assert rhetoric's separate character and unique contribution. Indeed, this insistence on rhetoric's discrete role as a result of its historical situation is in accordance with a principle endorsed by Stuart Hall (1992) in his evaluation of the development of cultural studies at Birmingham: that the institutional position of any academically situated project must never be ignored in assessing its potential for creating change. There is thus the additional consideration that, unlike some fellow travelers, workers in rhetoric enjoy a relatively secure institutional site from which to launch their projects for disciplinary reform. In short, we in rhetoric are convinced that our colleagues in theory and cultural studies have as much to learn from us as we have to learn from them. At the same time, we wish to join forces with these colleagues in working for revised conceptions of reading, writing, and teaching and, finally, for new models of English studies.

There is one other reason why the view from rhetoric is especially worth our scrutiny. The influence of structuralist and poststructuralist theories in the humanities, social sciences, and even the sciences—what Jameson has called the linguistic turn—can be seen as an effort to recover the tools of rhetoric in discussing the material effects of language in the conduct of human affairs. One of the supreme conquests of the Enlightenment has been to efface the unique work of language in carrying out the ideological projects of the new dominant group. This victory has been accomplished by denying the inevitable role of signification in affecting communication, insisting instead that signs can and must become neutral transmitters of externally verifiable truths—truths, that is, existing separate from language. This is the correspondence theory of truth, the notion that signs are arbitrary stand-ins for the things they represent, where ideal communication exists when there are, in the words of Thomas Sprat of the Royal Society, "almost as many words as there are things."

This theory insists that the signifying practices of the dominant class and its supporting intellectuals are identical with this purely representative language and that all other practices are to be rejected as deceptions. A central part of this effort was the dismissal of rhetoric by declaring the study of signifying practices and their effects on meaning a worthless undertaking. Those who know the true use of language—that is, those who speak in the manner of the bourgeoisie—do not, the theory argues, need rhetoric. Rhetoric is offered as serious study only by the enemies of truth, who wish to support their heresies through an unorthodox use of language. Speakers or writers in the true, to allude to Foucault, call on correspondence theories of language to support what are actually ideologically involved discourses on science and politics. Other uses of language are sanctioned only in literary discourse, a discourse that is, by definition, fictive and nonrepresentational.

The structuralist and poststructuralist influence can thus be seen as an effort to recover the view from rhetoric, the perspective that reveals language to be a set of terministic screens, to recall Kenneth Burke, that constructs rather than records the signified. Examining the ways that language carries out this activity is the purpose of structuralist and poststructuralist projects, as it has been the purpose of a variety of rhetorics throughout Western history—from Gorgias to Vico to Kenneth Burke to Susan Jarratt and Susan Miller.

All of this indicates the central place of rhetoric and its relation to poetic in this study as well as some of the more obvious reasons for featuring these terms in the book's title. But what of "culture"? Throughout the 1980s and into the 1990s, what to make of the term *culture* has been one of the most conspicuous arenas of debate in education. The right—as represented by such figures as Allan Bloom, E. D. Hirsch, William Bennett, and Lynne Cheney—has argued for a notion of culture commonly traced to Matthew Arnold. Here the term refers to "the best that has been thought and said" in the visual and written arts, placed in opposition to common or popular forms of pleasure. Culture thus resides in a certain aesthetic experience regarded as transhistorical, imparting immutable values to all people in all places and times. As such, it transcends the ephemeral concerns of economics and politics, addressing instead the universal and eternal in human nature.

This notion of "high" culture was constructed in the eighteenth and nineteenth centuries with the institutionalizing of certain ideologically interested notions of taste. It has frequently been contested by those who argue that high culture is in fact related to historically conditioned economic and political interests. In more recent years, this challenge has been strongly proffered by workers in the humanities, especially those in English studies. In place of a class-interested notion of culture, they have forwarded an anthropological formulation. Here, as in the work of Richard Hoggart and Raymond Williams, culture is seen as the entire lived experience of humans in response to concrete historical conditions. Culture is pluralistic, so that everyone is "cultured," whether their behavior reflects that associated with high culture or not. At the same time, this formulation avoids narrow economistic explanatory models associated with a certain orthodox Marxism. Thus, although culture involves economic and political conditions, it is not a mere reflection of them. Humans create the conditions of their experience as much as they are created by them.

This idea of culture as lived experience has subsequently been altered in response to the linguistic challenge to the humanities posed by structuralism and poststructuralism. With this challenge, culture is seen not simply as lived activity, but as the mediations of lived activity by language. In other words, culture is a set of historically variable signifying practices characteristic of diverse social groups. In recent times, this structuralist notion of culture has been integrated with the anthropological in the work of such figures as Raymond Williams, Stuart Hall, Lawrence Grossberg, and Paula Treichler. Thus, culture is both signifying practices that represent experience in rhetoric, myth, and literature and the relatively independent responses of human agents to concrete economic, social, and political conditions (Johnson 1986-87). It is, once again, a polysemic and multilayered category, best considered in the plural.

This alternative notion of culture is of course part of the turn to "cultural studies" in English departments today. Its strongest influences come from those who have continued the work of the Birmingham Center for Contemporary Cultural Studies (see Johnson 1986-87; Grossberg and Nelson 1988; and Grossberg, Nelson, and Treichler 1992), from workers in literary theory (Spivak, Jameson, Eagleton, and Leitch, for example), and from proponents of epistemic rhetoric (see Berlin 1991, "Composition and Cultural Studies," and Berlin 1993). The larger immediate point I wish to make, though, is that the use of *culture* as a contested key term by both the right and the left is a significant response to a set of far-reaching and pressing historical events.

At the most obvious level, an intense diversification of cultures and cultural experience has taken place in the United States in recent years. First, there has been a sharp increase in international residents. As Margaret L. Usdansky explains in a report on a Census Bureau study released in 1992, the "USA's largest 10-year wave of immigration in 200 years—almost 9 million people—arrived during the 1980s" ("Immigrant Tide Surges in the'80s," *USA Today,* 29 May 1992, 1A). Usdansky further reports that "1 in 4 people in the USA is black, Hispanic, Asian, or Native American. Fourteen percent speak a language other than English at home" ("'Diverse' Fits Nation Better Than 'Normal,'" *USA Today,* 29 May 1992, 1A). This infusion of cultures from abroad, primarily Asian and Hispanic, has been accompanied by a dramatic increase in the division between rich and poor in all populations. As median household income has increased, so has poverty, a strong indication, explains Usdansky, of an inequitable distribution of wealth. Finally, the family is undergoing great change. Usdansky reports, "Families headed by married couples make up just over half of USA households. One in 4 households is made up of a person living alone. One in 4 children is born out of wedlock" ("'Diverse' Fits Nation Better Than 'Normal,'" *USA Today,* 29 May 1992, 2A). And all of this cultural relocation is taking place within the context of dramatic transformations in national and international economic, political, and social conditions and the everyday experience of them in the United States, developments commonly discussed under the heading "post-Fordism" or the "regime of flexible accumulation" or, sometimes, postmodernism.

These obvious shifts in demography and daily experience, coupled with increased international economic competition, explain a great deal about the debate concerning the conception of culture that is to hold sway in schools and colleges. As the lived experiences and everyday language of citizens become more and more diversified, conservative forces insist on the imposition of a uniform set of texts and a monolithic set of reading and writing practices. These texts and practices are designed to reinforce the cultural hegemony of certain class, race, and gender groups at a time when this hegemony is being challenged in the daily encounters of ordinary citizens—citizens who inhabit a disparate array of cultural spaces. It is no wonder that the meaning of *culture* and its role in English studies are urgent issues today. The contentions surrounding these formulations and the role of English studies in addressing them will be a central concern of my study.

Overview

This book is divided into four sections. The first provides relevant historical background and explores the political uses of English as a discipline. Chapter 1 examines the relations of the larger economic, social, and political conditions of the eighteenth and nineteenth centuries to the formation of English studies, with a special concern for the uses of the literary text in securing hegemony for a newly dominant social class. It also outlines the continuation of this effort in the textual hierarchies found in contemporary U.S. English departments. Chapter 2 explores the formation of the English department at the turn of the century, paying special attention to its connections to changes in the workforce and education and to the special roles of women and immigrants in these transformations. The chapter closes with an overview of the competing reading and writing practices taught in the early college English department, with a special regard for their place in a curriculum attempting to produce a certain kind of modern graduate, a subject outfitted for a complex role in work, politics, and private life.

The second part of the book, "The Postmodern Predicament," shifts the focus to the contemporary scene. Chapter 3 explores the disruptions in the relation of English studies to the society it serves—disruptions occasioned by conditions that have come to be characterized as "postmodern." It traces the shift from a Fordist to a post-Fordist mode of production and the changes in economic and social conditions this shift has brought about, particularly as these changes appear in work activities and the experience of everyday life. This chapter argues that these alterations demand new educational approaches to preparing students for work, democratic politics, and consumer culture. Chapter 4 considers the changing conceptions of knowledge, language, interlocutors, and audiences at the center of current academic discussions, with a central concern for the radical consequences structuralist and poststructuralist speculation have held for the intellectual and political work of the humanities. Chapter 5 considers in detail the ways postmodern developments have influenced the rhetorical paradigm that has come to be called the "social-epistemic." The chapter also sketches out the recommendations of this rhetoric for a refigured English studies.

Chapter 6 opens the third section of the book, "Students and Teachers," by exploring the general guidelines I am recommending for the pedagogy of a refigured English studies. I argue that the classroom should become the center of disciplinary activities, the point at which theory, practice, and democratic politics interact. The materials and methods of all courses should be organized around text interpretation *and* construction—not, as previously, one or the other exclusively—leading to a revised conception of both reading and writing as acts of textual production. Chapter 7 describes in concrete detail two courses that exemplify the materials and methods of my proposal.

The book's final section, "Department Directions," looks at how versions of a refigured English studies are already taking shape in English departments today. Chapter 8 describes three English department programs that have introduced different versions of English studies that, despite their many divergences, include many of the recommendations of this book. It also glances at a debate over English studies that has recently emerged among teachers of creative writing, a confrontation that reproduces in many of its features the struggles outlined here. The chapter ends with a description of the kinds of research projects graduate students preparing for a career in a refigured English studies might attempt and, indeed, are already pursuing at some universities. Chapter 9 brings the book to a close with a brief comment on the complex uses of English studies in the United States.

I Historical Background

1

Building the Boundaries of English Studies

Rhetoric and poetic have been explicitly connected in discussions of discourse throughout Western history (see Burke 1978, Todorov 1982, Baldwin 1924, and Berlin 1987). Their relation to each other, however, has been variously formulated. At some historical moments—perhaps most—rhetoric has been the larger category, including poetry as one of its subdivisions. This configuration is not unexpected (except, of course, to the historically innocent) given the explicit focus of the rhetorical text on the management of political power, as discussed, for example, in Plato, Aristotle, Cicero, Quintilian, Augustine, Wilson, and, more recently, Kenneth Burke. At other times, poetic has been the master paradigm, including rhetoric as a minor subcategory within it, although this is almost exclusively a post-Romantic division, one designed to resist the actual lines of power in a society (although just as often tacitly complicit with them). The argument in this case is that the poet is superior to the rhetorician-politician—that is, more influential—precisely because he or she is outside the dominant power structures.

The ruling tendency in the English department since its inception some hundred years ago has been closest to this latter position. As I have explicitly argued in my history of twentieth-century writing instruction (1987)—and as Gerald Graff (1987) has tacitly indicated in his history of the English department (in which writing instruction is conspicuously absent)—for English studies, all that is important and central in the study of discourse falls within the domain of literary texts and all that is unimportant and marginal falls within the realm of rhetoric. The result has been singular. While previous generations of U.S. college students were prepared in the production of political texts that would enable them to take their rightful place as leaders in their communities (Guthrie 1946-49, 1951; Halloran 1982; and Berlin 1984), their descendants in this century have been as rigorously exercised in the aesthetic and putatively disinterested interpretation of literary texts said to be above the conflicts of politics. Meanwhile, the rhetorical text has been relegated to the limbo of first-year composition, a course offered only because of the alleged failure of the high school to do its job in what is now designated a "lower" level of study.

The explanation for this sharp departure can be found in examining the intersection of English studies and the historical formations that encouraged it. My argument here is that changes in economic and social structures during the eighteenth and nineteenth centuries led to a new conception of the nature of poetic, a conception that defines the aesthetic experience in class terms while isolating it from other spheres of human activity, most explicitly the political and the scientific. I will call upon the work of Raymond Williams extensively in this discussion. I will then locate this new division of the poetic and the rhetorical, the aesthetic and the political-scientific, in the formation of major schools of literary criticism in the college English department in this century, relying on Graff's description of this development. Since Graff implicitly endorses the analysis of the poetic-rhetoric binary that Williams offers while denying its origins in social class, I will invoke—by way of a corrective—the empirical work of Pierre Bourdieu. It compellingly demonstrates a corresponding inscription of this binary relation in the constitution of class relations in contemporary France.

I will conclude this historical analysis by considering the description of contemporary English studies found in Robert Scholes's *Textual Power* (1985), a work that responds to the current crisis in the English department's sense of professional purpose. While I do not plan to discuss the causes for the crisis in this chapter, it is not difficult to see reason for concern in the recent decline of undergraduate majors in many—although certainly not all—departments as well as in a loss of faculty positions due to budget cuts (a more nearly universal event, occurring even where student enrollment has increased). The Reagan-Bush agenda for education reflected a narrow utilitarian insistence on career training in schools and colleges and a corresponding relegation of the humanities to the margins, all the while defending their traditional objects and methods of study. This conservative challenge from outside English studies has been matched by a critique within it, as postmodern theoretical inquiry has questioned the disciplinary assumptions governing the field. Scholes's work represents one of the less radical of these internal responses, but a valuable one nonetheless. In it, he both affirms the poetic-rhetoric relationship described in the studies of Williams, Graff, and Bourdieu and presents a proposal for reformulating it. That is, he offers a program for reconstituting the relationship institutionally prescribed in our treatment of poetic and rhetorical texts, a program that reorganizes English studies under the rubric of cultural studies.

The Historical Trajectory

The best comprehensive discussion of the historical events that led to the conception of the rhetoric-poetic relationship now inscribed in the English department is in Raymond Williams's *Marxism and Literature* (1977). Williams explains that in the eighteenth century, the term *literature* "included all printed books. There was not necessary specialization to 'imaginative' works. Literature was still primarily reading ability and reading experience, and this included philosophy, history, and essays as well as poems" (47-48). Literature was thus little more than "a specialization of the area formerly categorized as *rhetoric* and *grammar:* a specialization to reading and . . . to the printed word and especially the book" (47). The nineteenth century, however, witnessed a significant change in the concept of literature. Most important, literature "lost its earliest sense of reading ability and reading experience, and became an apparently objective category of printed works of a certain quality" (48). Literary quality was thus in the text, not the reader. With this shift came three related tendencies: "first, a shift from 'learning' to 'taste' or 'sensibility' as a criterion defining literary quality; second, an increasing specialization of literature to 'creative' or 'imaginative' works; third, a development of the concept of 'tradition' within national terms, resulting in the more effective definition of 'a national literature'" (48).

Williams's explication of these tendencies is revealing. First, the move from literature as learning in general to literature as taste or sensibility was marked by a shift in structure and site from the old scholarly profession based in the church and in state universities—acknowledged by sharing classical languages—to the new scholarly profession defined in class terms. In other words, the new definition of literature accompanied the development of the bourgeoisie. Members of this dawning class made "taste" and "sensibility" characteristically bourgeois categories by seeing their class-determined experience of certain texts as objective qualities of the texts themselves. At the same time, the ability to experience subjectively these "objective" qualities became a sign of taste and sensibility, not class identification. The subjective experience was thus given objective status, made an inherent and universal—rather than a class-determined and historical—feature of consciousness. Criticism as it is understood today was a related development, shifting from learned commentary "to the conscious exercise of 'taste,' 'sensibility,' and 'discrimination'" (49). Significantly, criticism marked the class-biased move toward the consumption of printed works and away from their production. A certain notion of literary taste was thus enforced by class membership, as indicated, for example, by frequent references to the "reading public."

This notion of taste created a set of complementary binary oppositions valorizing the subjective over the objective, the unconscious over the conscious, and the private over the public. It also insisted on the "immediate" and "lived" qualities of literary discourse, as distinct from the learned tradition of the old university. These class concepts were eventually taken over as the central element of the new discipline of academic literary criticism, although "attempts to establish new abstractly objective criteria" (49) were made as well. Eventually, literary criticism was "taken to be a natural definition of literary studies, themselves defined by the specializing category (printed works of a certain quality) of *literature*" (49). Both literature and criticism in their modern senses are thus products "of a class specialization and control of a general social practice, and of a class limitation of the questions which it might raise" (49).

Second, Williams notes that the reservation of the term *literature* for the creative or imaginative was a response to the dehumanizing conditions of the new social order of industrial capitalism. Creative or imaginative works were placed in opposition to the horrors of social experience:

> The practical specialization of work to the wage-labor production of commodities; of 'being' to 'work' in these terms; of language to the passing of 'rational' or 'informative' 'messages'; of social relations to functions within a systematic economic and political order: all these pressures and limits were challenged in the name of a full and liberating 'imagination' or 'creativity.'(50)

This is, of course, a development of the Romantic period in English literary history, a time when these binary contrasts were being inscribed in the parlance of the educated. Thus, literature was set against the inhuman realm of work in a cruel, exploitative economic order—an order in which the language of currency was rational and informative discourse. It was this mechanical discourse to which rhetoric was relegated. The world of practical affairs was simultaneously identified with the denial of all that was in the best interests of the individual. The space for political discourse was obliterated, since neither mechanistic science nor the aesthetic poetic were to address the political dimensions of experience.

New terms—now commonplace for us—arose in connection with this semiotic: *art* moved from a general human skill to the special realm of *imagination* and *sensibility; aesthetic* was no longer a general perception but a special part of the *artistic* and *beautiful; fiction* and *myth* became marks of *imaginative truth,* not fancies or lies. Art objects were seen as mythic and aesthetic, possessing qualities that appealed to taste and sensibility. Furthermore, these were the qualities that were to be extended to everyday life and, when the destructiveness of capitalism had reached everywhere, to be preserved from everyday life. In other words, the attempt to introduce the aesthetic into ordinary daily experience in a material and social world made ugly by the ruthless pursuit of profit would eventually be declared impossible. All that could be hoped for was to keep the aesthetic safely apart from this fallen realm, untainted by its corruption.

These elevated qualities of art were, on the one hand, attributed "to the 'imaginative' dimension (access to a truth 'higher' or 'deeper' than 'scientific' or 'objective' or 'everyday' reality; a claim consciously substituting itself for the traditional claims of religion)." On the other hand, they were ascribed "to the 'aesthetic' dimension ('beauties' of language or style)" (50-51). Attempts were also made to fuse the two, setting literary discourse against all other experience and discourse: "not only against 'science' and 'society'—the abstract and generalizing modes of other 'kinds' of experience—and not only against other kinds of writing—now in their turn specialized as 'discursive' or 'factual'—but, ironically, against much of 'literature' itself—'bad' writing, 'popular' writing, 'mass culture'" (51). Thus was inaugurated the division between art and science, literature and politics, high culture and low culture—in general, the distinction between poetic and rhetoric. High literary culture was defined by the new discipline of criticism, discriminating the important from the less important and the unimportant, the critic becoming as necessary as the artist in making the authentically literary available for consumption. Political discourse, the language of social arrangements, was relegated to the world of the fallen and unregenerate, the intractable realm of the rhetorical.

Related to this discriminatory function of criticism is Williams's third element in the changing conception of the literary: the growth of a national literature. Criticism called upon this national literature in exercising its cultural judgments, but not without transforming it: "The 'national literature' soon ceased to be a history and became a tradition. It was not, even theoretically, all that had been written or all kinds of writing. It was a selection which culminated in, and in a circular way defined, the 'literary values' which 'criticism' was asserting" (52). The result was the formation of a canon, "the absolute ratification of a limited and specializing consensual process. To oppose the terms of this ratification was to be 'against literature'" (52). In other words, to argue that discourse other than this narrowly defined literary category be taken seriously—either for consumption or production—was to be hostile to the truly literary.

The Role of English Studies

Gerald Graff's discussion of the English department in the United States reveals the relevance of Williams's analysis. In *Professing Literature: An Institutional History* (1987), Graff clearly elucidates the manner in which successive schools of literary criticism in the U.S. university set themselves against the dehumanizing conditions of industrial capitalism. Furthermore, the evidence Graff presents indicates that most have embraced the binary oppositions that characterized the class-biased redefinition of literature described by Williams.

This embrace is seen vividly in the various charges leveled at those schools of criticism whose place was being usurped. Thus, Graff cites Edwin Greenlaw's 1931 list of accusations made by the New Critics against literary-historical research: "that it apes scientific method, that it is against ancient standards, that it is immersed in subjects of no possible use, that it destroys the ability to teach. It is neglectful of culture. It stifles creative art. It looks at facts rather than at the soul" (248). A similar litany is in turn recited by Douglas Bush in his 1948 attack on New Criticism itself, as he denounces its "aloof intellectuality," its "avoidance of moral values," its "aping" of the scientific, and its treatment of criticism as "a circumscribed end in itself" (248). Graff sums up the purport of the critiques leveled by one after another school of literary criticism at its predecessor: "scientism, preference for nit-pick-ing analysis over direct experience of literature itself, and favoring the special interest of a professional coterie over the interests of general readers and students" (249). Furthermore, we can be sure that the "general reader" indicated is an abstraction that closely resembles the class-determined "reading public" of an earlier age.

Clearly, all of these charges were intended to show that the critical school being attacked was guilty of conflating the literary text with the marginalized discourse of rhetoric, the discourse of science and society. In other words, each of these charges mirrors the binary opposition in which the exalted discourse of canonized literary texts—the imaginary, the aesthetic, the disinterested appeal to private taste and sensibility—is opposed to the discourse of rhetorical texts—the scientific, the objective, the practical and political, interested appeals to public intellect and reason.

Graff's discussion of literary criticism in the English department in *Literature against Itself* (1979) similarly demonstrates the institutionalization of these dichotomies. He cites R. S. Crane's dismissal of the New Criticism. The New Critic, explains Crane, "knows what the nature of 'poetic language' must be because he has begun by dividing all language into two opposing and incommensurable kinds—the language of 'logic' and the language of 'symbolism'—and then has deduced from this initial assumption that the 'symbolic' language of poetry must necessarily possess the contraries of all qualities commonly asserted of 'logical discourse'" (178). The same opposition is found in the work of Northrop Frye, of whom Graff says,

> Over and over in successive works, Frye asserts that there are two orders of reality, an objective order in which we invest our belief and a human order we impose on this other order in order to give it meaning. The first order is that of nature or things as they are, dead, neutral, inhuman, and unavoidable; the second is . . . the order of art, applied science, religion, culture, and civilization. (182)

The lifeless, meaningless material world is thus relegated to the language of logic; the humanly significant realm of art is contained in the language of myth. Graff makes the point more strongly by explaining that the natural world in Frye's scheme is that domain "the wrong sorts of people put unquestioned faith in—positivists, moralists, social engineers, superpatriots, bureaucrats" (185).

Graff earlier locates the same set of contrasts between culture and nature in the work of I. A. Richards and Paul de Man, saying of the latter, "De Man, too, deduces the nature of literature by dividing all language into two opposing and incommensurable camps, but instead of dividing language into 'paradoxical' vs. 'steno-language,' de Man divides it into language that deconstructs itself by calling attention to its own fictiveness and undecidability and language that presumes a naive confidence in its ontological authority" (178). Indeed, Graff's entire text is meant to demonstrate a set of binary oppositions inscribed in the institutional arrangement of literary studies: creation over representation; texts as open, indeterminate "invitation" against texts as determinate objects; voyages into the unforeseen against boundaries and constraints; risk against docility and habit; truth as invention and fiction against truth as correspondence; meaning as "process" against meaning as product" (24).

Graff denies that these binaries are supported by class structure, arguing that this

> thesis credits high culture and those who rule with a coherence of outlook neither any longer possesses. When the modernist revolution made Matthew Arnold's concept of culture seem outmoded, high culture lost what relative unity it may have had. A high culture which includes both Arnold and Artaud, Samuel Johnson and Samuel Beckett, has no ideological unity. As for those who rule, it is self-flattering but mistaken to think that these flexible pragmatists require high culture as a means of justifying or consolidating their power. (117)

Of course, Graff was writing before William Bennett and Lynne Cheney used their government posts as platforms for book-length defenses of high culture. Putting this aside for the moment, Graff's error, it seems to me, is in the assumption that the poetic-rhetoric binary must be explicitly invoked by all members of a class in supporting class divisions, his charge assuming a mechanistic base-superstructure model of cultural production. It is possible, however, that the poetic-rhetoric distinction can be used to reinforce class barriers by members of the academy who are themselves unconscious of any political intention. They can do so, moreover, despite disputes about the value of differing literary texts, since it is the response to the texts, and not the texts themselves, that counts. Here the work of Pierre Bourdieu becomes instructive.

Bourdieu and the Uses of Culture

In *Distinction: A Social Critique of the Judgement of Taste* (1984), Pierre Bourdieu reports the result of an empirical study in France of "the relationships between the universe of economic and social conditions and the universe of life-styles" (xi). His focus, as his title indicates, is on lifestyles as they are imbricated in cultural pursuits. Bourdieu's intention is no less than "giving a scientific answer to the old question of Kant's critique of judgment, by seeking in the structure of social classes the basis of the systems of classification which structure perception of the social world and designate the objects of aesthetic enjoyment" (xiii-xiv). Bourdieu's work, by his own admission, is subversive, since his study defies "the laws of academic or intellectual propriety which condemn as barbarous any attempt to treat culture, that present incarnation of the sacred, as an object of science" (xiii).

Bourdieu's study population consisted of men and women representing a full range of the social spectrum in terms of family background, education, and occupation. His method was to ask these subjects a series of questions about their responses to a variety of cultural experiences, including music, painting, photography, film, literature, and sports. It is perhaps not surprising that Bourdieu's study confirmed previous findings "that all cultural practices (museum visits, concert-going, reading, etc.) and preferences in literature, painting, or music, are closely linked to educational level (measured by qualification or length of schooling) and secondarily to social origin" (1). It is remarkable, however, to discover that Bourdieu located inscribed within French class relations the same binary oppositions regarding culture described by Williams in his historical study and by Graff in his investigation of academic literary criticism in the United States.

Bourdieu discovered that a "work of art has meaning and interest only for someone who possesses the cultural competence, that is, the code into which it is encoded" (2). Furthermore, this code is always historically specific. At present, the code is constituted by a set of opposing terms corresponding to the distinction between high culture and low culture, higher class and lower class. The first of these is the separation of form from function: "the primacy of the mode of representation over the object of representation demands categorically an attention to form which previous art only demanded *conditionally*" (3). The art that exists for itself, reproducing its own forms rather than the concrete objects of material existence, is thus valorized. This means that the artist must be autonomous, free to create in accordance with his or her own program, not restricted to traditional devices or the external world. Bourdieu explains that the "'open work,' *intrinsically* and deliberately polysemic," is thus preferred over the work that *lends* itself to a small range of interpretation. As he explains, to "assert the autonomy of production is to give primacy to that of which the artist is master, i.e., forms, manners, style, rather than the 'subject,' the external referent, which involves subordination to function" (3). The capacity to enjoy art that privileges creation over representation, the open text over the closed one, the unexpected and risky over the bounded and constrained, truth as *invention* over truth as correspondence (all binaries from Graff's scheme) involves a knowledge of the history of art, since art objects of the past serve as referents for this polysemic art. And while this mastery can be acquired by intensive study, it is continuous and long contact with art objects that separates the higher orders from their educated imitators.

Bourdieu characterizes this disposition toward art objects as the "pure gaze," a concept originating in the nineteenth century and appropriated in marking contemporary class distinctions. This response denies the continuity between art and life. Popular taste, he explains, is incapable of this pure gaze, preferring function to form, looking beyond the art object for its relation to actual material and social conditions, displaying a utilitarianism considered a part of the practical and political world. As Bourdieu explains, "working-class people expect every image to explicitly perform a function, . . . and their judgments make reference, often explicitly, to the norms of morality or agreeableness. Whether rejecting or praising, their appreciation always has an ethical base" (5). The counter to this position is the intellectual response, which prefers "the representation—literature, theatre, painting—more than . . . the thing represented" (5). This involves, of course, a distancing from the necessities of natural and social experience, often resulting in the extension of the privatized aesthetic experience to all features of life, as in "the ability to apply the principles of a 'pure' aesthetic to the most everyday choices of everyday life, e.g., in cooking, clothing or decoration, completely reversing the popular disposition which annexes aesthetics to ethics" (5). Thus, Bourdieu finds, for example, a statistical correspondence between class position, cultural practices, and eating habits.

Recalling for us Raymond Williams's language, Bourdieu sums up the disjunction between the disinterested cultural object that appeals to private taste and sensibility and the instrumental object concerned with the public, practical, and political: "The denial of lower, coarse, vulgar, venal, servile—in a word, natural—enjoyment, which constitutes the sacred sphere of culture, implies an affirmation of the superiority of those who can be satisfied with the sublimated, refined, disinterested, gratuitous, distinguished pleasures forever closed to the profane. That is why art and cultural consumption are predisposed, consciously and deliberately or not, to fulfill a social function of legitimating social differences" (7). These social differences are conceived by Bourdieu in terms of cultural or human capital, the accomplishments of class and education serving as a medium of exchange in social relations, a medium that performs the function of money in economic relations. The literary texts that are a part of this cultural capital can change over time without jeopardizing class unity and the exchange process. What is important is the way the texts are interpreted and used, not the texts themselves. Indeed, Bourdieu is himself mistaken in arguing for a particular version of the aesthetic as a constitutive element of the structure of social class. Aesthetic responses and the texts that evoke them are more accurately seen as appropriations in the service of class interests, reinforcing rather than creating differences more accurately attributed to economic and political categories.

Scholes Scrutinizes the Binary

In *Textual Power: Literary Theory and the Teaching of English* (1985), Robert Scholes offers an illuminating summary of the results in English studies of the historical and social developments charted here. Scholes argues that the "field of English is organized by two primary gestures of differentiation, dividing and redividing the field by binary opposition" (5). English departments "mark those texts labeled literature as good or important and dismiss those non-literary texts as beneath our notice" (5). Scholes sees this division as corresponding to the distinction between consumption and production and, recalling Williams's analysis, asserts that consumption is privileged over production "just as the larger culture privileges the consuming class over the producing class" (5). Nonliterary texts are thus relegated to the field of reading and the lower schools, since they lack both complication and disinterestedness. Scholes notes that "actual non-literature is perceived as grounded in the realities of existence, where it is produced in response to personal or socioeconomic imperatives and therefore justifies itself functionally. By its *very* usefulness, its non-literariness, it eludes our grasp. It can be read but not interpreted, because it supposedly lacks those secret-hidden-deeper meanings so dear to our pedagogic hearts" (6). Furthermore, the production of these non-literary texts cannot be taught apart from the exigencies of real-life situations, so that the field of composition is a sort of "pseudo-non-literature," just as the attempt to teach creative writing in the academy is an effort to produce "pseudo-literature," the product of attempting to teach what cannot be taught. Finally, Scholes uses this governing scheme of oppositions to characterize English department practices along the same lines seen in Williams and Bourdieu: the division between sacred and profane texts, the boundary between the priestly class and the menial class, the placing of beauty and truth against the utilitarian and commonplace.

Scholes's work is an intelligent and comprehensive attempt to address the destructively decisive oppositional categories on which practices in the college English department are based. His displacement and refiguring of them, however, are less successful, although certainly provocative. Scholes invokes the deconstructive challenge to these practices from Paul de Man, along with objections from the left offered by Terry Eagleton and Fredric Jameson. Yet he refuses to see texts as radically indeterminate and finally aesthetic, as does the former, while denying that they are unremittingly political, as the latter avow. Instead, he argues for the multiple determination of texts depending on the semiotic codes—that is, cultural codes—located in them through the specific set of reading practices invoked in their consideration. In other words, texts can mean many things depending on the codes applied to them as well as the codes inscribed in them, the two acting dialogically. Their polysemic meanings are the product of this interactive process.

There are, however, a number of shortcomings in Scholes's method. The choice of interpretive strategies—the code preferred in a particular reading, whether political or aesthetic or historical, for example—seems arbitrary. Scholes suggests no standard for choosing one in preference to another. The political and the ethical become just one more set of choices, in no way to be recommended over any other. In short, Scholes shows no concern for deciding among competing reading codes or, of equal importance, for integrating more than one of them. There is a fragmentation and arbitrariness at the base of this system. In addition, Scholes's attempt to deconstruct the current rhetoric-poetic opposition and its invidious distinctions focuses exclusively on literary texts, once again reinforcing the conviction that they alone merit close analysis. Scholes mentions nothing about the production of rhetorical texts—that is, the teaching of writing—assuming in the manner of those he opposes that learning to interpret literature will automatically teach students to master the methods of producing non-literary discourse. Finally, there is in *Textual Power a* political timidity, a reluctance to explore fully the subversiveness of the charges leveled at the English department. Thus, any reference to the role that the practice of college English studies plays in reinforcing the injustices of race, class, sexual orientation, age, ethnic, and gender bias is scrupulously avoided, even though it is not difficult to infer that this is part of Scholes's tacit agenda.

Williams, Bourdieu, and Scholes together, however, point to certain conclusions about the current role of the English department in the larger social scheme. A literary studies based on the poetic-rhetoric bifurcation found in English studies serves the interests of a privileged managerial class while discriminating against those outside this class. Furthermore, it does so through cruelly clandestine devices, refusing the political in the service of an aesthetic experience that implicitly reinforces discriminatory social divisions. All of this is occulted by its pretensions to disinterestedness. Thus, the English department's abhorrence of the rhetorical, of political and scientific texts, does far more harm than creating a permanent underclass of department members whose putative role is the remediation of the poorly prepared. It also works to exclude from the ranks of the privileged managerial class those students not socialized from birth in the ways of the aesthetic response, doing so by its influence on the materials and methods of reading and writing required for success in secondary schools, college admission tests, and the colleges themselves.

Thus, the English department both serves an important exclusionary function and mystifies the role it plays in precluding reading and writing practices that might address inequalities in the existing social order. In other words, by excluding reading practices that might discover the political unconscious of literary texts and by refusing to take seriously the production and interpretation of rhetorical texts that address political matters, English studies has served as a powerful conservative force, all the while insisting on its transcendence of the political. The enforcement of this invidious division of the literary from the non-literary has served to entitle those already entitled and to disempower the disempowered, doing so in the name of the sacred literary text.

As Immanuel Wallerstein (1988) points out, university professors occupy a strategic place in the distribution of cultural capital. Wallerstein argues that historically the bourgeoisie is rarely satisfied with its status as bourgeoisie. Instead, it aspires to the cultural conditions of an aristocracy. Soon after its wealth is accumulated (usually with the second generation), this class disengages from the direct management of economic enterprises, living on rent after the manner of an aristocracy. Those who take over the role of handling the quotidian tasks of making money are the salaried bourgeoisie, the managerial class. Because they lack capital, most in this class can never hope to achieve bourgeois status. They are, after all, only wage earners—although well-paid wage earners. As a result, this group becomes concerned with accumulating cultural or human capital, the marks of the educated middle class, the educational certifications and accomplishments that distinguish this class from wage earners lower on the social scale. Cultural capital thus becomes a commodity that can be passed on to children in the form of dispositions and practices learned at home (for example, the aestheticizing of experience discovered by Bourdieu) and the certifications acquired through advanced education. The latter are secured through managing the educational system so that it favors the offspring of the managerial class—through class-biased achievement tests and entrance requirements, for example. Furthermore, in its conceptions of art and literature, the managerial class emulates its aristocratic betters—not the entrepreneurial class, but those who have separated themselves from management to live a life of cultivation and leisure.

English teachers are the bankers, the keepers and dispensers, of certain portions of this cultural capital. Their value to society is defined in terms of the investment and reproduction of this cultural capital. Since this capital has been located almost exclusively in literary texts, it is small wonder that attempts to challenge the rhetoric-poetic binary in which the value of these texts resides is resisted. Surrendering this hierarchy of texts means questioning claims to preeminence and power both within and outside the classroom, challenging the very bases of professional self-respect. Changing English studies along the lines recommended here will thus require a reformulation of the very figuration of cultural capital on which our discipline is based.

The next chapter will consider the response to these larger developments displayed in the formation of the college English department in the United States during the last century. English studies at that moment became the center of a plethora of agendas in the changing economic, political, and cultural relations of the time.

2

Where Do English Departments Really Come From?

A college curriculum is a device for encouraging the production of a certain kind of graduate, in effect, a certain kind of person. In directing what courses will be taken and in what order, a curriculum undertakes the creation of consciousness and behavior. A curriculum does not do this on its own, free of outside influence. Instead, it occupies a position between the conditions of the larger society it serves—the economic, political, and cultural sectors—and the work of teachers-scholars within the institution. The students themselves are, of course, central to this circle of curricular influence, but, unfortunately, their impact has typically been limited in the United States, as institutional practices have succeeded in limiting their effectiveness (the most notable exception being the brief period of the late 1960s and early 1970s). In short, the curriculum serves as a mediator between the demands of those outside the institution—employers, government agencies, political groups—and. those within it—primarily faculty, the disciplines they serve, and students. The response of the curriculum to the exigencies of its historical moment thus represents a negotiation among forces both outside and inside the institution.

In this chapter, I want to survey the changes within the larger society and the changes within certain academic disciplines that took place at the end of the last century, changes that radically altered the nature of higher education in the United States. I want to situate the development of English studies within these larger formations, examining the role it played in the new curriculum. The chapter will close with a brief consideration of the shortcomings of this curriculum, shortcomings that have thrown into doubt its contemporary relevance.

In the nineteenth century, the college curriculum in the United States was monolithic and relatively uniform throughout the country. A college education was intended to prepare students—overwhelmingly white males until late in the century—for law, the ministry, and politics. Significantly, it was assumed that a single liberal arts curriculum based on certain standard texts served all professions equally well. Higher education was by and large meant primarily for those already financially secure, young men getting ready to take their rightful roles as professionals and community leaders. Meanwhile, the key to economic mobility in this period of competitive capitalism was in business, mainly the entrepreneurial venture. Colleges thus ignored the needs of commerce and manufacturing, arguing that higher education's mission was to prepare civic and moral leaders (most colleges were church-affiliated), not technicians. Practical scientific training was acquired in the world of work, after the college experience (Rudolph 1977). The center of the college curriculum was three to four years of rhetoric, courses in which students brought to bear the fruits of their learning in public performances and written essays (Wozniak 1978). Study in most colleges was capped by the senior-year course in moral philosophy taught by the college president.

Frederick Rudolph (1977) has detailed the tradition of complaint that surrounded the old liberal arts college. Attempts to introduce new scientific courses were successfully resisted at most schools. Those that did provide an alternative science curriculum commonly treated the students enrolled in it as less than full-fledged members of the college community (221-33). Dramatic, quick, and widespread changes in the curriculum, however, took place during the last twenty-five years of the century.

The major cause of the changes was the shift from entrepreneurial to corporate capitalism. The college was soon regarded as an institution designed to serve the economic and social needs of the larger society, or at least the needs of newly emergent power groups. Gradually, the small liberal arts college was replaced by the research university. This reformed institution was to conduct empirical study in the useful sciences, improving the techniques of farming, mining, manufacturing, and commerce. It was also to train professionals who could take their specialized knowledge into the larger society, providing both increased profits for businesses and an improved standard of living for all citizens—for example, through new techniques in health care and urban management. New land-grant colleges participated in this effort, but private schools—notably Harvard and Johns Hopkins—and other state schools—Michigan and Wisconsin, for example—actually led the way (Veysey 1965).

One of the central elements in the transformation from the old liberal arts college to the new research university was the emergence of

English—an area of study that simply did not exist in the old curriculum—as a disciplinary formation. As an introduction to considering this development, I would like to glance at one of the most widely read origin narratives of English studies, primarily because it prefigures some of the central disciplinary debates of the past and present.

In responding to the question posed in the title of his 1967 *College English* essay "Where Do English Departments Come From?" (reprinted in a popular collection by Tate and Corbett 1981), William Riley Parker engages in a number of slippery rhetorical strategies before settling into his argument. He begins by refusing the answer "out of the everywhere into the here," moves to a maxim from Cicero on the necessity of historical study, admonishes all students of English literature to learn Latin, and finally announces that college English departments are a recent arrival, less than a hundred years old. What follows this announcement, however, works with what precedes it to belie the parvenu status of English studies. Parker identifies the English department with what he declares to be its exclusive subject matter: literary texts in the authentic Anglo-Saxon line of historical descent. The need for an English department, in this account, clearly began with the first literary work in Anglo-Saxon, even though, as Parker admits, serious research in literature—and then without benefit of university status—began only with the Tudors in the 1560s.

Thus, even though he repeatedly concedes that the college English department is a recent affair, Parker forwards in defense of its appearance the historical succession of literary texts from the Anglo-Saxons to the present. English departments exist because literary texts exist. Parker underscores this point by repeatedly declaring the work of teaching writing to be an unfortunate historical accident, doing so even as he quite accurately observes that it "was the teaching of freshman composition that quickly entrenched English departments in the college and university structure" (11). He further acknowledges rhetoric as the grandmother of literary studies and oratory as its mother. (Paternity is attributed to philology figured as an early linguistics.) For Parker, however, rhetoric observes a strict division between oral and written discourse, with its rightful sphere as the former.

Parker thus works hard to dissever the task of teaching text production from that of teaching literary interpretation, doing so despite all the evidence to the contrary (see Berlin 1987)—some of which, as we have seen, he himself acknowledges. He does, however, for one brief moment wander into a consideration of the historical events surrounding the creation of English studies—and in a way that offers a far more plausible account. Parker describes the following elements as operative in defeating the classical curriculum: "There were the impact of science, the American spirit of utilitarianism or pragmatism, and the exciting, new dream of democratic, popular education, an assumed corollary of which was the free elective system" (11). He adds a fourth factor as well: "a widespread mood of questioning and experimentation in education, a practical, revisionary spirit that challenged all traditions and accepted practices" (11). Unfortunately, these events are relegated to the ranks of the merely ephemeral, partly responsible for the insertion of English studies into the university structure, but also culpable for having made these studies stray from their true purpose: the examination of the significant literary texts of the English language. One result, as already noted, has been the importance of what Parker calls the "slave labor" (11) of composition in the English department. For Parker, the genuinely significant social and political events that he correctly identifies as having influenced early English departments are finally mere ripples in the eternal sea of the literary tradition.

I will argue that the historical events Parker so blithely skips over, as well as those he does not consider, are indeed central to the formation of the college English department in the United States. These larger developments can be seen as formative of both the institutional shape of the department in all its diversity and of the literary tradition that it claims to stand for. English studies is a highly overdetermined institutional formation, occupying a site at the center of converging economic, social, political, and cultural developments at the end of the nineteenth century, developments that continue to affect it today. These forces have continually encouraged the diversity of English studies that Parker so deplored.

Making higher education the provider of scientifically trained experts and managers who would administer a corporate—as opposed to a laissez-faire—capitalist economy had widespread consequences. The modern university became the basis of a comprehensive certification process, setting requirements for credentials within the various new professions and determining who had met them. Compulsory education was one of the first effects of this new order, with colleges providing the trained teachers needed for the expanding public schools. Science and scientific modes of thought were at the center of the university's activities, since research—in addition to imparting knowledge—was seen as crucial to its mission. This scientific orientation was as influential in the English department as elsewhere, affecting methods of literary scholarship and study as well as methods of writing instruction. The professionalization of English studies in schools and colleges was also inextricably involved in the drive for equality of opportunity among women, as many of the new state universities adopted gender-equal admissions policies. Finally, this entire complex of occurrences was part of a reformation of class relations. The new credentialing process created a meritocracy, with the professional middle class at its apex. The period also evoked a call from a Brahminical elite for a reassertion of the Anglo-Saxon tradition. This group was engaged in a holding action against the challenge to its power and privilege posed by the arriviste professional middle class and, more important, the huge numbers of recent immigrants from eastern and southern Europe. The new professionals commonly joined their betters in uniting against the latest wave of foreigners, out-Anglicizing the Anglo-Protestant elite in their zeal for things English and old. All of this finally contributed to the institutional form that English studies assumed as well as to the varieties of poetics and rhetorics studied in the early English department.

The dramatic change in capitalism begun during the last quarter of the nineteenth century has been well documented by Ernest Mandel, Alfred Chandler, Michel Beaud, and others. During most of the nineteenth century, the path to economic success could be found in entrepreneurial activities. The dream of the ambitious worker was to own his or her own business, whether a farm or a small shop for manufacture or sales. By the 1890s, this dream was increasingly unattainable. The growth in the size of the farming, manufacturing, or retailing enterprise necessary to turn a profit led to a decrease in the rural population and an expansion of the city. Between 1860 and 1910, the percentage of Americans living in towns and cities grew from 25 to 40 percent (Noble 1984, 33). As Richard Ohmann (1987) indicates, "the value of manufactured goods increased sevenfold in the last four decades of the century, far outdistancing the value of farm products. The number of factories quadrupled, and the number of people working in them tripled. . . . [B]usinessmen were in command of the nation's future" (29). In both the city and the country, work meant wage labor. Unfortunately, the unskilled factory worker's wage increases peaked by the time the worker was twenty-five (Noble 1984, 52). Success for the middle class was redefined in relation to educational accomplishment. High schools provided the training for lower-level skilled labor, while colleges provided the expertise needed to succeed in the upper levels of the meritocracy. The changing job market dramatically reflected this transformation. Between 1870 and 1910, jobs in the professions increased from 230,000 to 1,150,000; those in trade, finance, and real estate increased from 800,000 to 2,800,000 (Noble 1984, 52). Success in these endeavors commonly required educational certification.

This need for credentials meant that schools and universities grew precipitously. As Joel Spring (1986) has indicated, "schooling as a means of developing human capital has become the most important goal of the educational system in the twentieth century" (185). The high school mushroomed as it became central to the management of this human capital. In 1890, there were 202,963 students in 2,526 public high schools. In 1900, these figures more than doubled to 519,251 students in 6,005 public high schools. By 1912, the enrollment level reached 1,105,360. And by 1920, 2,200,389 students, or 28 percent of fourteen- to seventeen-year-olds, were in high schools (Spring 1986, 194). These schools became, to use Spring's term, sorting machines, reinforcing class relations by determining the future occupations and income levels of young people. Indeed, so sharp was the change in the life experience of teenagers during this time that adolescence as a distinct life stage was invented by G. Stanley Hall to justify the prolonged periods of financial dependence on the family demanded by the new schooling requirement. Adolescence became the period when young males, psychologically immature although sexually adult, needed protection from the stress of sexual and economic decisions. Young women were simultaneously depicted as more spiritual, less intellectually able, and more controlled by their emotions and bodies. Their educational preparation remained focused around marriage, family, and the home. (This formulation, however, did not go unchallenged.) In keeping with the invention of adolescence as a distinct life stage, the high school created a youth culture and organized student behavior around the principle of "social efficiency" (Spring 1986, 198).

Universities also grew and changed during this time. While historical discussions of English studies have often focused on private institutions, transformations in these schools were commonly motivated by a fear of being outpaced by public universities. The passage of the Morrill Land Grant Act in 1862 began the use of federal funds for public higher education. By the 1890s, the contribution of Cornell, Michigan, and Wisconsin to the new developments in higher education easily matched that of Harvard and Johns Hopkins (Veysey 1965). The influence of German universities led to the research model for college professors—before all but unheard of in the United States. Of course, corporations began to look to the university for research to improve their profit margins as well as for instruction to train managers and researchers. The growth of colleges and the number of college teachers during this time indicates the effect of these forces. In 1870, there were 5,553 faculty members in 563 institutions; in 1880, 11,552 in 811; in 1890, 15,809 in 998; and in 1900, 23,868 in 977. In thirty years, the number of institutions had nearly doubled, and the number of faculty quadrupled (Bledstein 1976, 271).

Despite the fact that the new colleges and universities were committed to the ideal of scientific research and to the transferal of scientific knowledge in the service of corporate capitalism, English studies was at the center of the new curriculum in both secondary and higher education—and for a number of compelling reasons. As already mentioned, compulsory education was on the rise throughout this period, primarily as a device for preparing a trained and disciplined workforce. By 1917, 38 states had introduced compulsory schooling until age 16 (Noble 1984, 54). A significant motivation for requiring this schooling, especially in urban areas, was the determination to assimilate huge numbers of immigrants into cultural norms defined in specifically Anglo-Protestant terms. Much of the urban population growth in the United States from 1860 to 1910 was due to the arrival of some thirty million immigrants from Europe (Noble 1984, 33). Thus, between 1880 and 1920, 70 percent of city dwellers were foreign-born or children of the foreign-born (Noble 1984, 43). The leadership class during this time was predominantly Anglo-Protestant, and it intentionally designed the schools to serve as devices for indoctrinating the foreign-born and their offspring in a particular ideological version of the Anglo-American heritage (Noble 1984, 31, and Spring 1986, 167-69). The first requirement for doing so, of course, was the insistence on English as the official language of education. Many states introduced laws preventing immigrants from setting up schools that conducted instruction in their native language (Noble 1984, 98). Indeed, one measure of the importance of mastery in English was the ascendance of the Irish in the state and church hierarchies because of their command of English, while the various non-English-speaking Continental groups remained subordinate.

English teachers thus occupied a place at the center of the new high schools, and it was the business of the university to provide them with training and certification. College English departments as a result got a steady supply of students who needed their offerings. The students in these new teacher-training programs were most likely to be women, while their college professors were most likely to be men. The cult of true womanhood of the mid-nineteenth century, combined with the social gospel forwarded later, encouraged women to assume an assertive role in addressing the economically caused evils of the day, especially in the crowded cities. While the cult of true womanhood urged education for women to make good mothers of the republic, the lessons of the social gospel argued that women should enter the world to improve it—in the settlement house, for example. Women called on the contradictions in these codes to increase their access to the professions. Meanwhile, school systems realized that they could save money by hiring women, since they could pay them less without fear of opposition.

Between 1870 and 1900, a dramatic increase thus occurred in the number of women in colleges, from 21 percent to 35 percent of the total attendance (Solomon 1985, 58). Furthermore, these women were strongly motivated and at a number of schools were resented because they performed at higher levels than did men, outdoing the best men, for example, at the University of Chicago and Stanford University (Solomon 1985, 58-61). Women also tended to choose humanities courses over scientific offerings, doing so for a number of reasons involving social expectations, previous educational training, and hiring patterns in the workplace. As a result, women were from time to time blamed for the declining enrollments of men in the humanities, the charge being that they drove men away from courses in Latin, Greek, and modern languages (Solomon 1985, 60, and Holbrook 1991). In fact, women selected these courses—some until just a few years earlier thought too difficult for a woman's delicate constitution—because they provided employment opportunities in the schools as well as because they were generally more hospitable. The men left these studies because their paths to success lay elsewhere in the curriculum.

Nevertheless, the fear of feminization had its effects on the gender distribution in schools and colleges. As Sue Ellen Holbrook (1991) has argued, there was a markedly defensive effort among college teachers during the early years of English studies to characterize their study of language and literature as a manly enterprise, hoping thereby to keep it safe from the incursion of women. At the turn of the century, 94 percent of university and college professors were men, while 75 percent of school teachers were women. During the subsequent eighty years, women constituted more than 25 percent of the professoriate class over only a single decade—the 1930s, when they represented 32 percent. Meanwhile, women have on average constituted 70 percent of teachers in the schools, reaching a high of 84 percent in 1930 and a low of 68 percent in 1981 (Holbrook 1991, 220).

This masculinizing of English studies relates directly to the establishment of the literary texts that were to serve as the basis for study in English courses. Despite the diversity in the twenty English programs described in William Payne's *English in American Universities* (the results of a survey published in 1895), all agreed that the core concern in literary studies, regardless of the method used, was to begin with Anglo-Saxon, proceed through Middle English, and end with certain mid-nineteenth-century English literary texts. The overwhelming majority of the texts to be studied were written by men. Furthermore, while some texts in American literature were included, these were invariably by male New England poets who were thought to be extensions of a male-dominated Anglo-Saxon and Protestant heritage. It is neither chance nor historical inevitability that this heritage served as the source for coursework and that it all but excluded women.

It is also significant that during the last quarter of the nineteenth century there arose among the ruling elite in the East a fascination with the Anglo-Saxon origins of the United States. The result was the resurgence of a strong U.S. tradition of racial nationalism. As John Higham (1988) explains, this position was characterized by the view "that the United States belonged in some special sense to the Anglo-Saxon 'race'" (9). This notion of an "Anglo-Saxon tradition" originally appeared in England in the seventeenth and eighteenth centuries among supporters of Parliament. These Parliamentarians were, according to Higham, seeking "precedents and roots for English liberty in the ancient institutions and temperaments of the country before the Norman conquest" (9). They ended by calling on Tacitus's description of the Germanic barbarians, among other texts, to trace England's heritage of freedom to the "Goths," here standing for Angles, Saxons, Jutes, and the other tribes that invaded the Roman Empire. This racial nationalism arose in England again in the nineteenth century and was a part of Romantic literary lore, a longing for the organic richness of the Gothic against the urban horrors of a mechanical age. It was reflected in Sharon Turner's popular *History of the Anglo-Saxons* (1799-1805), which appeared in the United States in 1841, proclaiming "the supreme Anglo-Saxon virtue, a gift for political freedom." As Higham explains, Americans thus saw in "the Anglo-Saxons, or perhaps the Teutons, . . . a unique capacity for self-government and a special mission to spread its blessings" (10). This notion was first used in the United States to support expansionism. There were also those who evoked it to protest the Irish immigrants of the 1850s. This use, however, represents a minor note, since the predominant view was that the Anglo-Saxon heritage was destined to prevail over all other influences in the United States by virtue of its inherent excellence, not by force and exclusion.

This confidence waned during the 1870s and 1880s, and with this waning came a revival of the cult of the Anglo-Saxon. By this time, the social and political threats to the old elite came from two sources: the Catholicism and political radicalism of the immigrant working class and the social climbing of the new rich, the parvenus who had amassed wealth and were eager to enter the most select circles of power. As Higham notes, "Anglo-Saxonism became a kind of patrician nationalism" (32). The interest in things English—ideas, literature, and social standards—grew among the intellectual elite. Anglophilia was especially endemic among the Brahmin gentry of New England, as well as among their arriviste imitators, including those of the new professional middle class.

During the 1890s, this enthusiasm became a weapon turned against "the new immigrants," the groups from eastern and southern Europe who, unlike northern European immigrants, could not be worked into the myth of the Anglo-Saxon heritage. Nevertheless, the reason for this hostility toward the new arrivals was clearly economic. The severe depressions that marked each decade between 1870 and 1900 resulted in an increasingly militant workforce, a third of which in manufacturing between 1870 and 1920 consisted of immigrants (Higham 1988, 16). What had begun as a revival of a national heritage by a ruling group socially threatened by immigrants and parvenus thus became an economic and political weapon used against the working class. Furthermore, this effort was buttressed by "scientific" studies that established the "racial" superiority of the Anglo-Saxon tribes. These economic and political battles encouraged the forwarding of an Anglo-Protestant literary canon and the installing of Anglo-Saxon studies in the early English department as an attempt at once to duplicate and supplant the ancient authority of the old languages of learning, Latin and Greek.

Competing Paradigms

It was within this context that the early English department entered a debate on the materials and methods of its discipline. I thus want to consider briefly the major forms poetics and rhetorics assumed in early English studies. My purpose is to offer a sketch that will support my stand on the ways English studies serves larger economic, social, and political objectives. This is easier to see in the early days of the discipline, when the effort to divorce the aesthetic from the political and moral was less pronounced. I will rely on my own reading of the materials of the debate, offering an interpretation that often diverges from Gerald Graff's in his institutional history. I should add, however, that I have found his evidence useful, even as I arrive through it at a different understanding of the stakes involved in the early discussions. Once again, our differences come from the fact that I am arguing from the perspective that includes the history and theory of rhetoric.

We have already seen that the decision to focus on the Anglo-Saxon and Anglo-Protestant heritage in literature was made immediately. A minor challenge to this preoccupation was offered by those who wished to give equal emphasis to American literature, but this effort did not receive strong support until after World War I. The chief disagreement in considerations of the study and teaching of literature instead focused on methodology. The nature of the reading practices to be recommended in pursuing the study of the approved texts was a prominent preoccupation of early English studies. This preoccupation is hardly surprising, considering that Graff's disciplinary history demonstrates that this issue has been a continuous topic of debate in English studies.

The study and teaching of rhetoric was also at the center of the department's efforts and its disciplinary disputes. Some argued against including rhetoric in the projects of English studies in any form, despite its dominant place in the college curriculum of the United States throughout the nineteenth century. In fact, this dominance led to its censure, since proponents of literary study feared that their efforts to introduce new literary study would constantly be threatened by the oldest and most prominent discipline in Anglo-American and European education. As I have tried to show in my histories of writing instruction in U.S. colleges, however, despite the "tradition of complaint" against rhetoric, its study was never successfully banished from the department's disciplinary agenda. While those in literary studies in the English department may have argued that writing was an accomplishment easily mastered in the lower grades, the testimony of experience in the United States—from the Puritans to the pre-Revolutionary colonial colleges to the democratically inclined colleges of the nineteenth century—indicated otherwise (Guthrie 1946-49, 1951; Halloran 1982; and Berlin 1984, 1987). Rhetorical accomplishment acquired through direct instruction in the college classroom had always been an important fixture of the college curriculum in the United States, and it maintained a place in the new English studies.

The early English department, then, engaged in the study and teaching of literature and composition. Just as the method to be pursued in reading literary texts was a central issue, so was the method to be pursued in teaching the production of rhetorical texts. As I indicated earlier, a poetic and a rhetoric tend to appear together, the one giving significance to the other through a division of textual labor. During the last two hundred years or so, poetics have commonly provided a method for interpreting literary texts. They previously offered, as in Aristotle, advice for creating them as well. Rhetorics during this time have offered methods for both producing and interpreting texts of all kinds, except, recently, the poetic. Once again, however, in previous eras, rhetorics explicitly included advice on poetic texts as well—for example, George Campbell's *The Philosophy of Rhetoric* (1776), in which literary texts are regarded as a subcategory in a hierarchy of discourses that culminates in the rhetorical. Most English professors today, however, would see this relationship as reversed, with poetry standing for the apotheosis of human discourse. The point I wish to make is that while the domains of rhetoric and poetic are historically variable, these domains are usually established as a function of their relation to each other.

The early English department displayed a division of discourse in which each major poetic theory and each major rhetorical theory appeared in a binary and oppositional relationship with its counterpart. There were three major paradigms of the poetic-rhetoric binary in competition with each other. Another way of saying this is that there were three alternative conceptions of literacy, of reading and writing: the meritocratic-scientific, the liberal-cultural, and the social-democratic. Each offered a poetic, or theory of literary interpretation, and a rhetoric, or theory of textual production, united by a shared epistemology and ideology.

Literacy for the Scientific Meritocracy

The teaching of reading and writing practices designed specifically for the new scientifically trained professional middle class appeared primarily at Harvard and a number of the other new elective universities. These schools were to provide experts to control the vagaries of capitalism in the hope of avoiding the boom-and-bust cycle that haunted the economy at the end of the nineteenth century. They were devoted to implementing the scientific method in addressing the concrete problems of agriculture and commerce, providing researchers and managers to staff the new technical positions emerging in government and industry. In place of the nineteenth-century uniform curriculum, students specialized as undergraduates and received training for a particular profession, such as farming, geology, teaching, social work, engineering, or business.

The English department played an important role in this new university. Even in the most unrestrained elective system, first-year composition remained required of all students. At Harvard in 1897, it was the only course that all students had to take. No literature courses were required, but by the turn of the century, Charles William Eliot, Harvard's president, was surprised to discover that English was Harvard's most popular major. Very early, a knowledge of English and American literature and a certain competence in written discourse had replaced the classical languages as the mark of membership in the leadership class (Watkins 1989 and Douglas 1976). While these developments affected all three paradigms of English studies, they had a special relation to the new scientifically trained professional middle class.

Text production for the new scientific meritocracy has come to be called current-traditional rhetoric, a tribute to its prominence over the last hundred years. Its most conspicuous formulators were A. S. Hill and Barrett Wendell at Harvard and J. F. Genung at Amherst. Current-traditional rhetoric does not deal with probabilities—as do, for example, the major rhetorics of ancient Athens and Rome as well as those of the eighteenth century—but with certainties ascertained through the scientific method. There is no need to teach invention (classical *inventio*), since the truths of any matter under consideration reveal themselves to the correct application of scientific investigation, whether we are considering an engineering problem or a problem in government policy. Disagreements are easily resolved by an appeal to science or, more accurately, to a university-trained person who is a certified expert in the branch of scientific knowledge at issue. The major work of the rhetoric classroom, then, is to teach budding young professionals to arrange the materials (*dispositio*) their expertise has enabled them to locate and to express themselves in accordance with the highest standards of grammar and usage (an elementary form of *elocutio*).

This rhetoric forwards the correspondence theory of language. The linguistic sign is seen as an arbitrary invention devised to communicate exactly the external reality to which it corresponds. Writing becomes a matter of matching word to referent in a manner that evokes in the mind of the reader the experience of the referent itself. This rhetoric accordingly emphasizes four modes of discourse—narration, description, exposition, and argument—each of which is thought to correspond to a different faculty of the mind. The assumption, of course, is that word and faculties correspond in perfect harmony—so many discourses for so many faculties. In matters of style, the class markers of superficial correctness become the major concern, with A. S. Hill cautioning against "barbarisms, solecisms, and improprieties," all of which are avoided through careful word choice and correct grammar.

The literary criticism forwarded as the counterpart to this rhetoric was philology. Philology, of course, originated in Germany in response to the study of the language and literature of ancient Greece and Rome. It was intended to discover the national spirit of ancient civilizations, although it was eventually applied to modern cultures of western Europe and even the United States (Applebee 1974, 25-28). In the hands of academics in the United States, however, it often focused on language itself, especially Anglo-Saxon and Middle English. (As suggested earlier, these languages were commonly required for graduate study because they provided the cultural capital once afforded by the languages of ancient Greece and Rome.) Its other major preoccupation was the search for historical facts surrounding the creation of the literary text. Literary study thus became data-gathering rather than literary or cultural interpretation. The classrooms in which reading practices along these philological lines were taught accordingly emphasized linguistic—primarily grammatical—detail and historical data. This material was to be memorized and reproduced for exams. As Graff (1987) points out, through these practices, the new English studies could claim to be as difficult and rigorous as the old Latin and Greek studies (72).

Philological study, however, assumed another form under the influence of Herbert Spencer and Hippolyte Taine. Both attempted to trace the literary work to its historical and cultural milieu. The poetic of the meritocracy primarily emphasized the Social Darwinism of Spencer, applying evolutionary theory to all areas of human experience, including art. This view finds competition, natural selection, and survival of the fittest in all features of human behavior. The artist who—like the manager or doctor or lawyer—is most fit for the cultural moment emerges and survives. The literary critic studies the relations between the artist and the culture that produced him or her. John Rathbun and Harry Clark (1979) find this Spencerian influence in the work of Harvard's John Fiske and Thomas Sargent Perry. (Graff attributes this merger of philology and historical criticism to the influence of Taine, but, as I will argue a bit later, Taine's method encouraged a somewhat different response.)

It is not difficult to detect the ideological commitments that underwrote this conception of literacy. From this view, the real is always the factual and rational. The answer to all questions—scientific, social, political, cultural—can be found unproblematically in the facts of the material world. The method of investigation is inductive, amassing data for the analysis of university-trained experts. Power in society is put in the hands of professionals in a newly formulated misrepresentation of democracy. As Peter Carroll and David Noble (1979) explain, "Middleclass progressives argued that democracy depended on disinterested and objective voters who were able to see the concerns of the entire nation." Mere farmers and workers, although the majority of the population, could not do this, because they represented only their own interests: "But educated business people and professionals, although a small minority of the population, could establish a democracy for all the other people, because their education made it possible for them to see the concerns of all kinds of people" (350-51). In practice, this meant that elected representatives, themselves increasingly college graduates, came to rely on trained experts to identify and solve problems. It should not be surprising that the problems and solutions these experts discovered most commonly served the interests of their own class, a result they would attribute not to ideology but to their contact with the scientific truths of nature. Thus, class-based interests—including race and gender biases offered in the name of science and objective truth were at the center of the literacy of the meritocracy.

The Literacy of Liberal Culture

The liberal-cultural paradigm was found primarily at colleges that initially resisted the elective curriculum, most conspicuously its encouragement of an education in science. Certain old and established colleges—such as Yale, Princeton, and Williams—argued that there was a common core of liberal and humane ideas that all college graduates should share. Acknowledging the spirit of progress enough to admit this core was no longer located in the languages and literatures of ancient Greece and Rome, this group argued that its new home was to be found in the language and literature of the Anglo-Protestant tradition. Classical education in humane letters became literary education in the language and literature of England and, to a lesser extent, America.

For this position, writing is a manifestation of one's spiritual nature. Errors in superficial correctness, for example, are considered the result of deep spiritual maladies. Teachers must address the source of this disorder, not its symptoms. This is done through the correct study of the best literature. Only after undergoing the experience of great art is the student prepared to express himself (but hardly ever herself) in truth and beauty. Reversing the more common historical pattern, rhetoric becomes a branch of poetry.

Graff (1987) treats the members of this group under the heading "The Generalist Creed." He explains, "In social outlook, the generalist tended toward a 'mugwump' view that saw national leadership as the virtual birthright of the cultured classes" (83). Yet while his discussion of their approach to the classroom and their avoidance of literary scholarship is accurate, Graff fails to recognize the systematic character of their poetic. This group embraced a philosophical idealism similar to Emerson's emphasis on the spiritual in human affairs without his commitment to democracy. Truth, beauty, and goodness are located in a transcendent realm beyond the material, an unchanging substratum only partially, although progressively, unveiled on earth. The act of revelation is performed by the gifted seer in philosophy, politics, or art.

From this perspective, art is the product of genius, of the inspired visionary who reveals to lesser mortals the meaning of life. The essential features of human experience, found in all great literary works, are eternally true. Thus, in this system, the new is not excluded, but is always suspect until it can be proven to be in harmony with the old and established. Literature here provides the central study of education, addressing all areas of human experience. It offers the collective wisdom of humankind. Furthermore, it comes from the individual and is directed toward the individual, more specifically, from the best self of the author to the best self of the reader. The aim of art is thus self-discovery. for both artist and auditor, since the isolated individual is the central support of truth, virtue, and beauty as well as the foundation of a sound society. Most important, as Laurence Veysey (1965) notes, poetic texts cultivate taste, the sure mark of a gentleman and testimony to a whole range of political and personal convictions (184-91).

This group was distrustful of the philological methods they found in colleges because these methods reduced the work of literature to mere facts. This suspicion further extended to literary scholarship in general, since no research in literature could ever capture the actual experience of the text itself. Thus, as Veysey points out, Barrett Wendell of Harvard tried to teach literary texts "by creating a contagious mood of enthusiasm rather than by critical analysis. It is recorded that after reading a poem in the classroom Wendell would sit silently for a moment and then cry out: 'Isn't it beautiful?'" (222). Hiram Corson of Cornell and Charles T. Copeland of Harvard likewise put oral reading at the center of their classroom repertoire, since to those of taste the text spoke for itself. William Lyon Phelps, on the other hand, who taught Yale's first freshman course in English in 1892, was an animated lecturer who believed he must "inflame the imagination" (Veysey 1965, 225). Yet he scrupulously avoided the abstract, focusing on vivid imagery in his presentation instead. A passive receptivity to literature, rather than creative rigor, was usually preferred.

As Veysey indicates, professors in this camp were reluctant to publish. Irving Babbit even commented that "to get rid of laziness in college [threatens] the whole idea of liberal culture" (188). When they did write about literature, their criticism tended to be unsystematic and impressionistic, celebrating the eternal spiritual values in great literature—as in the work of Hiram Corson, George Woodberry, and Brander Matthews. These values, of course, confirmed the power and privilege of the old New England leadership class. Members of this group also wrote histories, influenced largely by Taine. Their purpose was usually to chart the rise, as in Matthews, or the fall, as in Wendell, of eternal values invariably embodied within the Brahminical version of the Anglo-Saxon literary tradition, even extending, as in Woodberry, to "race power."

The literacy of liberal culture is based on a conservative ideology that treasures continuity. While the new is not altogether rejected, longevity is the best recommendation for any concept or institution. Only a small minority can achieve the realm of higher truth, and it is this group that must be trusted for leadership in politics and culture. Education ought to be limited to this small group, a natural aristocracy with the potential for genius. While in theory this included the Platonic faith that the natural disposition for genius could arise among all groups, including women, in practice liberal culture distrusted the meritocracy. As Veysey explains, "Numbers, which democracy produced, interfered with standards, which it was the special task of culture to maintain" (191). Power ought to be lodged in the hands of the gifted and brilliant few. Democracy, even with the limitations of a meritocracy, allowed too many inferior souls into the center of power.

I should mention here that during the first two decades of the twentieth century, the literacy of the meritocracy and the literacy of liberal culture tended to move closer to each other, each compromising its position in deference to the other. As Veysey indicates, "Harvard under Eliot had strayed from the natural propensity of its region and its clientele" (248). Most Harvard students, after all, came from homes very much like those of the students at the bastions of liberal culture. In time, Harvard had to make concessions to the power of this privileged group. Meanwhile, schools such as Yale could not ignore the increasing importance attached to professional preparation, even among the privileged. Thus, by World War I, the two schools came to look very much alike, both pledging allegiance to a democratic meritocracy while upholding the time-tested values of background and breeding in their admissions policies.

Democratic Literacy

The social-democratic conception of rhetoric and poetic arose in response to the political progressivism that was an especially potent force in the Midwest, but it could also be found at schools such as Penn State, New York University, Reed College, and Vassar. This position agreed that universities should provide a group of trained experts to solve economic and social problems. These experts, however, existed to serve society as a whole, not their own narrow class interests. Power in a democracy must remain in the hands of common citizens, and citizens must finally decide on the courses that government and business are to take. While the voice of experts must be heard, the people must choose the heading the community should follow. This conception of literacy is the most committed to egalitarianism in matters of race, gender, and class—an objective to be encouraged through education.

Fred Newton Scott of Michigan and Gertrude Buck of Vassar, Scott's student, were the most conspicuous spokespersons for this position in rhetoric. Rhetoric in college should focus on training citizens for participation in a democracy. From this perspective, all institutions are social constructions continually open to revision. The democratic process always guarantees the right to change economic and political institutions to serve the interests of the governed. No class, race, or gender can thus claim ownership of the language. Accordingly, Scott and Buck rigorously argue for the students' right to their own language, paying special attention to the immigrants who were entering the public schools and universities.

Scott's essay "Rhetoric Rediviva" (1909) is an especially effective and succinct statement of this rhetoric. Here Scott criticizes both the rhetoric of the meritocracy and the rhetoric of liberal culture. The first is too concerned with winning, he explains, being more aware of the interests of the writer's discipline than of the community. The rhetoric of liberal culture is similarly committed to narrow and partisan class interests. Scott thus proposes a rhetoric that emphasizes service to the community and ethical commitment to the public good. Writing in this classroom must consider the entire rhetorical context—writer, audience, topic, and social and linguistic environment—in arriving at a statement that engages the student's interests as well as the community's. Students learn to write in a manner that will prepare them for participation in the political life of a democratic society.

This conception of literacy encourages a literary criticism that seeks to integrate the aesthetic response with a study of the social and historical milieu that generated works of art. This is seen, for example, in Fred Scott and Charles Mills Gayley's *An Introduction to the Methods and Materials of Literary Criticism* (1901), an attempt to catalog the vast range of critical work appearing in the university at the time while privileging the aesthetic response within its historical moment. Members of this group were inclined to favor the study of American literature—and in a manner most unlike their counterparts in the other two groups. America represented to them a unique set of social and historical conditions offering the potential for a new kind of art. This commitment can be seen in a brief glance at three representative histories.

In *A History of American Literature during the Colonial Period, 1607-1765* (1878, revised 1897), Moses Coit Tyler, a professor at Cornell and later the University of Michigan, explains that he plans to discuss writing of Americans that has "some noteworthy value as literature, and some real significance in the literary unfolding of the American mind" (v). In his preface to *The Literary History of the American Revolution, 1763-1783* (1897), he notes that he plans to set forth the period, "the history of its ideas, its spiritual moods, its motives, its passions, even its sportive caprices and its whims" (v). He also promises to trace "the several steps of thought and emotion through which the American people passed during the two decades of struggle which resulted in our national Independence" (vi). In *A History of American Literature* (1912), William B. Cairns of the University of Wisconsin offers "the course of literary development in America," placing "greatest emphasis on general movements because American literature is first of all important as an expression of national life" (v). Finally, in *The First Century of American Literature, 1770-1870* (1935), Fred Lewis Pattee explains that in his three histories of American literature (the previous two appeared in 1896 and 1899), "My fundamental conception has been that American literature during its century and a half of existence has been an emanation from American life and American conditions. But I have begun every case with the literary product rather than the historical background, my eye always upon the American people" (vi). In short, each literary historian is attempting to arrange an accommodation of the aesthetic with the political.

As is apparent, members of this group present their ideological commitments in a fairly straightforward way in their statements on writing and reading practices. While they tend to be social constructionists in their conception of economic and political arrangements, their unquestioned faith in the rational powers of ordinary people often includes a corresponding faith in the scientific expertise of the professional middle class. Their support for a redistribution of wealth and power in the hope that all will be assimilated into the middle class shares the liberal's confidence in economic progress and the wisdom of professional middle class values. Of course, the key to this effort is the extension of free education to all. The social theories of John Dewey best represent this comprehensive version of democratic literacy (Spring 1986, 172-75).

This group also offers the strongest support for an egalitarian and participatory conception of democracy. All political questions are open to debate, and all citizens should be allowed an equal opportunity to speak freely. This view unfortunately displays an excessive faith in existing democratic procedures and an innocence about economic realities and their effects on politics (Noble 1984, 71-75). For example, this view rarely considers limits to open and free discussion caused by differential access to the media. All too often, it innocently and mistakenly assumes that the conditions of participatory democracy already exist. Finally, this view does not adequately take into account the effects of economic and social arrangements—for example, the conflicts of capitalism and the existence of unjust class, gender, and race relations.

The Continuity of the Curriculum

The nature of the rhetorics and poetics found in the English department underwent dramatic changes in the years immediately after the turn of the century. Developments in literary theory and criticism have been considered by Gerald Graff (1987), Vincent Leitch (1988), and others, while related developments in rhetoric have been discussed in the work of David Russell (1991) and Robert Connors (1991), as well as in my own work. The point I wish to underscore in considering these changes is that up until about 1970, the reading and writing practices taught in the English department responded in appropriate fashion to a curriculum and an economy that remained relatively impervious to alteration. This is not to deny that change in these realms took place. As Frederick Rudolph's *Curriculum: A History of the American Undergraduate Course of Study since 1636* (1977) makes clear, however, the curricular questions that continued to appear tended to repeat a few basic themes. The most important of these was that the curriculum failed to provide a stable core of general studies that unified the educational experience of students. This objection was never in any satisfactory way resolved. Instead, it was simply revived and given token attention from time to time.

The major reason for this complacency about the curriculum was that, despite acknowledged shortcomings, it was indeed doing the job of fulfilling the demands of the groups it most directly served, both within and outside the institution. Designed to prepare a workforce of trained professionals who could enhance the profits of diverse corporate enterprises, it accomplished its mission admirably during a time when the characteristics of economic activity remained relatively stable. Indeed, as economists of both the left and right agree, the economy of the United States during most of the twentieth century—despite the immense historical upheavals of drought, depression, and wars—pursued a fairly constant course. Changes have amounted to adjustments in basic configurations rather than to a major overhaul of them.

For most of the twentieth century, a college degree has been a ticket to prosperity. Business enterprises increased their profits through an application of the skills of trained professionals, while government agencies looked to educated experts to fulfill progressive social policies (Carroll and Noble 1979, 350-54). The elective system was created so that students could freely select the curriculum appropriate to their career ambitions. The common core curriculum was simultaneously abandoned—so that by 1897, the only required course for all students at bellwether Harvard was first-year composition. Later, general education requirements and core studies were introduced to address this excessive move to specialization and to provide students with a common intellectual and cultural orientation. Unfortunately, these core courses were usually taught by isolated experts from different disciplines who rarely communicated. Thus, at most schools, the only genuinely common and unifying experience in the curriculum remained first-year composition. At times, this course did try to bring an organizing force to bear, proposing a sense of common values along with instruction in writing (see Berlin 1987). This, however, is difficult to do within the frame of one or two semesters. Furthermore, teachers were more and more rewarded for being specialists, for disseminating knowledge that constituted their range of expertise, not for being liberal thinkers who explained the value of their discipline to society as a whole.

For the most part, there was no great concern about the fragmented curriculum. The Enlightenment conception of the unified, autonomous subject and confidence in the coherent metanarrative of progress governing the unfolding of historical events argued that the individual could make sense of the fragmented elective curriculum. It was left to the student to organize the smatterings of knowledge gathered from different departments. All of these would, taken together, finally provide a coherent formulation, because the universe was an organized whole, and the disciplines, after all, simply studied the various parts of this unified structure. In fact, this system did work well throughout most of the twentieth century, as graduates called on their specialized knowledge and their generalist courses in writing and speaking to serve the needs of the corporate workplace.

This period of stability ended in the 1970s. As has been repeatedly noted, capitalism underwent a major transformation at this time—a development characterized as a move from a Fordist to a post-Fordist node of production. Along with this rupture came a loss of faith in the effectiveness of the current college curriculum to prepare students in ways adequate to new conditions. Today, a new set of criticisms is being leveled at the curriculum. Along with this crisis in confidence in the larger educational structure has come a challenge to the work of English studies, the caretaker of reading and writing practices in the larger society. The major questions universities are asking themselves today thus revolve around the adequacy of their curriculum to the demands of the economic conditions of the moment. Related to this is an interrogation of the relevance of a college education to the political and cultural transformations of what has come to be called the postmodern era. In the next chapter, I will consider the convergences of these larger economic and social changes with the college curriculum and English studies.

II The Postmodern Predicament

3

Postmodernism, the College Curriculum, and English Studies

There is today considerable uncertainty about the value of the elective curriculum to students and society alike. This doubt is cultivated by the economic and social conditions of our moment. We daily witness dramatic changes in the nature of work and the configuration of the workforce. At the same time, intellectual revolutions are taking place in academic circles that are no less disruptive of the established practices of the various disciplines. These alterations have been commonly discussed under the rubric of the postmodern, a term found nearly as easily in the daily newspaper as in the abstract theoretical explorations of a Jean-François Lyotard, a Jurgen Habermas, or a Fredric Jameson—major disputants in a well-attended debate in academic journals and books.

In this chapter, I will discuss the economic and cultural conditions of the postmodern that are challenging traditional practices in the educational mission of colleges and universities. I will rely especially on the discussions of the postmodern found in David Harvey's *The Condition of Postmodernity* (1989) and in a collection of essays titled *New Times: The Changing Face of Politics in the 1990s* (1990), edited by Stuart Hall and Martin Jacques. Both texts consider this central historical concept in terms of its place in the development of international capitalism as well as its manifestations in the cultural arenas of art, philosophy, and forms of popular entertainment. In doing so, they take into account the various competing versions of the postmodern, offering an intelligent and articulate statement of the conflicting elements of this complex phenomenon.

Harvey and the contributors to Hall and Jacques's collection are especially useful in helping us understand the changing economic conditions for which we are preparing our students. The consequences of today's shift from a Fordist mode of production to the post-Fordist "regime of flexible accumulation" are dramatic and complex. And although most would argue that this shift represents an extension of the forces of modernism—an inevitable development of the trajectory of twentieth-century capitalism rather than a new stage of it—its disruptions nonetheless call for radically new responses at every level of our experience.

Fordism

In "Fordism and Post-Fordism" (1990), Robin Murray offers a succinct description of the mass production systems perfected (though not invented) by Henry Ford at his Michigan auto plants early in the twentieth century. These systems, Murray explains, were based on four principles. First, products and the parts and tasks that went into them were all standardized. Second, this standardization allowed many of the tasks needed for production to be mechanized. Third, the remaining jobs were "Taylorized" (after the efficiency principles articulated by Frederick Winslow Taylor), that is, "redesigned by work-study specialists on time-and-motion principles, who then instructed manual workers on how the job should be done" (39). Finally, factory production was organized along a nodal assembly line so that the products being assembled flowed past the workers. This method of production led to an economy of scale. As Murray explains, "although mass production might be more costly to set up because of the purpose-built machinery, once in place the cost of an extra unit was discontinuously cheap" (39). Of course, this mode of mass production depended on mass consumption, a pattern of buying in which consumers were accustomed to purchasing standardized products. It also demanded protected national markets so that companies could recover their production costs at home before any attempt to compete internationally.

Fordism created new kinds of workers. Unlike the craft mode of production, Fordist work was de-skilled and fragmented into a set of mechanized movements. This made for a rigid division between manual workers and mental workers. For the most part, manual workers were essentially interchangeable parts of the production machine and were paid according to the job they performed. As Murray explains, the "result was high labour turnover, shopfloor resistance, and strikes" (40). Managers constantly sought new laborers from rural areas, among immigrants, and from the marginalized in the cities. The Fordist mode of production also gave rise to a distinct group of managers, employees who were more and more likely to hold a college degree. Taylorism, however, was applied even at this level. Murray notes, "Fordist bureaucracies are fiercely hierarchical with links between the divisions and departments being made through the centre rather than at the base. Planning is done by specialists; rulebooks and guidelines are issued for lower management to carry out" (40). The bureaucratic structuring of mental work meant that even managers were often extensions of the machine, performing tasks that required little skill and training and that allowed almost no initiative. In this scheme, very few managers were required to display creativity or imagination in the implementation of their areas of expertise. Finally, the most important consequence of the Fordist regime was that an accommodation was reached between management and labor in which higher wages were exchanged for managerial control of production. After World War II, this system of collective bargaining on a national scale led to a period of growth and prosperity for large numbers of workers.

Fordism is finally based on these three interacting strands: "standardized production and consumption," "the semi-skilled worker and collective bargaining," and "a managed national market and centralized organisation" (Murray 1990, 41). Its practices were eventually extended to all parts of the economy, including agriculture and the service industries, and even to sectors of the state. As a number of commentators in *New Times* as well as Harvey (1989) and Jameson (1984, 1991) argue, its application of Enlightenment rationality also appears in politics and the diverse fields of culture, such as sports, dance, architecture, and art. Murray finally concludes his description of Fordism with a harsh evaluation: "The technological *hubris* of this outlook, its Faustian bargain of dictatorship in production in exchange for mass consumption, and above all its destructiveness in the name of progress and the economy of time, all this places Fordism at the centre of modernism" (41).

Post-Fordism

The Fordist mode of production still survives, of course, but it is rapidly being challenged by the regime of flexible accumulation, or post-Fordism. Their differences fall into three general categories. First, production becomes an international rather than a national process, a development made possible by technological changes in transportation and communication. Today a company might have its assembly plant in one country, its parts production in two or three other countries, and its markets in all of these and still others. Communication and the movement of technical experts, parts, and products among these various divisions are made possible by advances in electronics technology and modes of rapid transportation. Second, the small-batch production of a variety of goods replaces the mass production of homogeneous products. While corporations are larger, production operations are smaller and responsive to demand, not, as in the Fordist mode, to resources, the means of production, and the workforce. Subcontractors are more common, and they now share the risks of overproduction and underdemand, saving the larger corporation manufacturing capital. Third, the internationalization of corporations through the decentering of operations is in turn accompanied by the decentralizing of urban areas. Regional industrial zones and inner cities are abandoned in favor of "green sites" that come with tax concessions and promises of a better quality of life. Once again, all of this is made possible through the rapid means of communication and transportation facilitated by the technological compression of time and space. Clearly, the managers in this dispersed system must display extraordinary ability in communicating in written form, usually through the mastery of various electronic media.

There are two other central features of the new regime of flexible accumulation that are especially important. First, the financial system has been restructured on a global scale, so much so that, as Harvey (1989) explains, the result is "a single world market for money and credit supply" (161). The ties of capital to nation-states are accordingly weakened. Of equal importance, the role of the state in the economy has changed significantly. While under the Fordist-Keynesian regime governments were to intervene in the economy to redistribute wealth, "the easy accommodation between big capital and big government" is no longer operative (Harvey 1989, 170). The state must somehow manage to moderate the actions of capital in the interests of the nation while creating an attractive business climate that will not send businesses fleeing to the more generous policies of other countries.

These developments have had dramatic effects on the workforce. Well-paying unskilled manufacturing jobs continue to decline, accompanied by a destruction of the balance of power between management and workers. Employers now exert control over labor not seen since a much earlier period of capitalism. Harvey explains, "Flexible accumulation appears to imply relatively high levels of 'structural' (as opposed to 'frictional') unemployment, rapid destruction and reconstruction of skills, modest (if any) gains in the real wage, . . . and the rollback of trade union power—one of the political pillars of the Fordist regime" (147, 150). In the era of flexible accumulation, workers who hope to earn an adequate wage must perform multiple tasks, train on the job, and work well with others—requiring at once more adaptability and responsibility than under the Fordist mode.

At the same time, the workforce has been radically restructured. At the center is a core group of full-time managers. They enjoy job security, good promotion and reskilling prospects, and relatively generous pensions, insurance, and other fringe benefits. In return, they must be adaptable, flexible, and geographically mobile. This group is made up primarily of college graduates. Its numbers are kept small, however, as many companies now subcontract management tasks that under Fordism they performed themselves—advertising, for example. The competition for these safe jobs is becoming more and more intense, so that today a college degree provides only a permit to compete, not, as previously, a voucher for a more or less guaranteed position. Thus, in contrast to the modernist era, a college education no longer promises automatic upward mobility.

The consequences of not making it into this increasingly smaller upper tier are bleak. In the new employment pattern, the remaining workforce consists of two large groups. The first is made up of clerical, secretarial, routine, and lesser-skilled manual work positions. Since these jobs offer few career opportunities, there is great turnover in them. Their numbers are thus easily controlled in response to business conditions. The second group is composed of even less secure part-timers, casuals, temporaries, and public trainees. These jobs are the most unstable and offer the least compensation. While obviously some employees might enjoy the flexibility they provide, the effect for most workers is discouraging in terms of wages, insurance coverage, pension benefits, and job security. The net result of this new industrial organization has thus been a significant reduction in the ability of workers to organize for better wages, benefits, and conditions, particularly since they are isolated by the conditions of their employment.

The efforts of women to achieve parity in the workplace have been especially damaged by these developments. Women are central to this entire process. Since they are still the primary caregivers for the home and family throughout the industrial world, they are more likely to seek part-time work. As a labor force, they are thus easier to exploit, as they are substituted for their better paid and more secure male counterparts. Furthermore, this exploitation takes place in underdeveloped nations as well as industrialized countries. In many advanced capitalist nations, women make up 40 percent of the labor force, their numbers increasing at a time when well-paying, secure jobs are in decline and low-paying, unstable positions more and more prevalent.

One of the most obvious features of the employment picture today is the decreasing number of jobs in manufacturing and the increasing number in the service sector. The vast majority of the latter fall into the two unstable employment tiers and offer few attractions for most workers. There are, however, conspicuous exceptions. One obvious feature of flexible accumulation is that accelerating cycle time in production requires accelerating cycle time in consumption. The result is the growth of well-compensated workers—almost exclusively educated workers—in the business of producing the artifices of need inducement: advertising, public relations, and the like. As Harvey explains, the media, through advertising and other means, have encouraged "a postmodernist aesthetic that celebrates difference, ephemerality, spectacle, fashion, and the commodification of cultural forms" (156). Additional well-compensated service jobs have been created by new information industries that meet the increasing need for data to coordinate decentered operations as well as provide up-to-date analyses of market trends and possibilities. In flexible accumulation, markets are as much created as they are identified and so "control over information flow and over the vehicles for propagation of public taste and culture have likewise become vital weapons in competitive struggle" (Harvey 1989, 160).

So far we have seen that the managerial job market our students wish to enter values employees who are expert communicators, who are capable of performing multiple tasks, who can train quickly on the job, and who can work collaboratively with others. In sum, today's workers must combine greater flexibility and cooperation with greater intelligence and communicative ability. Any consideration of the postmodern, however, must also examine its social and cultural manifestations. These, I would argue, are largely a response to the changing economic forces I have just discussed and are, like them, both continuations of the modern and a sharp break with it. Recent social and cultural developments especially demonstrate the results of space-time compression.

We have the feeling we live in a decentered world, a realm of fragmentation and incoherence, without a nucleus or foundation for experience. Cities are without centers, except for shopping centers and industrial centers, neither of which is at the center of anything but itself. Our national culture seems decentered as we see more differences among our members than similarities. Furthermore, this perception is not without foundation. The 1980s witnessed the largest wave of immigration to the United States in two hundred years, totaling nearly nine million immigrants. The result is that 43.8 percent of the foreign-born in the United States arrived after 1980 (Margaret L. Usdansky, "Immigrant Tide Surges in the '80s," *USA Today,* 29 May 1992, 1A). Anxiety about this recent influx may be partly responsible for the lament for the lost Anglo-Saxon ideal—for example, in the insistence on the literary canon to ensure national unity through a common discourse (see Hirsch 1987, for example). Indeed, not since the huge immigrant influx at the turn of the century has there been such alarm about the endangered Anglo-Protestant cultural heritage, as we daily encounter the internationalization of our cities and experience a variety of international cultures on TV and in other media. We even have an "English Only" movement in some states, as if legislation could somehow undo the work of economic and social forces, changing a group's culture in the swipe of a pen. Space has been compressed so that the geographic borders of the United States no longer provide the security and simple-minded insularity they once did. Multiculturalism is a reality of daily experience, not a mere politically correct shibboleth of the left.

We also experience time compression in the world of fast foods, fast cars, and fast fads. Ours is declared the age of image and spectacle, and we are daily bombarded by a variety of sensory assaults—from the shopping center to the TV. Manners, modes, and styles are constantly in flux. This compression extends to history, too, as styles of earlier times in clothing, architecture, and art are freely appropriated, merging the past and present in "pastiche" (Jameson 1984, 1991). The most ordinary shopping expedition encounters the random arrangement of products from different societies and times. We live in the culture of the "simulacrum," of simulations that take on a life of their own, appearing more "real" than what they represent—even more real than immediate material conditions. The cultivated images and spectacles of other eras and places are celebrated as an opportunity to live from one intense experience to another (Baudrillard 1988). For those with the means and time, life becomes a rich succession of manufactured events, a simulation of the past or future, the end being detachment from the concrete material and social conditions of one's own historical moment. One defeats time and space and escapes the depressing features of daily life—the dark side of the new regime—through manufactured public performance.

Much of this, I would argue, is facilitated by the regime of flexible accumulation. The decentering of the city is, in large part, a response to the international economy and its time and space compression. The constant bombardment of advertising images is a result of the need to create new demands and desires to sell products. There is little that advertisers will not exploit to sell commodities—from classical music to high art to canonical drama. Advertisements continually create narratives for us to enter. On the other hand, the processes of decentering and fragmentation have shaken the foundations of our experience. Our faith in the universal laws of reason and the centrality of the Western cultural heritage in the larger world has eroded. Much of the chauvinism and the nostalgia for traditional forms of art and experience in the United States may in part be an elaborate reaction to this erosion, an effort to will into existence a world that is no more.

These larger economic, political, and cultural transformations are accompanied by dramatic disruptions in traditional conceptions and practices in philosophy, history, art, and science. Postmodernism in the academy has led to challenges in our understanding of the subject, language, epistemology, history, and the relation of all of these to each other. I will consider this shift in detail in the next chapter. Here I want to interrogate the adequacy of the modernist curriculum to the economic and cultural conditions I have just described.

The modified elective curriculum, which has been the center of a college education since around the turn of the century, was able to resist criticism because it delivered what graduates, government leaders, and employers most wanted: a secure class of skilled managers whose well-compensated expertise would increase profits. Any accusation that universities failed to provide an educated citizenry or cultivated patrons of the arts or well-rounded individuals could be ignored as long as both employers and workers were pleased with the economic benefits of higher education. As we have seen, the configuration of the workforce today has threatened this happy arrangement. In the post-Fordist environment, a college degree no longer ensures a secure job and a comfortable way of life. It is more likely instead to be no more than a certificate qualifying a graduate to compete for one of the comfortable positions at the center of the job circle. A Labor Department study released in 1992, for example, indicated that between 1984 and 1990, 20 percent of college graduates were underemployed or unemployed. This figure is expected to rise to 30 percent between 1993 and 2005 (Greenwald 1993, 36).

Discontent on the part of graduates facing an uncertain job market after the effort and expense of four or five years in school is meanwhile echoed by the dissatisfaction of employers with the educated workers they are hiring. In 1987, Badi G. Foster, president of Aetna Life and Casualty Company's Institute for Corporate Education, charged that "universities have become decoupled from the needs of business and industry," largely because professors spend too much time in research and too little time on "education of the kind that we need" (quoted in Blitz and Hurlbert 1992, 10-11). Speaking on the same occasion, Owen B. Butler, former chairman of the Proctor and Gamble Company, explained that he thought there were "two essentials for employability, and only two." The first was "the ability to speak and to hear, to read and write the English Language fluently and with true comprehension and true ability to articulate ideas." The second was "work habits, attitudes, and behavior patterns" (quoted in Blitz and Hurlbert 1992, 9). On both scores, he found American education wanting. College graduates, employers commonly tell us, are technically competent, but they lack the ability to communicate and are reluctant to seek out and solve problems creatively. Thus, neither graduates (with the exception, of course, of those who land the decreasing number of good positions) nor employers are particularly happy with the relationship of the college curriculum to the conditions of work life. Experts on the workforce are meanwhile convinced that major reforms in education are needed to meet the needs of the new economy.

There is no simple way to address this dissatisfaction. College graduates argue that the university should offer better preparation for the workforce. This suggests consultations with prospective employers about bringing the curriculum more in line with job demands. Unfortunately, these efforts offer little help. In "Cults of Culture" (1992), Michael Blitz and C. Mark Hurlbert analyze the script of nine days of hearings held by the Subcommittee on Education and Health of the Joint Economic Committee of the United States Congress in 1987. It is immediately obvious from these hearings that many of the complaints leveled against schools and colleges are often simply an attempt to shift to new workers the blame for the failures of top managers or the vagaries of the market. Congressman James H. Scheuer, for example, explained that the goal of literacy education must be "to provide our industries with adequately trained and educated workers and to halt the deteriorating position of our nation in world commerce" (quoted in Blitz and Hurlbert 1992, 89). For Scheuer, workers and schools, not inappropriate management responses to the changing conditions of the post-Fordist economy, were responsible for the economic losses of the 1980s. Ronald Reagan's Secretary of Labor, William E. Brock, warned that if schools continued to ignore the advice of business and military leaders, "We're going to leave our people without the kind of skills that are going to be needed to hold a job in the United States. If we don't change, we're going to have to import those people" (quoted in Blitz and Hurlbert 1992, 11). Once again, unemployment is not the result of the massive "downsizing" (read "huge layoffs") of the workforce brought about by automation, the use of temporary workers, and the loss of manufacturing jobs to cheaper labor markets, but of the failure of workers to bring with them the necessary literacy skills to compete in the new high-tech economy.

I do not wish to suggest that schools are blameless in the recent economic crisis. They must indeed reexamine what they are doing. Yet expecting business to provide ideas and direction for the effort is a mistake. First of all, when corporate leaders attempt to dictate what ought to take place in universities—in order, that is, to prepare better workers—they commonly offer a host of contradictions. As Blitz and Hurlbert found time and again, the standards voiced by corporate leaders call for workers who are at once creative and aggressive in identifying and solving problems and submissive and unquestioningly cooperative in carrying out the orders of superiors. According to Richard E. Heckert, chairman of DuPont Corporation, workers must display "good work habits and attitude; and an understanding of American economic and social life. The essence of this is learning how to learn, and learning how to behave" (quoted in Blitz and Hurlbert 1992, 9). The two sets of demands simply do not always square with each other. Furthermore, the frequently voiced charge that college professors should teach traditional knowledge rather than searching out and disseminating new discoveries flies directly in the face of the need of the workforce for up-to-date information and training.

The changing complexity of the workforce, with its three-tiered hierarchy, further complicates any simple effort to adjust the curriculum to the employment market. As Samuel Bowles and Herbert Gintis (1976) have demonstrated, higher education is already organized along hierarchical lines. Job placement and earnings correlate with the kind of school a person attends: community college, low-prestige private or state college, or high-prestige private or state college. These divisions are partly the result of the conscious vocational choices students make. For example, dental technicians make less than teachers, who make less than engineers or doctors, but those who choose these careers are aware of these differences in advance. More, however, than individual choice is involved in these disparities. A degree, say, in engineering from MIT or Cal Tech or Purdue is worth more on average over a career than a comparable degree from a less prestigious program. Such differences are based on conditions that will be difficult for any change in curriculum to address and so are outside the present discussion.

The larger point I wish to make is that no one ought to expect that colleges should build into the curriculum, particularly in their offerings in the humanities, such hierarchical divisions and vocational choices—say, one set of texts and reading practices for one tier of students and another set and reading practices for another tier. In other words, while professional training may vary from school to school, there is every reason to expect that the kind of knowledge and competencies that English studies provides will be fairly consistent. Trying to adjust the college curriculum exactly to the minute configurations of the job market is out of the question.

At the same time, I do not think that we in the academy can simply ignore the advice of employers. We must finally provide a college education that enables workers to be excellent communicators, quick and flexible learners, and cooperative collaborators. Indeed, many of the recent changes in the English department reflect this effort. The increase in the number of undergraduate writing courses as well as graduate programs in rhetoric and composition has been encouraged by college administrators responding to the appeals of graduates, employers, and professional schools. The emphasis on learning diverse writing practices in literature courses is also on the rise, as indicated, for example, by almost any issue of *College English.* Furthermore, as Lester Faigley (1992) has demonstrated, courses that prepare students for the dispersed electronic communication characteristic of the post-Fordist economy are also increasing. One of Faigley's mid-level writing courses at the University of Texas at Austin, for example, relies on a networked computer system. Students spend half of the term conducting large-group discussions through the system, learning the difficulties of communicating exclusively through electronically produced texts.

In addition, Mas'ud Zavarzadeh and Donald Morton (1992) have argued that the abstract mode of thinking encouraged in postmodern literary studies prepares students for the decentered conditions of the new economy. I would concur in this judgment and will later explore its consequences for the classroom. (I will also consider reservations I share with them about some of the unfortunate effects of this development.) Writing courses have also encouraged collaboration both through peer-editing and group-composed assignments, the latter a common feature of courses in professional communication. Even some literature courses are experimenting with group efforts. An openness to the differences of other cultures, both at home and abroad, is also fostered in literature courses that extend the reading list beyond the more or less traditional western European and American literary canon as well as in writing courses that take as their subject cultural differences. All of these developments promote both the kinds of literacy and the quick and flexible learning required in the postmodern workplace.

In short, English departments are indeed moving in the direction of preparing students for work in the postmodern economy. I would argue once again, however, that this can never be a simple accommodation to the marketplace. It can never be simply a matter of "learning how to learn, and learning how to behave," as Heckert would have it. We must instead measure our efforts against a larger institutional objective. Colleges ought to offer a curriculum that places preparation for work within a comprehensive range of democratic educational concerns. Regardless of whether students are headed for the highest or lowest levels of the job market, we ought to provide them with at least an understanding of the operation of the workforce as a whole. This will require preparation in dealing with the abstract and systemic thinking needed for the dispersed conditions of postmodern economic and cultural developments, in distinct contrast to the atomistic, linear, and narrowly empirical mode often encouraged by modern conditions. Students need a conception of the abstract organizational patterns that affect their work lives—indeed, comprehensive conceptions of the patterns that influence all of their experiences.

In addition, students deserve an education that prepares them to be critical citizens of the nation that now stands as one of the oldest democracies in history. The United States has seldom considered it sufficient to educate students exclusively for work. The insistence that students also be prepared to become active and critical agents in shaping the economic, social, political, and cultural conditions of their historical moment has been a valuable commonplace in this nation's educational discussions. And while I will admit that this position has not always been overwhelmingly dominant, it has never been altogether absent in curriculum formation in U.S. schools and colleges (Spring 1986, 45).

From this democratic political perspective, knowledge is a good that ought to serve the interests of the larger community as well as individuals (a prime motive, incidentally, for the formation of land-grant colleges in the last century). It must be situated, however, in relation to larger economic, social, political, and cultural considerations. Students must learn to locate the beneficiaries and the victims of knowledge, exerting their rights as citizens in a democracy to criticize freely those in power. I realize that we have just been through a period in which the end of education was conspicuously declared to be primarily the making of money. The counterproposal offered here, however, is in keeping with one of the oldest notions of education we in the United States possess, eloquently proclaimed in the American pragmatist philosophy of John Dewey. Here, the interests of the larger community and the integrity of the individual must be paramount. This is true whether we are discussing the activities of government or of large corporations. This educational scheme is designed to make human beings and their experience in a community the measure of all things—in this, as Susan Jarratt (1991) indicates, echoing the sophist Protagoras. In short, education exists to provide intelligent, articulate, and responsible citizens who understand their obligation and their right to insist that economic, social, and political power be exerted in the best interests of the community. If pursuing this objective somehow renders our students less acceptable to employers, then the flaw can hardly be located in the students or their schools. To use the term proffered by Henry Giroux (1988), the work of education in a democratic society is to provide "critical literacy."

I would also invoke in support of my position the many liberal critics who propose economic democracy as the most appropriate response to present global conditions. One of the best arguments is offered by Robert N. Bellah, Richard Madsen, William M. Sullivan, Ann Swidler, and Steven M. Tipton in *The Good Society* (1991). They propose an alternative to the radically individualistic and hierarchical modes of production and work relations found in both entrepreneurial and Fordist regimes. Indeed, invoking Robert Reich, Michael Piore and Charles Sabel, Shoshana Zuboff, and others, they argue that post-Fordism requires new forms of cooperation in production, distribution, exchange, and consumption that call for democratic arrangements throughout the workplace. While the argument of Bellah's group is too complex to rehearse in detail here, I would like to summarize its major features.

This recommendation would require comprehensive planning to take into account the quality of life of all members of society. Such planning demands that the interaction of the political and the economic be recognized so that the economic not be treated as beyond the intercession of the public in serving its own good. Corporations, we are reminded, are legal entities that must be held accountable for the consequences of their acts on the environment, workers, and citizens. Furthermore, given the radically collaborative nature of the post-Fordist production process, corporations must themselves participate in this decision making to ensure maximum productivity. At the same time, the division of the workforce into a small group of the comfortably secure, on the one hand, and a large group of the poorly compensated and expendable, on the other, must be challenged in the name of social justice. Finally, the new economic democracy would require consumers whose buying habits are intelligent responses to the needs of the community, not simply an extension of personal interest. The proposal for refiguring English studies that I am offering here is meant to encourage the program of Bellah's group for economic democracy and to simultaneously insist that the promise of our political democracy be met. This notion of education's mission leads to a consideration of the cultural conditions of the postmodern economy and their relation to English studies.

I would argue that our colleges, despite the inadequacies of the modernist curriculum, are much better equipped to prepare workers for the new job market than they are to prepare citizens for the quotidian cultural conditions of our new economy. In other words, our students are more likely to acquire the abilities and dispositions that will enable them to become successful workers than the abilities and dispositions to make critical sense of this age of image and spectacle, to understand their daily experience in a postmodern culture. When it comes to understanding the creation and fulfillment of desire through the use of the media, for example, our students receive virtually no guidance from their schools. Students in the United States ought to be formally prepared to critique the images that today occupy the center of politics, as students are, for example, in parts of Canada and the United Kingdom (see Brown 1991). While there is no denying that many of our young people arrive at sophisticated strategies for negotiating the messages of the media on their own (see McRobbie 1984, for example), negotiating these messages is too important a part of daily life to be left to chance. In this age of spectacle, democracy will rise or fall on our ability to offer a critical response to these daily experiences.

A key argument of this book is that English studies has a special role in the democratic educational mission. It is, after all, the only discipline required of all students in the schools, even including in most states four years in high school. The college English department prepares the teachers who staff these English classrooms, so that its influence always extends far beyond its own hallways. Furthermore, for the vast majority of college students, first-year composition is a necessary ritual of passage into higher education (Bartholomae 1985). English studies has also historically served as the center of liberal education, assuming the role the rhetoric course played in the nineteenth-century college. English courses have been looked upon as the support and stay of certain ethical and political values since at least the turn of the century. They have even served in times of crises—for example, major wars, the Great Depression—as rallying points for encouraging certain values. As Applebee, Graff, and I have indicated in our disciplinary histories, Matthew Arnold's call for literature as the surrogate for religion in a secular society was embraced with great seriousness of purpose in the United States.

I would like to close this chapter with an example of one of the important societal functions of English studies. Harvey (1989) has deplored what he calls the "aestheticization of politics," by which he means the insertion of a myth between the realm of truth and the realm of ethical action. This myth is a highly clichéd and simplistic narrative that, nevertheless, provides a coherent basis for action. For Harvey, this process is suspect, because the coherence is purchased at the price of ignoring the contradictions posed by actual material conditions, privileging a misguided and partial narrative, most commonly about a nation-state and its destiny. Such a narrative escapes critique since it is accepted without reflection, by its nature immune to self-analysis and investigation in its obliviousness to historical events. The aestheticization of politics thus prevents us from forming adequate cognitive maps, to use Jameson's phrase, that represent economic, social, political, and cultural conditions in a manner more nearly adequate to their complexity. Cognitive maps are for Jameson (1991) "something like a spatial analogue of Althusser's great formulation of ideology itself, as 'the Imaginary representation of the subject's relationship to his or her Real conditions of existence"' (415). In other words, cognitive maps provide our imaginary conception of the larger conditions that influence our daily lives.

I would like to consider a number of observations about this aestheticization. First of all, as Terry Eagleton (1990) has demonstrated, Kant was the first to theorize the aesthetic as the mediator between the realm of knowledge and the realm of morality. Renato Barilli (1989) in his history of rhetoric has indicated that in this move Kant was installing the newly formulated concept of the aesthetic in the position that rhetoric had historically played. In other words, the mediator between the realm of what we know to be true and the realm of what we know to be virtuous was historically found in the deliberation of public discourse—as in Aristotle, for example. (The ancient Athenians also allowed for the role of the aesthetic in politics, at certain times even paying citizens to attend the theater. Rhetorical deliberation in the agora, however, was always the center of political life.) Public discourse thus provided the means for enacting a practical course of action, a course always considered to be contingent and probable in nature, as distinct from the greater certainty of philosophical knowledge, including ethics. Kant's insertion of the aesthetic in place of the rhetorical was quite self-conscious on his part, since Kant, never guilty of democratic sympathies, was extremely distrustful of public discourse as a means for resolving political questions. This Kantian wariness of rhetoric has been a permanent fixture of the English department, which has historically forwarded the aesthetic text, the rhetorical characterized as merely scientific and so lacking a human dimension or as failed art and so inherently suspect.

The important consideration here, contrary to what Harvey would argue, is that this aestheticization of politics is a normal feature of our response to political events today. Indeed, the political is always in one sense aesthetic, and the aesthetic is always political. As Roland Barthes has so ably demonstrated in *Mythologies* (1972) and elsewhere, placing the incidents of a particular moment within the context of a narrative that offers an explanatory frame for them is one of the key features in our interpretation of daily occurrences. And if we do indeed customarily shape our understanding of everyday affairs in terms of certain narratives that guide us in our responses, then the role of English studies in suggesting and reinforcing possible narratives for us to call upon in responding to our experience is crucial. Thus, in choosing the texts we are to read and in providing the interpretive strategies we are to use in responding to them, English studies plays an immensely important role in consciousness formation. The danger is not that we will see events in terms of narrative patterns. A central purpose of this book is to insist that such narratives are inevitable in responding to the complex conditions of our experience, enabling us to make sense of the myriad and confusing details of the postmodern. The danger here—and now we are back to Harvey's fear—is that our narrative patterns will be dangerously simplistic, concealing conflicts and contradictions in the name of self-interest. As a result, rhetoric must always be a part of our narrative frames, providing a critique of their operation.

Harvey locates an obvious failed narrative in the recent turn to simplistic myths of localism and nationalism as a response to the internationalization of economics and politics, culminating in "charismatic politics (Thatcher's Falklands War, Reagan's invasion of Grenada)" (306)—and, more recently, I might add, the Persian Gulf War. These are clear cases in which the narrative frame provided for a certain set of events concealed the complex interests that were actually at stake. What was needed in these cases was a more inclusive narrative, one able to take in the vast materials that the current narrative simply removed from view. In the following chapters, I will consider the work of a refigured English studies in supplying such narratives.

4

Postmodernism in the Academy

John Schilb (1991) has explained that postmodernism "can designate a critique of traditional epistemology, a set of artistic practices, and an ensemble of larger social conditions" (174). I have already discussed a number of the larger economic, social, and cultural developments at stake in the concept and related them to the college curriculum in general and to English studies in particular. The challenge to traditional epistemological notions today is no less dramatic. At first glance, these matters seem to be of concern solely to isolated academics and intellectuals. After all, businesspeople, government policy makers, purveyors of popular culture, and even most artists are less concerned with discussing the theoretical consequences of the changes we are witnessing than in devising ways to respond to them. I would argue, however, that the theoretical discussions so central to intellectual debates in the human sciences today are in fact directly encouraged by the economic, social, and cultural changes that surround us. In other words, these discussions are necessary responses to the changing world in which we live. Far from being the self-indulgent musings of careerist academics, these theoretical discussions respond to alterations in our basic understanding of self, society, and the nature of human value fostered by today's economic and cultural conditions.

This chapter is divided into three parts. In the first, I will summarize the major theoretical developments at issue in postmodern philosophical discussions, calling on a broad range of thinkers. These developments involve revised notions of the nature of signifying practices, the status of the experiencing subject, and the role of metanarratives in responding to human affairs. In the second part, I will argue that these concepts are capable of a broad range of uses, extending across the entire ideological spectrum. My main concern here will be to outline the ways these concepts have been called upon both explicitly and implicitly to deflect any critique of current economic and political conditions. In the third part, I will offer a theoretical response to the disruptions of postmodern theory, indicating a way challenges to signification, subject formation, and explanatory metanarratives can be addressed so as to encourage critical literacy rather than a passive acquiescence to things as they are.

Postmodern Theory

Postmodern theoretical discussions radically alter our conception of the nature and function of signifying practices, of language in its broadest designation. Language is no longer a set of transparent signifiers that records an externally present thing-in-itself, a simple signaling device that stands for and corresponds to the separate realities that lend it meaning. Language is instead a pluralistic and complex system of signification that constructs realities rather than simply presenting or reflecting them. Our conceptions of material and social phenomena, then, are fabrications of signification, the products of culturally coded signs.

Saussure (1966), the prime influence in structuralist formulations in Europe, first demonstrated the way language functions as a set of differences. The sounds that are significant in any given language are arbitrary, deriving their meaning not in relation to any external referents but in a contrastive relation to other sounds. For example, the sound *t* is significant in English because it contrasts with *d*—making for a difference in meaning between such words as *to* and *do* or *tip* and *dip*. The sound contrasts necessary for meaning in a given language are thus arbitrary selections from the entire repertoire of sounds available to the human vocal system and constitute only a fraction of the possibilities. This principle of structural significance—that is, meaning as a function of the relation of contrasting elements in a larger structure—is also found in the vocabulary and grammar of a language. Thus, a term has meaning because it stands in oppositional relation to other terms of its class—for example, other nouns. A term's meaning is also significant by virtue of its contrastive relation to other structures within a sentence. For example, in English a noun appears in a distinct position and form in relation to the position and form of a verb in making a meaningful sentence.

The revolutionary conclusion of Saussure's work was that signifiers have meaning as a result of their relation to other signifiers in a structured system of signs, not by virtue of their relation to external signifieds. Languages thus organize and communicate experience in different, arbitrary, and unpredictable ways. Saussure remained confident, however, that the speaking voice, as distinct from the written, was capable of directly representing features of the external world. In other words, while language was arbitrary in its sounds and grammar, it could be made to stand for concepts corresponding to external realities, concepts that could be shared by subjects speaking face to face.

During the course of his career, Saussure suggested that it might be possible to develop a science of signs that would extend his understanding of linguistic structure to the entire range of human behavior, indicating that culture might be arranged in the organized manner of a language. This project was successfully taken up by the French anthropologist Claude Levi-Strauss. Levi-Strauss (1963) demonstrated that, just as a sound or term or grammatical marker has meaning by virtue of its contrastive relation to other elements in its category, so do the key signifiers of a culture fall into binary relations with each other in the formation of cultural grammars or codes of behavior. For example, the term *man* in a particular society derives its meaning from its binary relation to some other term or terms in the society's language, not from the biological characteristics of a person. Thus, terms are socially indicated, not produced by simple material determinants. To be a "man" in one society often differs radically from being a "man" in another. Levi-Strauss also demonstrated that the key binaries of a culture are arranged hierarchically, so that one term is privileged, considered more important than its related term. His work finally demonstrated the ways these important terms form narratives—what he called myths—that govern the behavior of a culture in its everyday operations. These narratives indicate what is important to the life of the culture and instruct its members in behavior appropriate to their place in the social hierarchy.

Roland Barthes applied these methods of structural anthropology in an analysis of a set of everyday cultural experiences in Paris. In *Mythologies* (1972), he demonstrated the ways that signs form semiotic systems that extend beyond natural language to all realms of a culture—film, television, photography, food, fashion, automobiles, even professional wrestling. Using key terms and levels of connotation, he analyzed ordinary cultural events to reveal their encouragement of race, class, and gender codes as well as larger economic and social narratives guiding human behavior. Writing as a Marxist, Barthes was especially interested in displaying the dominance of bourgeois ideological categories of thought and action.

Yet these structuralist modes of investigation in the human sciences were soon seriously challenged. Indeed, Barthes himself was a part of this effort. The most formidable of these challenges came in the work of Jacques Derrida. Since Derrida's work is extensive, complex, and still in progress, I will consider only the barest of its elements, focusing in particular on the central place that *différance* holds in his system. This term is a neologism that, as Vincent Leitch (1983) points out, stands for at least three meanings: "(1) 'to differ'—to be unlike or dissimilar in nature, quality, or form; (2) 'differre' (Latin)—to scatter, disperse; and (3) 'to defer'—to delay, postpone" (41).

For Derrida (1976), *différance* describes the relations of terms in binary opposition to each other. He acknowledges that this opposition gives a term its significance within a larger system of meanings. At this point, however, Derrida parts company with the structuralists. For Derrida, the term is detached from its signified, indeed, so much so that it is always and evermore different from what it represents. This detachment means that signifiers are never in contact with things-in-themselves, but are constructions totally formed of their own operation. In other words, a term has significance only in relation to the term with which it is contrasted and is not in any way related to the signified it claims to represent.

This principle leads to Derrida's critique of "logocentrism," the insistence that the spoken word is in direct contact with reality, establishing the presence of a genuine signified, while the written word offers only a distant shadow of the real. Derrida denounces this founding principle of structuralist linguistics. He first of all argues that there is no presence of the thing-in-itself in the concept uttered, only the play of differences. This makes writing the primary form of language, because writing demonstrates the system of differences on which meaning is based. In other words, in examining the larger system of language necessary to write and read, we come into contact with the principle of difference that underlies all language. Writing becomes a metaphor for *différance,* displaying the systemic nature of language in its total reliance on other elements within its confines and its total difference from that which it is supposed to represent. Writing comes to stand for the very act of making meaning in language. Derrida's charge of logocentrism is most forcefully leveled at philosophical discourse, since philosophers claim to offer the foundations of all knowledge, the essential principles that underlie the universe. For Derrida, they instead offer only the play of language in its eternal difference from that which it represents and, finally, in its eternal difference from itself.

Derrida's second use of *différance,* to scatter or disperse, is meant to demonstrate that significance is never in a term itself but in its relation to another term. Thus, meaning is never found in the presence of a single term but in its relation to a term not present, an absent term. At the most obvious level, when we use a term, we do not indicate its binary opposite, although this term too is at play in establishing meaning. We now see Derrida's second means of denying presence. Just as meaning is not present in the relation of the spoken term to that which it represents, it is also not present in the signifier itself, since the meaning of this signifier is always located in a relation to an absent signifier. This leads to Derrida's third meaning of *différance,* to defer, as in delaying or postponing. The total meaning of a signifier is never fully established, since it always points to another signifier to establish its claim. The signifier is thus always deferring, putting off meaning. Likewise, it always occupies a position of deference in relation to an absent term that is necessary for its existence. Signs, therefore, are always traces of other signs, never offering the presence of the signified.

Derrida further destabilizes signification by insisting that *différance* cannot be controlled. A signifier's difference from its signified and from itself, its scattering and dispersal of signification, and its deferral of meaning make up the inevitable operation of all language acts. This process is aleatory and thus unpredictable, beyond the control of any person or group. Just as a speaker never has the entire significance of a term available to consciousness even as he or she uses it, a speaker can likewise never predict the significance the term will have for an audience, since listeners will receive it differently. We are thus all spoken by language as much as language is spoken by us. In short, language has an uncontrollable life of its own.

All of this constitutes a devastating critique of both Saussure and Levi-Strauss. From the Derridian perspective, Saussure is guilty of logocentrism in his privileging of the spoken voice over the written text. Thus, while he insists on the arbitrary relation of the signifier to the signified, Saussure sees a warrant for true discourse in the presence of the speaking subject referring to the actual concept in consciousness. Writing offers no authorizing subject that can attest to the actual presence of the signifieds represented, but speech gives the thing-in-itself. Yet Derrida denies that the signifier can ever capture the external signified. He also argues against the notion of a unitary concept, seeing in all concepts the free play of linguistic difference. A concept signifies by virtue of what it does not signify, which is not present and, indeed, can never be totally brought to presence. Derrida also faults this privileging of orality over literacy because it fails to realize that all signification is based on the operation of the system as a whole, a system best discovered in the scheme of writing.

Derrida finds in Levi-Strauss this same privileging of the spoken voice over writing. Levi-Strauss further denigrates writing by identifying it with the corruptions of civilization. This in turn points to his continual preference for nature over culture, locating in "primitive" societies the realization of natural truths corrupted by civilization. For Derrida, the nature-culture binary is still another attempt to locate presence, the foundation for some essential truths that are the same everywhere and always. It is finally simply another device to locate some external origin for humanly constructed knowledge. Still, despite this tendency toward privileging origins, Levi-Strauss begins the work of deconstruction by frequently acknowledging the arbitrariness of such binaries. From Derrida's perspective, Levi-Strauss starts the effort of breaking down the artificially imposed boundaries of nature-culture, subject-object, speaking-writing, center-margin, origin-imitation, and their logocentric correlatives.

The structuralist and poststructuralist conceptions of signification have dramatic consequences for our understanding of the self and its formation. The unified, coherent, autonomous, self-present subject of the Enlightenment has been the centerpiece of liberal humanism. From this perspective, the subject is a transcendent consciousness that functions unencumbered by the social and material conditions of experience, acting as a free and rational agent that adjudicates competing claims for action. In other words, the individual is the author of all his or her behavior, moving in complete freedom in deciding the conditions of his or her experience. The critique of this Enlightenment subject has been offered by a host of thinkers, most prominently Emil Benveniste, Jacques Lacan, Roland Barthes, Michel Foucault, and, of course, Derrida. Here I will offer a brief sketch of the major consequences of their positions for our understanding of the subject, although I realize that in doing so I imply a coherence among them that does not exist.

The speaking, acting subject is no longer considered unified, rational, autonomous, or self-present. Instead, each person is regarded as the construction of the various signifying practices, the uses of language and cultural codes, of a given historical moment. In other words, the subject is not the source and origin of these practices but is finally their product. This means that each of us is formed by the various discourses and sign systems that surround us. These include not only everyday uses of language (discursive formations) in the home, school, the media, and other institutions, but the material conditions (nondiscursive formations) that are arranged in the manner of languages—that is, semiotically—including such things as the clothes we wear, the way we carry our bodies, and the way our school and home environments are arranged. These signifying practices are languages that tell us who we are and how we should behave in terms of such categories as gender, race, class, age, ethnicity, and the like. The result is that each of us is heterogeneously made up of various competing discourses, conflicted and contradictory scripts, that make our consciousness anything but unified, coherent, and autonomous. At the most everyday level, for example, the discourses of the school and the home about appropriate behavior ("Just say 'No'") are frequently at odds with the discourses provided by peers and the media ("Go for it"). In short, we are constituted by subject formations and subject positions that do not always square with each other. To state the case in its most extreme form, each of us is finally conflicted, incoherent, amorphous, protean, and irrational in our very constitution.

These anti-foundational, anti-essentialist assaults on Enlightenment conceptions of the subjects and objects of experience are also demonstrated in the critique of Enlightenment claims for the power of reason in arriving at universal truths. The two most conspicuous figures in this effort are Foucault and Jean-François Lyotard, although Derrida is of course involved too.

Foucault's effort as a philosopher of history and as a practicing historian was to dispute attempts to locate simple continuities and identities in the past. In "Nietzsche, Genealogy, History" (1980), he argues that traditional historians impute one of two narratives to the events of history. The first involves a progressive improvement in the human condition over time, with the present representing the culmination of human achievement. The other argues that the past represents a perfect origin from which humankind has strayed, so that history will be fulfilled only with a return to the old ways. Both narrative patterns are based on a confidence in subjects as completely free makers of history and in reason as the principle undergirding human action. Against these stories of continuity, Foucault demonstrates historical irruptions, dramatic changes in historical conditions that cannot be accounted for in terms of either coherent narratives or rational principles.

When Foucault analyzes the role of humans in the historical process, he finds anything but freedom and reason. This is particularly the case in his examination of the Enlightenment and its aftermath. In his discussions of the formation of prisons, schools, hospitals, and asylums, Foucault depicts individuals as the instruments of impersonal institutions, structures designed to serve their own interests, not the interests of those who pass through them. Human subjects are thus products of power-knowledge formations. In other words, discursive and non-discursive structures are organized to create conditions of knowing that produce regimes of power. Reason and truth are shibboleths that conceal the irrational forces of domination and discipline that rule human institutions. Foucault is particularly interested in exploring those historical events that represent resistance to the dominant power-knowledge formations, stories of the victims of history that have been ignored. Here the coherent narratives of conventional histories are especially repudiated.

In *The Postmodern Condition* (1984), Jean-François Lyotard considers the disruptions in Enlightenment epistemology that mark contemporary intellectual activity. He explains the loss of faith in metanarratives that see history as the work of freedom and progress, as found, for instance, in Hegel, Marx, or in liberal accounts of inevitable economic or scientific betterment. The large narratives of both capitalism and socialism are discredited in Lyotard's description, depicted as misguided attempts to control nature and humans in the service of particular interests, not enactments of foundational truths. Even science is called into question as just one more metanarrative credible only because of what it excludes. In short, Lyotard argues that the postmodern condition denounces the Enlightenment faith in reason, totalizing truth claims, and historical coherence. Lyotard proposes that these be replaced by the *"petit recit,"* a limited and localized account that attempts to come to terms with features of experience that grand narratives exclude. As we have seen, structuralist and poststructuralist analyses of sign systems look for the binary opposites of key terms, the unspoken marginalized signifiers that usually go unmentioned. Similarly, postmodern investigations in the physical and human sciences should look for dissensus rather than consensus, for what traditional accounts of knowledge have excluded and ignored. Most important, attempts to offer sweeping metanarratives should be abandoned. Finally, Lyotard relates his analysis of the postmodern to the conditions of post-industrial society—the age of computers, information technology, and space-time compression, all of which challenge traditional epistemological notions.

Assessing the Damage

These theoretical claims have evoked a broad range of responses. As Lester Faigley (1992) has demonstrated, conservatives have often simply denounced them as egregious errors that must be resisted or ignored at all costs (28-30). Maxine Hairston (1990), former chair of the College Composition and Communication Conference, for example, asserted in a *College English* essay that postmodern theoretical discussions should be banned from NCTE publications. Leftists, meanwhile, have often demonstrated a similar response, declaring the challenge to Marxist positions offered by the new theory just one more bourgeois mystification. Even so incisive a theorist as Terry Eagleton, for example, initially displayed unrestrained hostility to postmodern speculation. Such dismissive reactions, however, cannot be given too much credibility, since I am convinced they will eventually fall by the side as workers in English studies begin to see the important consequences of postmodern theory for their discipline. This thought is simply too compelling to hope that ignoring it, banning it, or directing spleen in its direction will make it go away. Indeed, the position on postmodern theory that I am convinced needs the most careful response at this time is far removed from denial or extreme skepticism. Embracing what is sometimes called "ludic postmodernism," a number of observers have uncritically welcomed the new thinking, finding it an exhilarating and liberating ingredient of our historical moment. Because of the important consequences of this position for English studies, I would like to examine it a bit more carefully.

David Harvey opens *The Condition of Postmodernity* (1989) with a discussion of Jonathan Raban's *Soft City*, an account of upper-middle-class life in London in the early 1970s. Harvey finds the work significant because it both describes the cultural experience of the city under the regime of flexible accumulation and celebrates its effects. All of the characteristics of the postmodern city we have discussed—its decenteredness, fragmentation, incoherence—are hailed as opportunities, in Harvey's words, for "a widespread individualism and entrepreneurialism in which the marks of social distinction [are] broadly conferred by possessions and appearances" (3). In Raban, the city is "more like a theatre, a series of stages upon which individuals could work their own distinctive magic while performing a multiplicity of roles" (3, 5). The urban landscape becomes an invitation for self-fashioning in a domain of unstable subjects, free-floating signifiers, and unstable truths. In its very material and social structures, the city provides a concrete manifestation of postmodern anti-epistemology. Harvey's analysis of this phenomenon is useful because it both describes the conditions that give this version of contemporary life plausibility and offers a telling critique of its unstated dangers.

As Harvey demonstrates, this decentering of sign, subject, and value is closely related to changes encouraged by the regime of flexible accumulation. Money as the key sign of economic value has always been a central feature of capitalism. In a sense, money has itself been something of a free-floating signifier, always standing for something else, the absent other that constantly changes depending on the commodities involved in the way this or that money was earned or spent. Nonetheless, up until the early 1970s, Fordism made the U.S. dollar a relatively stable center of value in the world economy, based officially on the solid gold standard and unofficially on the unquestioned strength of U.S. productive capacity. In the post-Fordist world, however, the indeterminacy of the value of money assumes vertiginous proportions. The internationalization of economic activity means that the value of any national currency now constantly changes relative to other currencies as well as relative to the value of the commodities it is supposed to represent. Furthermore, money now not only has to represent goods and production capacity, but it must also stand for services, such as knowledge and communication capability. Money even becomes a commodity in itself, bought and sold on the open market. Thus, the value of money, like the meaning of a signifier, is never totally determinate in flexible accumulation, instead always residing in a relation that can never achieve full presence.

As we have seen, space-time compression has led to new technologies in production and the decentering of organizational forms. Production is sped up and downsized as international capital responds quickly to changing international markets. This means that other places and cultures are constantly before us in the ordinary experiences of daily life, particularly in the media, giving us an encounter with the shifting of values over geographic locations. Further indeterminacy is introduced by the conditions of the domestic market. In an economy that requires quick cycle time in production to increase profits, markets are as much created as they are discovered, particularly by encouraging media-manufactured subject formations through advertising images. Self-identity is established through the visual symbols associated with the commodities of the image. Images of commodities thus become the free-floating signifiers of subject formation that advertisers convince us lead to the fulfillment of "basic" needs and desires, both of which are themselves often concoctions of media advertising. Meanwhile, the advertising image is as important to corporations as to individuals "because of various associations of 'respectability,' 'quality,' 'prestige,' 'reliability,' and 'innovation'" (Harvey 1989, 288), all of which are as necessary for obtaining financing in the international marketplace as they are for selling products. The manufacturing of images even becomes a central feature of politics, as the persona of a candidate is created like any other advertising image to persuade voters of his or her authenticity. The simulacrum, as Baudrillard (1988) argues, becomes the real.

The constant and rapid changes in the images constructed to represent human subjects and commodities thus act as another effect of space-time compression in the new economy. These changes also serve to accustom us to the continual dislocations in our everyday lives that result from disposable goods, disposable industries, and disposable labor. Indeed, as Raban's *Soft City* shows, such instability is celebrated by those of means as an opportunity to construct new subject formations. This is the environment in which the esoteric theories of deconstruction are domesticated. As Harvey argues:

> If it is impossible to say anything of solidity and permanence in the midst of this ephemeral and fragmented world, then why not join in the [language] game? Everything, from novel writing and philosophizing to the experience of labouring or making a home, has to face the challenge of accelerating turnover time and the rapid write-off of traditional and historically acquired values. The temporary contract in everything, as Lyotard remarks . . . , then becomes the hallmark of postmodern living. (291; brackets in original)

Harvey concludes by arguing that for many city dwellers, the incoherent conditions of daily experience, postmodern fiction, and philosophical thought all converge in a mimicry of the incoherent conditions of flexible accumulation. Thus, the loss of the unified subject, stable signifiers, and reliable truths is celebrated as a triumph of contemporary civilization.

There are a number of dangers in this uncritical celebration. Most important, it is a narrative told from the limited and exclusive point of view of a small segment of the comfortable classes. The vast majority of workers are outside this circle of professional security, so that glorying in the possibilities of floating subjects and indeterminate signifiers is unthinkable. Space-time compression for them most often means out of work and out of luck, not the frolic of simulated experiences from other places and times. Even for those within the inner confines, security can never be taken for granted, as change becomes the first principle of daily economic life. It is difficult, then, for most of us to assume that all is for the best in an economy that treats so many so harshly.

This ludic postmodern stance also makes for a curious array of political responses. Those who celebrate "simulacra as milieux of escape, fantasy, and distraction" (Harvey 1989, 302) are obviously little interested in a democratic politics of critique and engagement. At best, theirs is a fragmented, privatized, and self-absorbed stance incapable of intervening beyond the personal level of experience. Those who deplore the postmodern inducements of the city are susceptible to an equally ineffective tendency. Faced with the fragmentation and indeterminacy of daily experience, many turn to a reactionary politics that calls for a return to a time of secure and stable values—whether the values of the small town or of "the real America" or of an earlier economic era. These nostalgic appeals are rendered powerless because they are based on an inadequate grasp of the causes and consequences of our historical conditions. Massive economic and cultural changes cannot be so easily willed out of existence. A third response to the postmodern is more promising, calling on postmodern difference to forward "a fragmented politics of divergent special and regional interest groups" (Harvey 1989, 302). This too often fails, however, because it falls prey to the fragmentations that are a part of the economic and cultural moment. Without some broader conception of the relation of special interests to global economic and political conditions, action can easily become partial and ineffectual.

In short, an effective democratic politics must somehow call on the very abstract and systemic thinking that the economic and cultural conditions of postmodernism call into question. The same must be said of the kind of reading and writing practices taught in preparing students for these conditions. A literacy limited to the mastery of atomistic skills renders students incapable of responding to the complex conditions that go into influencing them and the "global village," to use the current designation, in which they live. At the same time, it is clear that Enlightenment liberal humanist responses will no longer serve. In what follows, I wish to propose a reaction to the postmodern interrogation of signification, subject, and value that neither totally celebrates nor totally rejects its conclusions. My position is that postmodern theory contains within it important challenges to our traditional notions of reading and writing that we ignore at our own peril. At the same time, even as we answer these challenges, we must not suspend our counter-critique of its consequences, particularly for school and society.

The Rhetorical Response

From one perspective, the postmodern theoretical turn is an attempt to recover the services of rhetoric, the study of the effects of language in the conduct of human affairs. In fact, postmodern discussions have put rhetoric back on the agenda of virtually all of the human sciences. After all, the primacy of signifying practices in the formation of subject and society means that language can no longer be seen as the transparent conduit of transcendental truths. Under interrogation are the mystifications that resulted from the effacement of signifying practices and their role in constructing a world that corresponds to an interested version of things-in-themselves. In the United States, as in most Western nations, this mystification has been especially carried out by the professional middle class. This group has invoked the reputedly disinterested, objective language of experts in a manner that obscures the implementation of its own political interests. The realization that discourse is constitutive of knowledge rather than a mere instrumental transcription device challenges all such efforts. If the perceiving subject, the object perceived, and the community of fellow investigators are all in large part the effects of linguistic practices, then every discipline must begin with a consideration of the shaping force of discourse in its activities.

Of course, rhetorics have historically been concerned with the power of signification in public discourses of power, that is, in the provisional and probable realms of politics, law, and social ceremony. At present, however, no inquiry can be regarded as unquestionably outside the sphere of the provisional and probable. Even the physical sciences are coming to understand the rhetoricity of their own activities, as celebrated studies by Thomas Kuhn (1970) and Paul Feyerabend (1975) indicate. More practically, Donna Haraway (1989) and Greg Myers (1990) in biology and Donald McCloskey (1990) in economics have shown the effects of discourse in the conduct of their respective disciplines.

In what follows, I will offer what I take to be promising possibilities for responding to the postmodern challenge to traditional conceptions of subject, society, and material conditions in a refigured English studies. In doing so, I have tried to take into consideration the criticism of my earlier attempts at this project posed by Victor Vitanza, the thinker who has most shown us the vexing problems postmodern thought creates (see, for example, Vitanza 1991). In his incisive and witty explorations (the paralogical *petit recits* recommended by Lyotard), he has investigated the fragmentation of the subject, the death of foundational metanarratives, and the perils of converting theory into immediate educational practice. In so doing, he has shown us the formidable challenges of constructing a postmodern rhetoric. And while I know that my proposals will still seem rationalistic and excessively systematic to him, I have nonetheless attempted to provide space for the indeterminacy that he has shown us must now be taken into account in all our speculations and actions. I will, however, indicate the points at which we most clearly part company.

The loss of liberal humanism's autonomous subject is seen by many traditional thinkers as the death of democratic politics. From this perspective, the hope that human agents will transform economic and political arrangements so as to distribute more equitably the products of human labor (the call of the left) or enable individuals to achieve more freely their personal choices (the call of the right) is dashed. If humans cannot operate with at least some measure of freedom and individuality, both sides argue, they cannot be said to act at all, serving as mere puppets of the discourses that have constituted them as subjects. This response, however, is an overreaction that Paul Smith has effectively addressed in *Discerning the Subject* (1988).

Smith's discussion of the possibility of agency in the postmodern subject is instructive. Calling especially on the work of Luce Irigaray and Julia Kristeva, Smith argues for the organization of the subject as a contradictory complex of subject formations that makes for a negotiation among different positions. It is neither possible to remove all conflicts among these formations nor to freely choose among competing alternatives. Instead, a dialectic among them is created, and out of this emerges the possibility of political action, more specifically, the possibility of "a praxis of resistance (39). This dialectic even provides for a certain conception of individuality and self-interest. The content and development of the different subject positions will differ from one person to another as the negotiation among them takes place. Since each agent enjoys a unique set of interacting formations, each of us has a "specific history" (58). In other words, we are indeed different from each other, although never completely unique.

Keep in mind, however, that these negotiations among subject positions take place within a social context. Thus, a person's subject positions at any one moment are interacting with the subject positions of others. Our specific history is thus situated within a larger social history—the economic, political, and cultural conditions of the time. This concept of the subject as a dialectical process of subject positions within a specific social history as well as within a broader shared social history accounts for the possibilities of agents actively changing the conditions of historical experience (and in a way which recalls, or at least resonates with, Burke's conception of rhetoric as the achievement of persuasion through identification). Of course, this does not lead to the complete autonomy of the humanist subject, so that anything is possible. But neither does it lead to a subject for which nothing is possible. In short, acting is always circumscribed by material and discursive constraints, but acting against these conditions is feasible. The important implication of this scheme is that the more diverse and varied the subject positions of any agent and the more free and open the political environment, the greater the possibilities for action.

A complementary theoretical treatment of the question of postmodern political agency is presented by Susan Jarratt (1991) in a formulation she labels "Rhetorical Feminism." She argues that the efforts of Toril Moi, Linda Alcoff, and Gayatri Chakravorty Spivak converge with that of the sophists in that "all work their way out of [the] deconstructive dilemma" (69). Moi, explains Jarratt, responds to the contradictions of subject formations and their attendant conflicted political choices by offering the alternative of the rhetorical stance, "the choice of a position, in full knowledge that the 'economy' of her selection leaves out other, less usable truths" (70). In other words, any stance is contradictory, since all are marked by difference. Rather than leading to paralysis, however, this recognition must lead to an acknowledgment of what is deferred as well as what is foregrounded. Jarratt also calls on Alcoff's conception of positionality, "a construction of subjectivity as historicized experience" (70). While the subject is constructed of "a complex of concrete habits, practices, and discourses," she will select "gender as a position from which to act politically, while at the same time rejecting a universal, ahistorical definition of gender" (70). Alcoff argues for the position of woman as a resistant site from which she can act against her oppression, an agency possible because historical discourses seek to control the category of the feminine without allowing it to utter its own discourse. It thus arrives at an awareness of its own denial as subject, and from this stance outside official discourse, resistance becomes possible. Finally, Jarratt invokes Spivak's "kairotic discourse—i.e., suitable for the time" (70)—where one finds, in Spivak's terms, "strategic 'misreadings'—useful and scrupulous fake readings" (quoted in Jarratt 1991, 70). Spivak's gesture is a call for readings of culture from woman's position of marginalized other, the subaltern who is not allowed to speak. Out of such strategies comes the rewriting of history along less oppressive lines.

Once again, the discussion of the subject turns to *différance,* to what is left out of dominant discourses, the overlooked margins. We are asked to locate heretofore silenced voices. While from one perspective the liberal education curriculum has historically committed itself to this project, aspiring to a comprehensiveness in the positions it examined, its logocentrism limited the range considered. In other words, the liberal humanist determination to forward truths as universal certainties rather than as historical and contingent provisionalities narrowly constricted the curriculum. Thus, the subject positions of certain groups were simply unspeakable. A postmodern conception of the subject requires that the dialectic of subject formation and the strategic selection of standpoints be the result of encounters with a diverse set of subject positions, cutting across the entire range of the social and intellectual spectrum.

The comprehensive role of signifying practices in constructing the relations of subjects to the material and social conditions of experience can also be construed in a manner that need not induce despair. From the position of rhetoric, the notion that material conditions are constructed through signifying practices is not surprising. Kenneth Burke (1966) some time ago argued for the difference between the sheer physical motion of the material and the symbolic action of the human. This, of course, is not to propose an idealism that denies the limits material conditions impose on human affairs. People need to provide for physical needs, create refuge from the elements, deal with death. These limits, however, are continuously negotiated and defined differently over time and place. As Derrida (1976) reminds us, the distinction between nature and culture can never be determined with certainty. The interventions of culture prevent humans from ever knowing nature-in-itself. In other words, experiences of the material are always mediated by signifying practices. Only through language do we know and act upon the conditions of our experience—conditions that are socially constructed, again through the agency of discourse. Ways of living and dying are finally negotiated through historically and culturally specific signifying practices, the semiotic codes of a time and place. The economic, social, and political conditions of a historical period can be known and acted upon only through the discourses of the moment. Thus, both the subject who experiences and the material and social conditions experienced are products of discursively constituted and historically specific negotiations with genuine material constraints.

In an interview, Cornel West (1988) offered a telling criticism of the extreme form of postmodern epistemological skepticism sometimes found in Baudrillard, a proposal that argues for the complete abandonment of any concern for the non-discursive:

> Baudrillard seems to be articulating a sense of what it is to be a French, middle-class intellectual, or perhaps what it is to be middle class generally. Let me put it in terms of a formulation from Henry James that Fredric Jameson has appropriated: there is a reality *that one cannot not know.* The ragged edges of the Real, of *Necessity,* not being able to eat, not having shelter, not having health care, all this is something that one cannot not know. The black condition acknowledges that. It is so much more acutely felt because this is a society where a lot of people live a Teflon existence, where a lot of people have no sense of the ragged edges of necessity, of what it means to be impinged upon by structures of oppression. To be an upper-middle-class American is actually to live a life of unimaginable comfort, convenience, and luxury. Half

> of the black population is denied this, which is why they have a strong sense of reality. (277)

Here West acknowledges the inevitable claims of the material conditions of experience. At the same time, he admits the role of representation in forming subjects who bring to these conditions interpretive frames. Once again, the position of the subaltern is forwarded to expose the contradictions of the hegemonic discourse of dominant groups, this time to underscore that signification can never by itself cure hunger and want. The meaning of the messages of those in power can be understood only by examining what gets left out of their discourse, the marginalized and excluded others of their pronouncements.

The signifying practices of a given time and place are always marked by this contention and contradiction. In the effort to name experience, different groups—class, racial, gender, ethnic—constantly vie for dominance, for ownership and control of terms and their meanings. As Stuart Hall (1980) has pointed out, a given language or discourse does not automatically belong to any group, however powerful it may be. Following Volosinov and Gramsci, Hall argues that language is always an arena of struggle to make certain meanings—certain representations—prevail. Cultural codes are thus constantly in conflict. They contend for hegemony in constructing and directing the formations of material conditions as well as consciousness. The signifying practices of different groups compete in forwarding different agendas for the ways people are to regard their historical conditions and their modes of responding to them.

This leads to a consideration of the possibility of comprehensive narratives in explaining human events. I have already noted the turn to limited narratives in historical accounts—for example, in the form of history from the point of view of previously excluded class, race, gender, and ethnic groups. Here I wish to elaborate on this response, taking a somewhat different tack. Against the plea for the abandonment of comprehensive historical accounts and the denial of any significance in the myriad details of everyday life, I would propose the necessity for provisional, contingent metanarratives in attempting to account for the past and present. Here Vitanza and I totally part company. While history may be marked by no inherent plan or progression, it is the product of complex interactions of disparate groups, social institutions, ideologies, technological conditions, and modes of production. To abandon the attempt to make sense of these forces in the unfolding of history is to risk being victimized by them.

At the most obvious level, those who have the most to gain from historical explanations that validate present economic and political arrangements, the most recent victors of historical battles, will continue to sponsor histories from their point of view, framing master narratives that authorize their continued power and privilege. (This, of course, is seen today in the revival of Hegel's end-of-history thesis, which is said to have occurred with the dissolution of the Soviet Union and the triumph of a market economy in eastern Europe, a triumph as yet more imagined than realized.) In other words, dominant groups will always attempt to make sense of history, at the very least to account for the justice of their access to power. These histories will, of course, deny the ideological commitments of their master narratives, usually in the name of an innocent empiricism, an insistence that the facts of the matter, not any ruling narrative codes, make the case. The postmodern recognition of the inaugurating role of signification in all human activities, however, challenges this account. After all, the events contributing to the formation of current social and political arrangements will always be too numerous to present in their entirety. Some principle of organization and selection must be invoked. The ruling narrative can be found in these choices.

The postmodern turn demands that the role of such narratives be acknowledged, while cautioning against the temptation to posit any as essential or universal. All are provisional and contingent, always subject to revision or even rejection. West (1988) offers a similar proposal in distinctly rhetorical terms, looking upon provisional and contingent notions of the total as a necessarily heuristical and synecdochal way of proceeding:

> Without "totality," our politics become emaciated, our politics become nothing but existential rebellion. Some heuristic (rather than ontological) notion of totality is in fact necessary if we are to talk about mediations, interrelations, interdependence, about totalizing forces in the world. In other words, a measure of synecdochal thinking must be preserved, thinking that would still invoke relations of parts to the whole. . . . It is true, on the other hand, that we can no lon-

> ger hang on to crude and orthodox "totalities" such as the idea of superstructure and base. (270)

Despite their conditionality, these heuristical, synechdocal narratives are always preferable to atomistic responses that, in the words of Stanley Aronowitz and Henry Giroux (1985), "run the risk of being trapped in particularistic theories that cannot explain how the various diverse relations that constitute larger social, political, and global systems interrelate or mutually determine and constrain each other" (70). Contingent narratives thus become heuristics that open up "mediations, interrelations, and interdependencies that give shape and power to larger political and social systems" (70). To use Jameson's formulation (1991), such narratives provide cognitive maps that, at the simplest level, are indispensable to daily experience, providing "that mental map of the social and global totality we all carry around in our heads in variously garbled forms" (415).

For projects as complex as the estimation of history, complex cognitive maps that serve as provisional guides for responding to the vast array of data are indispensable. Indeed, in a remarkable departure from Marxist tradition, Jameson even concurs with West in placing the concept of the base-superstructure relationship in this category, identifying it as "a starting point and a problem, an imperative to make connections, as undogmatic as a heuristic recommendation simultaneously to group culture (and theory) in and for itself, but also in relation to its outside, its content, its context, and its space of intervention and effectivity" (409). The guiding narratives to be invoked in writing history that I am recommending similarly offer this capacity to provide connections while never determining in advance exactly what those connections will be. The narrative and the details it discovers engage in a dialectical interaction in which the two terms of the encounter are always open to revision, the narrative revealing data while the data revises the narrative.

Before closing this chapter, I would like to offer one more model of the kind of historical thinking I am recommending, a proposal that offers an extremely useful conception of the value of a provisional totality within a postmodern frame. Teresa Ebert (1991) has provided a feminist model of what she calls "resistance postmodernism," a formulation meant to contrast with the focus on the indefinite play of difference found in feminist "ludic" postmodernism (to be distinguished from the nonfeminist ludic postmodernism discussed earlier). She explains,

> There are two radically different notions of politics in postmodernism. Ludic politics is a textual practice that seeks open access to the free play of signification in order to disassemble the dominant cultural policy (totality), which tries to restrict and stabilize meaning. Whereas resistance postmodernism, I contend, insists on a materialist political practice that works for equal access for all to social resources and for an end to the exploitative exercise of power. (887)

While Ebert is thoroughly appreciative of the critique offered by feminist ludic postmodernism, she finds it wanting. It is not enough to examine difference and the excluded other in an effort to reverse or displace hierarchical binaries, however valuable this may have been at some historic moment: "Instead it needs to inquire into the power relations requiring such suppression" (889).

Ebert offers a scheme for regarding the central role of signifying practices in the formation of subject and society that is a useful summary of the position I have sketched here. Like Stuart Hall, she regards "the sign as an ideological process in which we consider a signifier in relation to a matrix of historically possible signifieds. The signifier becomes temporarily connected to a specific signified—that is, it attains its 'meaning'—through social struggle in which the prevailing ideology and social contradictions insist on a particular signified" (897). Language is thus the arena of struggle for determining the meaning of key signifiers, signifiers which then operate in the formation and maintenance of economic and political conditions as well as in the construction of social subjects. The important point is that resistance is always possible, since the contradictions between signified and signifier—for example, the promises of supply-side economic policies and the actual living conditions of those now referred to as "the bottom ninety percent" of the population—continually provoke opposition to hegemonic ideologies.

Ebert also offers a reading of difference that leads to a conception of the inevitability of provisional and contingent notions of a constantly changing totality:

> But a postmodern materialist feminism based on a resistant postmodernism, I contend, does not avoid the issues of totality or abandon the struggle concept of patriarchy; instead, it *rewrites* them. Totality needs to be reunderstood as a system of relations, but such a system is not a homogeneous unity as the Hegelian expressive totality proposes: *it is an overdetermined structure of difference.* A system—particularly the system of patriarchy—is thus always self-divided, different from itself and multiple; it is traversed by 'differences within,' by differ*ance.* (899)

Difference here involves the constantly changing conflicts of social and material contradictions conceived as a totality of shifting relations between the economic, political, and cultural:

> If totalities are structures of differences and thus multiple, unstable, changeable arenas of contradictions and social struggle, then they are open to contestation and transformation. But such transformations are themselves contingent on analyzing the ways in which the operation of power and organization of differences in a specific system are *overdetermined* by other systems of difference, because systems of difference are also situated in a social formation—which is itself a structure of differences made up of other systems of differences, including the social, economic, political, cultural, and ideological. (899)

All of this means that none of these last named categories of investigation can be given an unquestioned first place in analysis. Each instead must be considered in its complex relations to other mutually influencing categories within a complex and shifting totality of differences. This shifting totality means that any study must be historically specific in its methods and materials, never resting secure in any transhistorical and universal mode of thought. At the same time, this study must continually forge and reforge a method of analysis that takes into consideration a comprehensive standpoint, one that avoids stasis by observing the changing interactions of the various elements of the whole.

This chapter has set forth the major postmodern challenges to the ruling theoretical principles of the humanities and offered a response to them. This response, however, can be complete only in examining its consequences for new conceptions of reading and writing practices in English studies. In the next chapter, I will turn to the rhetoric that describes these practices, exploring its intersections with postmodern speculation.

5
Social-Epistemic Rhetoric, Ideology, and English Studies

Social-epistemic rhetoric is a recent development unique to the United States, growing out of the singular experiences of democracy in this country. Its roots are in the social constructionist efforts of pragmatism that first appeared around the turn of the century, but it offers a dramatic departure from its forebears. This rhetoric has responded to the challenge posed by postmodernism. It has two corresponding but separate historical trajectories, one in English and the other in communication departments, in both instances acting independently of European influences, at least until just recently. To understand its development, I will briefly examine predecessors in the English department and then show the details of its departure from them. I would then like to consider some of the broader implications of this scheme for the work of a refigured English studies.

Social-epistemic rhetoric is the study and critique of signifying practices in their relation to subject formation within the framework of economic, social, and political conditions. This is a dense formulation, and it will be the business of this chapter to unpack it. Indeed, I have elsewhere argued that certain earlier paradigms in rhetoric and composition studies have from their start, before the turn of the century, attempted to constitute themselves along these lines. While none succeeded, I want to look briefly at the most fruitful of these unsuccessful efforts. Before doing so, however, I must take up the question of ideology in rhetoric.

Ideology in Rhetoric

In considering any rhetoric, it is necessary to examine its ideological predispositions. As the last chapter made clear, no set of signifying practices can lay claim to a disinterested pursuit of transcendental truth; all are engaged in the play of power and politics, regardless of their intentions. In discussing ideology, I will call on a scheme based on the work of Goran Therborn in *The Ideology of Power and the Power of*

Ideology (1980), a book I have discussed at greater length in "Rhetoric and Ideology in the Writing Class" (1988). Therborn is especially useful because of his inclusion of structuralist and poststructuralist formulations, including the strengths of both Althusser and Foucault, as well as the speculation on hegemonic discourse found in Gramsci. As a result, his method is at every turn rhetorical, by which I mean he considers ideology in relation to communicators, audiences, formulations of reality, and the central place of language in all of these.

From this perspective, ideology interpellates subjects—that is, addresses and shapes them—through discourses that offer directives about three important domains of experience: what exists, what is good, and what is possible. Significantly, it also promotes versions of power formations governing the agent in his or her relation to all of these designations. As Therborn explains, directives about what exists deal with "who we are, what the world is, what nature, society, men, and women are like. In this way we acquire a sense of identity, becoming conscious of what is real and true" (18). Discourses about the good indicate what is "right, just, beautiful, attractive, enjoyable, and its opposites" (18). This concerns the linked realms of politics, ethics, and art. Finally, the possible tells us what can be accomplished given the existent and the good. It gives us "our sense of the mutability of our being-in-the-world, and the consequences of change are hereby patterned, and our hopes, ambitions, and fears given shape" (18). Thus, the recognition of the existence of a condition (homelessness, for example) and the desire for change will go for nothing if ideology indicates that change is simply not possible (the homeless freely choose to live on the street and cannot be forced to come inside). This consideration of the possible is closely related to the question of power and its distribution and control.

Ideology always brings with it strong social and cultural reinforcement, so that what we take to exist, to have value, and to be possible seems necessary, normal, and inevitable—in the nature of things. This goes for power as well, since ideology naturalizes certain authority regimes—those of class, race, and gender, for example—and renders alternatives all but unthinkable. In this way, it determines who can act and what can be accomplished. Finally, ideology is minutely inscribed in the discourse of daily practice, where it emerges as pluralistic and conflicted. A given historical moment displays a wide variety of competing ideologies, and each subject displays permutations of these conflicts, although the overall effect is to support the hegemony of dominant groups. From this perspective, the subject is the point of intersection and influence of various conflicted discourses—discourses about class, race, gender, ethnicity, sexual orientation, age, religion, and the like. Of equal importance, the subject in turn acts upon these discourses. The individual is the location of a variety of significations, but is also an agent of change, not simply an unwitting product of external discursive and material forces. The subject negotiates and resists codes rather than simply accommodating them.

Social Constructionist Rhetoric

As I have demonstrated in *Rhetoric and Reality* (1987), social constructionist rhetoric appeared around the turn of the century, primarily in the Midwest, but also at a number of colleges in the East, especially women's schools. Growing out of democratic populism and progressive politics—the latter itself a response to the cruelties of capitalism in cities—this position acknowledged the influence of social forces in the formation of the individual. Furthermore, it argued that each person is first and foremost a member of a community. Thus, any claim to individuality can be articulated only within a social context. Here, the existent, the good, and the possible are determined by consulting the welfare of the populace as a whole. All citizens must learn reading and writing to take part in the dialogue of democracy. Moreover, these activities call on a social hermeneutic, measuring the value of a text in relation to its importance to the larger society. This means that the expertise of the meritocratic class must be employed in the service of the community, and the community, not the experts themselves, must finally decide on solutions to economic, social, and political problems. In the schools, this rhetoric was strongly influenced by Dewey's pragmatism, placing reading and writing practices at the center of communal decision making. It was the counterpart of a literary criticism that regarded poetic texts in relation to their social and cultural context, as, for example, in the work of Fred Newton Scott, Gertrude Buck, Vida Dutton Scudder, Moses Coit Tyler, and Frederick Lewis Pattee.

During the twenties, this rhetoric spawned the "ideas approach," an attempt to regard the writing course as training in political discourse. Students read contradictory points of view on contemporary social problems and wrote essays stating their own positions. During the Depression, socially oriented approaches took a leftist turn. For example, the hope voiced by such figures as Warren Taylor (1938) of

Wisconsin was that the rhetoric course would provide students with the means to examine their cultural experience—"advertisement, editorial, newsreel, radio speech, article, or book" (853)—so as to detect threats to the democratic process at a time of national crisis. Fearful that an elite might prevail against the claims of the community, this rhetoric saw the critical examination of the subtle effects of signifying practices as key to egalitarian decision making. A similar effort was taken up after World War II, when the communications course—combining writing, reading, speaking, and listening—was forwarded as a safeguard for democracy, particularly against the threat of propaganda. General semantics was especially prominent here, arguing for a scientific notion of signifying practices that enabled a discrimination of true political discourse from the deceptive. During the 1960s and 1970s, responses to racial injustice, poverty, and the Vietnam War once again encouraged a rhetoric of public discourse that demanded communal participation in decision making—for example, in the work of Harold Martin, the early Richard Ohmann, and Kenneth Bruffee.

Despite considerable attractions, the flaws in these social rhetorics when viewed from the postmodern perspective cannot be denied. While this rhetorical approach emphasizes the communal and social constitution of subjectivity, it never abandons the notion of the individual as finally a sovereign free agent, capable of transcending material and social conditions. Furthermore, although it does look to democratic political institutions as the solution to social problems, it lacks a critique of economic arrangements, arguing for the political as primary and in the final instance determinative. The critique of capitalism occasionally found during the thirties was thus abandoned after the war. This rhetoric also displays an innocence about power, lacking the means to critique it and exhibiting a naive faith in the possibility of open public discourse and the ballot box. It cannot, for example, problematize the obvious inequities in access to public discourse or the failures of the elective process when candidates do not offer genuine alternatives. And while this rhetoric sees the manipulative power of discourse, it never abandons its faith in the possibilities of a universal, ahistorical, rational discourse. As a result, it regards itself as a disinterested and objective arbiter of competing ideological claims, occupying a neutral space above the fray of conflict. In other words, it is incapable of examining its own ideological commitments, mistaking them for accurate reflections of eternal truths. It accepts its own signifying practices as finally indisputably representative of things-in-themselves.

Social-Epistemic Rhetoric

Social-epistemic rhetoric retains much that is worth preserving from these earlier social rhetorics. Most important, it has maintained a commitment to preparing students for citizenship in a democratic society. Public discourse openly and freely pursued also remains a central commitment. Its departures from its predecessors, however, are significant.

The first of these was part of the revival of rhetoric that took place in the 1960s and 1970s, especially—and most important—the move to regard composing as a process. While the discussion surrounding the process approach to teaching writing was in no way univocal, more than one competing group insisted that text production constructed knowledge, rather than simply reproducing it. The emphasis on heuristics in the work of Janice Lauer, Richard Larson, and Richard Young, for instance, was an attempt to argue that writing discovered orders of meaning previously unacknowledged in a particular discourse community. By offering students open-ended questioning strategies for exploring issues, teachers encouraged methods for arriving at new perspectives, conceptions, and modes of behavior. Writing is thus discovery and invention, not mere reproduction and transmission. Indeed, as I argued in the closing chapter of *Rhetoric and Reality* (1987), this turn in rhetoric and composition studies created a ready audience for discussions of epistemic rhetoric today.

The second departure from earlier social constructionist rhetorics arose out of rhetoric's encounter with the postmodern critique of Enlightenment conceptions of signification, the subject, and foundational narratives. The result has been a convergence with poststructuralist speculation in a mutually enriching effort. To say this differently, poststructuralism provides a way to more adequately discuss fully operative elements of social-epistemic rhetoric. At the same time, social-epistemic rhetoric offers poststructuralism devices for studying the production as well as the reception of texts, particularly since text production has long been at the center of rhetoric's project. I want to explore these convergences by discussing the elements of the rhetorical situation—interlocutor, audience, conceptions of the existent, and signification—as they occur in a social-epistemic rhetoric informed by poststructuralism. My main concern will be an analysis of the kinds of writing and reading practices this rhetoric encourages.

Social-epistemic rhetoric is self-reflexive, acknowledging its own rhetoricity, its own discursive constitution and limitations. This means that it does not deny its inescapable ideological predispositions, its politically situated condition. It does not claim to be above ideology, a transcendent discourse that objectively adjudicates competing ideological claims. It knows that it is itself ideologically situated, itself an intervention in the political process, as are all rhetorics. Significantly, it contains within it a utopian moment, a conception of the good democratic society and the good life for all of its members. At the same time, it is aware of its historical contingency, of its limitations and incompleteness, remaining open to change and revision.

We have already seen that the subject of the rhetorical act is not the unified, coherent, autonomous, transcendent subject of liberal humanism. The subject is instead multiple and conflicted, composed of numerous subject formations and positions. From one perspective, the protean subject is a standard feature of many historical rhetorics in their concern for the speaker's *ethos,* his or her presentation of the appropriate image of his or her character through language, voice, bearing, and the like. For a postmodern rhetoric, the writer and reader or the speaker and listener must likewise be aware that the subject, or producer, of discourse is a construction, a fabrication, established through the devices of signifying practices. This means that great care must be taken in choosing and constructing the subject position that the interlocutor wishes to present. Equally great care must be taken in teaching students the way this is accomplished. It will not do, for example, to say "Be yourself" in writing or interpreting a particular text. Each of us has available a multiplicity of selves we might call on, not all of which are appropriate for every discourse situation.

This is not, I hasten to add, to deny that each of us displays a measure of singularity. As I indicated in the last chapter, our own separate position in networks of intersecting discourses makes for differences among us as well as possibilities for political agency, for resistance and negotiation in responding to discursive appeals. Yet we cannot escape discursive regimes, the power-knowledge formations of our historical position. Political agency, not individual autonomy, is the guiding principle here.

But if the subject is a construct of signifying practices, so are the material conditions to which the subject responds. Social-epistemic rhetoric starts from Burke's formulation (1966) of language as symbolic action, to be distinguished from the sheer motion of the material. Only through language do we know and act upon the conditions of our experience. Ways of living and dying are finally negotiated through discourse, the cultural codes that are part of our historical conditions. These conditions are of an economic, social, and political nature, and they change over time. But they too can be known and acted upon only through the discourses available at any historical moment. Thus, the subject that experiences and the material and social conditions experienced are discursively constituted in historically specific terms.

The roles of signifying practices in the relations of subjects to material conditions are especially crucial. From the perspective offered here, signifying practices are always at the center of conflict and contention. In the effort to name experience, different groups constantly vie for supremacy, for ownership and control of terms and their meanings in any discourse situation. In "The Rediscovery of 'Ideology': Return of the Repressed in Media Studies" (1982), Stuart Hall points out that a given language or discourse does not automatically belong to any class, race, or gender. Following Volosinov and Gramsci, he argues that language is always an arena of struggle to make certain meanings—certain ideological formulations—prevail. Cultural codes are thus constantly in conflict. They contend for hegemony in defining and directing the material conditions of experience as well as consciousness. In this argument, Hall takes a distinctly rhetorical turn, as he situates signifying practices at the center of politics. Signification is described as a material force that must be studied in its complex operations of enforcing and challenging power arrangements. Social-epistemic rhetoric is in accord with this perspective, pointing out that rhetoric was invented not because people wanted to express themselves more accurately and clearly, but because they wanted to make their positions prevail in the conflicts of politics. In other words, persuasion in the play for power is at the center of this rhetoric, and studying the operation of signifying practices within their economic and political frames is the work it undertakes.

The receivers of messages—the audience of discourse—obviously cannot escape the consequences of signifying practices. An audience's possible responses to texts are in part a function of its discursively constituted subject formations—formations that include race, class, gender, ethnic, sexual orientation, and age designations. These subjectivities are often constructed with some measure of specificity as membership in a specific discourse community—in a particular union or profession, for example. But they are never discretely separate from other subject positions that members of an audience may share or, on the other hand, occupy independent of each other. In other words, members of an audience cannot simply activate one subject position and switch off all others. Members of an audience are thus both members of communities and separate subject formations. The result is that the responses of an audience are never totally predictable, never completely in the control of the sender of a coded message or of the coded message itself. As Stuart Hall demonstrates in "Encoding/Decoding" (1980), audiences are capable of a range of possible responses to any message. They might simply accommodate the message, sharing in the dominant or preferred code of the message and assenting to it. Alternately, an audience might completely resist the message, rejecting its codes and purposes altogether. Finally, the receiver might engage in a process of negotiation, neither accommodating nor resisting but engaging in an interaction of the two. Indeed, negotiation is the most common response, as audiences appropriate messages in the service of their own interests and desires. These are often themselves contradictory and conflicted, so that a completely reliable prediction of an audience's response is never possible. On the other hand, the members of an audience are never totally individualistic in these negotiations.

The work of social-epistemic rhetoric, then, is to study the production and reception of these historically specific signifying practices. In other words, social-epistemic rhetoric enables senders and receivers to arrive at a rich formulation of the rhetorical context in any given discourse situation through an analysis of the signifying practices operating within it. Thus, in composing or in interpreting a text, a person engages in an analysis of the cultural codes operating in defining his or her subject position, the positions of the audience, and the constructions of the matter to be considered. These function in a dialectical relation to each other, so that the writer must engage in complex decision making in shaping the text. By dialectic I mean they change in response to each other in ways that are not mechanically predictable—not presenting, for example, simply a cause-effect relation, but a shifting affiliation in which causes and effects are mutually interactive, with effects becoming causes and causes effects simultaneously. Here we are in the realm of difference and overdetermination, as shifting structures of differences—of gender, race, class, age, sexual orientation, ethnicity—continually interact with each other. For example, the different forms that patriarchy assumes in different social classes make for correspondingly different patterns of behavior and consequences for power and privilege. The reader must also engage in this dialectical process, involving coded conceptions of the writer, the matter under consideration, and the role of the receiver in arriving at an interpretation of the message. Writing and reading are thus both acts of textual interpretation and construction, and both are central to social-epistemic rhetoric.

Dislodging the Binaries

This brings us to a consideration of the writing-reading relationship. As I argue throughout this book, English studies in the United States is based on a privileging of literary texts and a devalorizing of rhetorical texts. This opposition in turn rests on a hierarchical division of activities in English departments that bears large consequences for the kind of teaching and research that takes place in them. I would like to reiterate briefly the terms of this division, explain their displacement in social-epistemic rhetoric, and offer an overview of the role the aesthetic will play in this revised scheme. Finally, I will explore briefly the consequences of this displacement for a refigured English studies.

In *Literature against Itself* (1979), Gerald Graff argues that English studies in the United States is based on a preference for the literary over the non-literary, the latter identified with the language of science and politics, that is, the rhetorical (although Graff does not use this term). Literary discourse is associated with the imaginative and the aesthetic, with disinterested appeals to taste and sensibility. The rhetorical is found in the scientific, objective, practical, and political—all regarded as inferior because they represent interested appeals to the public intellect and reason. Graff demonstrates that schools of literary criticism in English studies, regardless of their differences, offer a set of binary oppositions in which the literary text is preferred over the non-literary in consistent terms: creation against representation; texts as open, indeterminate "invitations" against texts as determinate objects; voyages into the unforeseen against boundaries and constraint; risk against docility and habit; truth as invention and fiction against truth as correspondence; meaning as "process" against meaning as "product" (24).

Robert Scholes examines the effects of enforcing these binaries in *Textual Power* (1985). He acknowledges the invidious distinctions that privilege the study of literary texts over the study of other texts and text interpretation over text production. He traces these distinctions to the division between production and consumption in a capitalist society, with consumption consistently favored. In the English department scheme, non-literary texts are relegated to the field of reading and the lower schools, since they lack both complication and disinterestedness. The non-literary, as Scholes explains in a passage that bears quoting again, is "grounded in the realities of existence, where it is produced in response to personal or socio-economic imperatives and therefore justifies itself functionally. By its very usefulness, its non-literariness, it eludes our grasp. It can be read but not interpreted, because it supposedly lacks those secret-hidden-deeper meanings so dear to our pedagogic hearts" (6). Moreover, the production of these non-literary texts cannot be taught apart from the exigencies of real-life situations, so that writing instruction produces merely a sort of "pseudo-non-literature." The attempt to teach creative writing is similarly regarded as an effort to produce "pseudo-literature," a futile attempt to teach what cannot be taught. Finally, Scholes uses this governing scheme of oppositions to characterize English department practices along the same lines found in Graff: the division between sacred and profane texts, the division between the priestly class and the menial class, the placing of beauty and truth against the utilitarian and commonplace.

We can now see the ways in which a social-epistemic rhetoric figured along poststructuralist lines refigures these binary relationships. It refuses the inherent distinction between representational and creative texts. From this perspective, language in all its uses structures, rather than simply records, experience. Thus, language never acts as a simple referent to an external, extralinguistically verifiable thing-in-itself. It instead serves as a terministic screen, to use Burke's phrase, that forms and shapes experience. That is, it comes between the perceiver and the perceived in a way that shapes the interpretation. All language use is thus inherently interpretive. All texts involve invention, the process of meaning formation. Note, however, that this structuring of experience is never undertaken by a unified, coherent, and sovereign subject who can transcend language. No single person is in control of language. Language is a social construction that shapes us as much as we shape it. In other words, language is a product of social relations and so is ineluctably involved in power and politics. Language constitutes arenas in which ideological battles are continually fought. The different language practices of different social groups are inscribed with ideological prescriptions, interpretations of experience that reinforce conceptions of what really exists, what is really good, and what is politically possible. The discourse of any given group tacitly instructs its members in who they are and how they fit into this larger scheme, as well as in the nature of the scheme itself.

Thus, language practices engender a set of ideological prescriptions regarding the nature of "reality": economic "realities" and the distribution of wealth; social and political "realities" regarding class, race, age, ethnicity, sexual orientation, and gender and their relations to power; and cultural "realities" regarding the nature of representation and symbolic form in art, play, and other cultural experience. These ideological prescriptions are in continual conflict for hegemony, with the groups in ascendance calling on all of their resources of power to maintain dominance in the face of continual opposition and resistance. This conception of the constructive capacity of language completely negates the distinction between referential and creative discourse and the binary oppositions they have been made to enforce.

This leads to reconfiguring the opposition between the production and consumption of texts. Producing and consuming are both interpretations (as all language is interpretive), requiring a knowledge of semiotic codes in which versions of economic, social, and political predispositions are inscribed. Since all language is interested, the task of the rhetor as well as the poet—and their readers—is a working out of semiotic codes. These codes are never simply in the writer, in the text, or in the reader. They always involve a dialectical relation of the three, a rhetorical exchange in which writer, reader, text, and material conditions simultaneously interact with each other through the medium of semiotic codes. This encounter in language is never totally free, since semiotic codes are themselves already interpretations. Thus, the signifying practices of a poetic or rhetoric are always historically conditioned, always responses to the material and social formations of a particular moment.

This conception of the production and consumption of texts deconstructs and reformulates the binaries of the rhetoric-poetic relationship. The sharp oppositions between disinterested and interested, private and public, contemplative and creative, high culture and low culture no longer hold up. There are no strictly disinterested uses of language, since all signifying practices—both in writing and reading—-are imbricated in ideological predispositions. We saw, for example, how Bourdieu's study (1984) of cultural practices in France uncovered the relationship of class and politics to aesthetic judgment. The private-public distinction is likewise broken down as we realize that language is a social device that is inherently public, collective, and communal. Individuals are indeed constituted by this public discourse, but, as I indicated earlier, individuals become differentiated sites of converging discourses that enable agency and change. The subject as discursive formation acts as well as reacts, the private and the public interacting dialectically. The private is neither totally separate from the public nor totally identical with it. The distinction between action and contemplation likewise collapses as we recall that all texts are involved in politics and power—all tacitly or explicitly underwrite certain platforms of action. Finally, from this point of view, the division between high culture and low culture becomes merely a validation of the class structure—a hierarchy of texts created from the perspective of a group devoted to representing its own interests.

This perspective does not obliterate all distinctions between rhetoric and poetic. But the aesthetic cannot be regarded as a category functioning apart from and beyond all other considerations. Historically determined aesthetic codes are essential elements in literary production and interpretation, but they can function only in relation to other codes. They are never isolated and innocent. I have in mind here the sort of practice recommended by Bakhtin and Medvedev (1985), who argue that literary study "is concerned with the concrete life of the literary work in the unity of the generating literary environment, the literary environment in the generating ideological environment, and the latter, finally, in the generating socioeconomic environment which permeates it" (27). Social-epistemic rhetoric continues to distinguish rhetoric and poetic, but it does so on the basis of the writing and reading practices involved in each—the semiotic, culturally indicated codes appropriate to each. This means an end to the invidious valorization of the literary because of its rich organic complexity and its satisfaction of the aesthetic need and the dismissal of the rhetorical because of its purported practicality and mechanical simplicity. Both are rich and complex in their expression of meaning, and both are necessary in the continued health of a society. The work of English studies is to examine the discursive practices involved in generating and interpreting both. The English classroom should therefore provide methods for revealing the semiotic codes enacted in the production and interpretation of texts, codes that cut across the aesthetic, the economic and political, and the philosophical and scientific, enabling students to engage critically in the variety of reading and writing practices required of them.

The Aesthetic Code

At this point, I want to examine the revised role of the aesthetic in a refigured English studies. As I indicated earlier, the aesthetic as a unique response to art objects separate from all other human responses was an invention of the eighteenth and nineteenth centuries and was related to the emergence of a new ruling class. Claims for the powerful effects of this notion of the aesthetic that both reinforce and challenge its contentions have been frequent during its two-hundred-year history. In "'The Aesthetic Ideology' as Ideology; or, What Does It Mean to Aestheticize Politics" (1992), Martin Jay offers a useful summary of some of these claims. Jay's treatment is especially relevant to this discussion, because he relates his critique of the historical tyrannies of the aesthetic to its destruction of the sphere of public discourse, the realm of rhetorical debate and dialogue in politics. In so doing, he endorses many of the assertions offered here.

Jay first considers the destructive effects of the aesthetic in the "aestheticization of politics" (a concern taken up earlier in relation to Harvey's analysis of postmodernism). Jay traces this practice in Hitler's efforts to make fascism seductive through "the conflation of artistic form-giving and political will" (42). Thus, Hitler presented fascism as a historical narrative compelling because of its aesthetic satisfaction, its fulfillment of certain formal and thematic elements so aesthetically gratifying that they appear indisputable. Jay traces the concept of the aestheticization of politics through a variety of manifestations. Calling on Walter Benjamin, he locates one source in "the *l'art pour l'art* tradition of differentiating a realm called art from those of other human pursuits, cognitive, religious, ethical, economic, or whatever" (43). This move justifies human sacrifice in the service of beauty, as in the case of Oscar Wilde and Laurent Tailhade—or Mussolini, who saw himself as a sculptor and the people as his clay. The result is the "reduction of an active public to the passive 'masses,' which is then turned into pliable material for the triumph of the artist/politician's will" (45). Jay pays particular attention to the reliance on the pleasures of the sensory image, rather than rational deliberation, in this aestheticization of politics, resulting in "the victory of the spectacle over the public sphere"—a practice, once again, seen in the example offered by Harvey in his analysis of postmodernism. Jay sums up the charges against these cruel practices: "In this cluster of uses, the aesthetic is variously identified with irrationality, illusion, fantasy, myth, sensual seduction, the imposition of will, and inhumane indifference to ethical, religious, or cognitive considerations" (45).

These are not the only charges made against the tyrannies of the aesthetic. The aesthetic ideology criticized by such figures as Paul de Man, Terry Eagleton, and other literary critics is characterized quite differently in Jay's analysis:

> The aesthetic in question is not understood as the opposite of reason, but rather as its completion, not as the expression of an irrational will, but as the sensual version of a higher, more comprehensive notion of rationality, not as the wordless spectacle of images, but as the realization of a literary absolute. In short, it is an aesthetic that is understood to be the culmination of Idealist philosophy, or perhaps even Western metaphysics as a whole, and not its abstract negation. Bourgeois culture at its height rather than at its moment of seeming decay is thus taken as the point of departure for aestheticized politics (46).

This impulse spawns a "quasi-religious metaphysics of art" whose function is to overcome "differences, contradictions, and disharmonies" (46) in political discourse, encouraging totalitarianism.

De Man traces the source of this failed aesthetic to Kant and Schiller, seeing in their totalization of the aesthetic a concealment of the violent denial of difference that makes it possible. Thus, Jay explains, "for all their emancipatory intentions, Kant and even more so Schiller spawned a tradition that contained the potential to be transformed into a justification for fascism" (47). For de Man, Kant and Schiller deny "literary language's resistance to closure, transparency, harmony, and perfection that could be pitted against the aesthetic ideology" (48). This ideology also calls upon sensual pleasure in a way that conceals values of truth and falsehood. Truth and virtue are simply assumed to be inevitably inscribed in any manifestation of the aesthetic. That the genuinely and sensuously beautiful may underwrite immorality is simply unthinkable. Finally, de Man resists the aesthetic ideology's appeal to metaphors of organic wholeness, because they, once again, conceal conflict and difference. Jay, admittedly following Jonathan Culler, sees de Man's concern for the aesthetic's denial of difference as a tacit critique of economic and political effects, tracing the consequences of the denial of difference far beyond the reading experience.

Eagleton launches a related but somewhat different critique of aesthetic ideology. For him, the aesthetic becomes through Schiller a device for constructing bourgeois consciousness that will more self-consciously conceal the contradictions of the economic, social, and political. Jay explains,

> The modern subject is thus more aesthetic than cognitive or ethical; he is the site of an internalized, but illusory reconciliation of conflicting demands, which remain frustratingly in conflict in the social world. As such, the aesthetic functions as a compensatory ideology to mask real suffering, reinforcing what the Frankfurt School used to call 'the affirmative character of culture.' (49)

At the same time, Eagleton admits that the aesthetic can provide a utopian dimension, offering a critique of the bourgeois social order. He thus finally attempts to recover the value of the aesthetic for politics, finding in Marx an endorsement of the aesthetic impulse: "For what the aesthetic imitates in its very glorious futility, in its pointless self-referentiality, in all its full-blooded formalism, is nothing less than human existence itself, which needs no rationale beyond its own self-delight, which is an end in itself and which will stoop to no external determination" (quoted in Jay 1992, 50).

Other discussions of the relations between the aesthetic and the political are less monological. Jay discusses Josef Chytry's history of the aesthetic, in which Chytry finds discontinuities in the inheritance from Schiller, locating political uses of the aesthetic that were not fascist in intent. Among these Jay cites Schiller's awareness of the role of the aesthetic in fulfilling the purposes of Greek democracy, manifested in the notion of *phronesis,* or practical wisdom. This is, of course, the contingent realm of politics situated between the more certain realms of morality and philosophical truth. Jay goes on to argue that Kant's treatment of the aesthetic in his Third Critique can be interpreted as supporting "a kind of uncoerced consensus building that implies a communicative model of rationality as warranted assertability" (52).

Kant is thus rehabilitated as amenable to support for a democratic political order of rhetorical discussion and debate.

Jay finally concludes that the boundary between the aesthetic and the political "is always to be breached (although not completely effaced)" (53). He cites de Man, Jean-François Lyotard, and Hannah Arendt as offering possibilities for reconceiving the relationship between the two domains. These possibilities are especially worth exploring because of their close relation to the reading and writing practices recommended in this chapter.

De Man's proposal for reading literary texts deconstructively offers one weapon against the insidious uses of the aesthetic in politics as well as art. In other words, through examining literary texts for indeterminacy and difference, the reader will develop strategies of critique for interpreting political events. In locating the unsaid and excluded elements that constitute a text's meaning, the reader develops a sensitivity to the gaps, inconsistencies, and disparities that are an element of all signifying practices. This is akin to the reading and writing practices recommended in this chapter, practices similarly committed to locating conflicts and contradictions in the literary and poetic texts that students encounter. The larger purpose is to encourage students to be better readers of the signifying practices that shape all of their experiences—economic, social, and political.

Lyotard's *Just Gaming* advocates a skepticism about totalizing theory that is derived from Kant. As Jay explains:

> Kant's exposure of the dangers of grounding politics in transcendental illusions, of falsely believing that norms, concepts, or cognition can provide a guide to action, is for Lyotard a valuable corrective to the terroristic potential in revolutionary politics in particular. The recognition that we must choose case by case without such criteria, that the conflicts Lyotard calls *differends* cannot be brought under a single rule, means that political, like aesthetic practice, is prevented from becoming subservient to totalizing theory. (54)

Lyotard's use of the aesthetics of the Kantian sublime also promotes the notion that the unrepresentability of certain political ideals prevents the forcing of "theoretically inspired blueprints for political utopias" (54). The sublime avoids "Ideas of Reason or the Moral Law" and instead "follows aesthetic judgment in arguing from analogies, which preserve differences even as they search for common ground" (54). Lyotard also cautions against conceiving a political community in the manner of an organic work of art, a unified and coherent whole without any internal division.

Jay recognizes, however, that Lyotard, like de Man, finally lacks a positive politics. The aesthetic of the sublime, he explains, "may be useful as a warning against violently submitting incommensurable differends to the discipline of a homogenizing theory, but it doesn't offer much in the way of positive help with the choices that have to be made" (54). In the end, Jay echoes Eagleton's critique, a critique also found in the proposals I have made here, that the absence of any larger narratives for reading history or for arriving at decisions leads to "a politics of raw intuition, which fails to register the inevitable generalizing function of all language" (54). However provisional our organizing categories of investigation may be, to be without them is to be victimized by the categories of others.

Arendt conceives of the production of the aesthetic text in rhetorical terms. As Jay indicates, this means "not the imposition of an artist's arrogant will on a pliable matter, but rather the building of a *sensus communis* through using persuasive skills comparable to those employed in validating judgments of taste. Here the recognition that politics necessitates a choice among a limited number of imperfect alternatives, which are conditioned by history, replaces the foolhardy belief that the politician, like the creative artist, can begin with a clean canvas or a blank sheet of paper" (55). Equally important, Arendt emphasizes the intersubjective basis of judgment and the need for communication. For Arendt, the aesthetic experience can provide the ability to see events through the perspectives of others while "invoking paradigmatic examples rather than general concepts" (55). It thus "avoids reducing all particulars to instantiations of the same principle" (55). The aesthetic experience can encourage the perception of the differences of the other while not destroying the conception of community. The kind of judgment encouraged by this intersubjective and communicative conception of the aesthetic finally "mediates the general and the particular rather than pitting one against the other" (55). This conception of the aesthetic also underscores the rhetorical and political nature of all texts.

This discussion of aesthetics is meant to stress the multiple uses of the aesthetic—for both evil and good. The aesthetic is not a universal characteristic of the best literary texts, always and everywhere the same. The aesthetic is a coded feature of reading and writing practices that must be considered in relation to the other codes with which it customarily appears. Its purport will vary across time, even during a single moment, as its function is created and construed along a variety of lines (Bennett 1990). Certainly one purpose of an English studies course is to examine the different uses to which the aesthetic has been put, considering both the theoretical and critical discussions of the function of the aesthetic as well as its manifestations in particular poetic texts. The English studies class will promote a variety of reading practices that will finally encourage the uses of the aesthetic in the service of a politics of democratic openness and tolerance, a politics dedicated to discussion and the discovery of difference, of the excluded other that our interpretive strategies often conceal. This does not mean, however, that we must avoid the critical investigation of other ways of reading and writing, methods, for example, that have been designed to foster an aesthetic ideology in the service of a totalitarian politics. Our students must see the aesthetic in its polysemic historical formations and arrive at the means for examining the political consequences of its operation. Finally, we must realize that the poetic text is neither more nor less important than the rhetorical text simply because it offers an aesthetic dimension. Throughout history, one never makes sense without the other. Of equal importance, the effects of the two are never mutually exclusive. There is, after all, an aesthetic of the rhetorical text just as there is a rhetorical dimension to the aesthetic.

Conclusion

All of this has important consequences for the English studies classroom. Given the ubiquitous role of discourse in human affairs, instructors cannot be content, on the one hand, to focus exclusively on teaching the production of certain kinds of utilitarian texts—the academic essay, the business letter, the technical report, the informal essay. On the other hand, they cannot restrict themselves to reading bona fide works of the literary canon. Our business must be to instruct students in signifying practices broadly conceived—to see not only the rhetoric of the college essay, but also the rhetoric of the institution of schooling, of politics, and of the media, the hermeneutic not only of certain literary texts, but also the hermeneutic of film, TV, and popular music. We must take as our province the production and reception of semiotic codes, providing students with the heuristics to penetrate these codes and their ideological designs on our formation as subjects. Students must come to see that the languages they are expected to speak, write, and embrace as ways of thinking and acting are never disinterested, always bringing with them strictures on the existent, the good, the possible, and the resulting regimes of power.

If English studies is to be a consideration of signifying practices and their ideological involvement—that is, their imbrication in economic, social, political, and cultural conditions and subject formations—then the study of signs will of course be central. A large part of this effort will be to provide methods for describing and analyzing the operations of signification. Just as successive rhetorics for centuries furnished the terms to name the elements involved in text production and interpretation of the past (inventional devices, arrangement schemes, stylistic labels for tropes and figures), social-epistemic rhetoric will offer English studies terminologies to discuss these activities for contemporary conditions and conceptual formulations. Workers in structuralism, poststructuralism, semiotics, rhetoric, and literary theory have all begun this effort. Members of the English department must take up this work with a special concern for its place in the classroom. It is here that theory, practice, and politics will intersect in an enlightened conception of the role English studies plays in preparing students for their lives as citizens, workers, and sites of desire.

III Students and Teachers

6
English Studies: Surveying the Classroom

Now we can consider the work of social-epistemic rhetoric in the English classroom. In this chapter, I want to explore the conceptions of teacher and learner and the methods of writing and reading that the social-epistemic classroom encourages. At the heart of this discussion will be an examination of the role of English studies in preparing critical citizens for a participatory democracy. I will invoke the concept of "critical literacy," a term used by Ira Shor, Henry Giroux, and Peter McLaren, among others, in responding to the critical pedagogy of Paulo Freire, a figure central to my discussion. I plan to place Freire in a postmodern frame, following the lead of feminists such as Carmen Luke, Jennifer Gore, Elizabeth Ellsworth, and Patti Lather and rhetorical theorists such as Susan Miller, Susan Jarratt, and John Trimbur. In other words, I want to read Freire's critical pedagogy across an epistemology that takes into account the indeterminacy of signification, the fragmentation of the subject, and the interrogation of foundational truth. My reading is meant as an emendation to Freire rather than as a wholesale rejection of his work. This discussion will be followed by an outline of the reading and writing practices pursued in the social-epistemic classroom. The entire chapter thus serves as a preface to the next chapter's description of two specific courses incorporating these insights and practices.

Critical Literacy

Freire's abiding preoccupation is teaching ways of reading and writing the world. His work has always emphasized the central place of this activity in the life of a society. He provides a rich rationale to support those who argue that literacy ought not be treated as merely an instrumental "skill," a mechanical activity acquired as a useful tool in the mastery of more significant and substantive academic subjects. For Freire (1970), to learn to read and write is to learn to name the world, and in this naming is a program for understanding the conditions of our experience and, most important, for acting in and on them. Everywhere reminiscent of Kenneth Burke, Freire insists that language is at the center of our knowledge of ourselves and others. Furthermore, language is a social construction, a constantly changing set of formations whose meanings emerge as people engage in written and spoken dialogue with each other. Language is thus always prior to individuals, always already in place as it works to form consciousness, to shape subjects.

Freire acknowledges that the concrete material and social conditions of our experience shape and limit us. He sees in the mediating power of language, however, the possibility for the change and transformation of these conditions. While language indeed serves as a means for control and domination, it can also serve as an instrument of liberation and growth. Language in its positioning between the world and individual, the object and the subject, contains within its shaping force the power to create humans as agents of action. Each individual occupies a position at the intersection of a multitude of discourses, which Freire, in the manner of Barthes, calls codes. These codes can define subjects as helpless objects of forces—economic, social, political, cultural—that render them forever isolated and victimized by the conditions of their experience. These discourses can also, however, form individuals as active agents of change, social creatures who acting together can alter the economic, social, and political conditions of their historical experience. The codes, scripts, or terministic screens that define individuals as helpless ciphers must thus be replaced by narratives that enable democratic participation in creating a more equitable distribution of the necessities, liberties, and pleasures of life.

As Luke and Gore (1992) and Ellsworth (1992) have indicated, critical pedagogy in the United States has failed in this last instance, the moment of democratic politics. The tendency instead—sometimes encouraged by the Enlightenment vestiges of Freire himself—is to privilege a unified, rational, and unmistakably male subject, to define discussion and action in naive and simplistic terms so as to obscure difference, and to offer a rationalistic conception of power and a politics of narrow group interests. A compelling response to the inadequacies of this conception of democracy is found in the work of Iris Marion Young. In a volume aptly entitled *Justice and the Politics of Difference* (1990), she offers a version of democracy that, in her terms, addresses "postmodern philosophy's challenge to the tradition of Western reason" (3).

Postmodern Democracy

Young begins with a critique of the notion of distributive justice as a basis for democratic action: "The distributive paradigm defines social justice as the morally proper distribution of social benefits and burdens among society's members" (16). While this distributive paradigm includes "nonmaterial social goods such as rights, opportunity, power, and self-respect," it tends to emphasize "wealth, income, and other material resources" (16). The result is that both categories are collapsed into the latter, with property becoming the central concern of the paradigm. Distributive justice thus regards individuals as isolated "consumers, desirers, and possessors of goods" (36) in a static social relation with others, alienated figures who regard their fellow humans only in "a comparison of the amount of goods they possess" (18). Individuals in this scheme are thus "logically prior to social relations and institutions" (27). As Young explains, "all situations in which justice is at issue are analogous to the situation of persons dividing a stock of goods and comparing the size of the portions individuals have" (18). Significantly, Young finds this paradigm in socialist as well as liberal capitalist notions of justice.

Young criticizes this model on two scores. First, it ignores the economic and social institutions—"state, family, and civil society, as well as the workplace" (22)—involved in material distributions. It accepts them as natural and inevitable by failing to take them into account (liberal capitalism) or by attributing all lapses to class relations and the mode of production (socialism). Second, this paradigm misrepresents the logic of distribution of nonmaterial goods. For example, rights are not objects to be statically possessed but relationships that involve action. Thus, the paradigm includes no provision for justice as an ongoing process of conflict and change, seeing instead a static social ontology. In this, the individual is separated from the social and made prior to it. Young concludes, "Such an atomistic conception of the individual as a substance to which attributes adhere fails to appreciate that individual identities and capacities are in many respects themselves the products of social processes and relations. Societies do not simply distribute goods to persons who are what they are apart from society, but rather constitute individuals in their identities and capacities" (27).

Young forwards a conception of justice that moves from a model of distribution to one that focuses on democratic participation, deliberation, and decision making. One consequence is that in Young's model "the concept of justice coincides with the concept of the political" (34). Young's conception of justice is thus based on two values that provide for conditions that allow individuals to engage in activities that make for a just society: "(1) developing and exercising one's capacities and expressing one's experience . . . and (2) participating in determining one's actions and the conditions of one's action" (37). The two, Young acknowledges, do not grow out of human nature, nor are they universal truths.

They are instead assumptions based on the democratic notion that all persons are of equal moral worth. In other words, they are grounded in a conception of human nature necessary for democracy, not foundational grounds. Injustice, then, corresponds to two social conditions: "oppression, the institutional constraint on self-development, and domination, the institutional constraint on self-determination" (37). Freedom from oppression involves the removal of institutional limits on engaging in learning, satisfying skills, play, and communication. Freedom from domination means the opportunity to engage in action and the conditions that make for action. Most important, "thorough social and political democracy is the opposite of domination" (38).

This postmodern conception of justice leads to a definition of democracy based on the recognition of difference. The idea of impartiality is immediately abandoned. In other words, there are no disinterested observers who can arrive at objective decisions in matters of public policy. Instead, democracy requires "real participatory structures in which actual people, with their geographical, ethnic, gender, and occupational differences, assert their perspectives on social issues within institutions that encourage the representation of their distinct voices" (116). Traditional notions of civic discourse have constructed fictional political agents who leave behind their differences to assume a persona that is rational and universal in thought and language. In a postmodern world, no such subject exists.

Democracy, then, becomes radically participatory, as the heterogeneous voices that constitute any historical moment are allowed a hearing: "All persons should have the right and opportunity to participate in the deliberation and decision making of the institutions to which their actions contribute or which directly affect their actions" (91). For Young, these democratic sites go beyond government institutions to include "production and service enterprises, universities, and voluntary organizations" (91). Decision making is here based on the traditional social contract theory of collective activity: "If all persons are of equal moral worth, and no one by nature has greater capacity for reason or moral sense, then people ought to decide collectively for themselves the goals and rules that will guide their action" (91). This participation ensures that the interests and needs of the heterogeneous groups competing for a hearing at any moment will be taken into account in arriving at decisions: "In the absence of a philosopher-king with access to transcendent normative verities, the only ground for a claim that a policy or decision is just is that it has been arrived at by a public which has truly promoted the free expression of all needs and points of view" (92-93). As for the protection of minority interests, Young invokes the primacy of certain constitutional rights: "democracy must indeed always be constitutional: the rules of the game must not change with each majority's whim, but rather must be laid down as constraints on deliberations and outcomes, and must be relatively immune to change" (93-94). These rights must cover economic, political, and civic domains. Finally, this conception of democracy is based on a politics of deliberatory discourse in which rhetoric is at the center of public life. As Young indicates in criticizing the exclusive emphasis on rational discourse in Habermas's theory of communicative action, deliberation must also include "the metaphorical, rhetorical, playful, embodied aspects of speech that are an important aspect of its communicative effect" (118).

The Democratic Classroom

The classroom in which writing and reading are seen from this perspective is preeminently participatory and democratic. It is, of course, disconcerting that a nation so justifiably proud of its democratic and activist legacy is currently so reluctant to extend the fruits of this legacy to its schools. For example, conspicuously lacking in the report of the 1989 governors' summit on education was any mention of citizenship preparation. A literacy that is without this commitment to active participation in decision making in the public sphere, however, cannot possibly serve the interests of egalitarian political arrangements. For democracy to function (as we are now reminded in eastern Europe), citizens must actively engage in public debate, applying reading and writing practices in the service of articulating their positions and their critiques of the positions of others. To have citizens who are unable to write and read for the public forum thus defeats the central purpose of the notion of democracy we have just examined: to ensure that all interests are heard before a communal decision is made.

Placing Freire within a postmodern frame enables us to relate this silencing of citizens through literacy education to the formation of subjects as agents. Without language to name our experience, we inevitably become instruments of the language of others. As I am authorized through active literacy to name the world as I experience it—not as I am told by others I should be experiencing it—I become capable of taking action and assuming control of my environment. In more direct terms, literacy enables the individual to understand that the conditions of experience are made by human agents and thus can be remade by human agents. Furthermore, this making and remaking take place in communities, in social collections. The lessons of postmodern difference remind us, however, that the individual must never be sacrificed to any group-enforced norm. All voices must be heard and considered in taking action; the worth of the individual must never be compromised.

In teaching people to write and read, we are thus teaching them a way of experiencing the world. This realization requires that the writing classroom be dialogic. Only through articulating the disparate positions held by members of the class can different ways of understanding the world and acting in it be discovered. This is important whether students are studying text interpretation or production. As I have already indicated, all responses to texts are engaged in production and critique. Differences among students organize themselves around class, race, gender, age, and other divisions, and it is the responsibility of the teacher to make certain that these differences are enunciated and examined. At the same time, those of us who have experienced the dialogic classroom know how reluctant many students are to engage in public debate. Their years of enduring the banking model of education, the model of teacher as giver of knowledge and student as passive receiver, have taken their toll. Many would rather sit quietly and take the notes that they will later gladly reproduce for an exam. When pressed to active dialogue, they may deny the obvious social and political conflicts they enact and witness daily. For example, the majority of male students I have encountered at Purdue have in our first discussions assured me that race and gender inequalities no longer exist in the United States and simply do not merit further discussion. Thus, the works of Kate Chopin or Virginia Woolf, for example, are mere historical curiosities of no contemporary relevance. Any inequalities that do remain, they insist, are only apparent injustices, since they are the result of inherent and thus unavoidable features of human nature (women are weaker and more emotional than men, for example) or are the product of individual failure (the "glass ceiling" that is supposed to prevent women from rising in the corporate world is an illusion fabricated by women who have not worked hard enough).

It is at the moment of denial that the role of the teacher as problem poser is crucial, providing methods for questioning that locate the points of conflict and contradiction. These methods most often require a focus on the language students invoke in responding to their experience. The teacher attempts to supply students with heuristic strategies for decoding their characteristic ways of representing the world. Here we see why the literacy teacher, the expert in language, is at the center of education in a democratic society (and not just because English studies has historically been used in U.S. schools to reinforce hegemonic ideological positions). The questions the teacher poses are designed to reveal the contradictions and conflicts inscribed in the very language of the students' thoughts and utterances. The teacher's understanding of structuralist and poststructuralist assertions about the operations of language in forming consciousness here comes to the fore. At the minimum, this involves an examination of the various hierarchical binary oppositions on which the key terms in any discourse are based, the various connotative levels on which these terms function, and the larger narrative patterns of which the terms form a part. The movement is thus from the concrete and specific conditions of the student's experience to the larger economic, social, political, and cultural systems with which these conditions coalesce. A student's attitude toward women in the workplace, for example, is often a part of a larger conceptual formulation regarding reproductive responsibilities, the family, work in the community, and the realities of the economic conditions that govern our lives.

The relation between the teacher and students is crucial at this point. Although the classroom is to be democratic and participatory, this does not mean that the teacher surrenders all authority. As Freire points out, the authority of the teacher is never denied. On the other hand, it should never be exercised so that it destroys the student's freedom to critique. The teacher must resist the obvious institutional constraints that in the typical college classroom make the teacher the center of knowledge and power and deny the student's active role in meaning formation. In a participatory classroom, the teacher shares the right to dialogue while never relinquishing the authority to set certain agendas for class activities. Certain matters are always debatable—for example, all positions on issues, whether the teacher's or students'—but certain others are not—the participatory and dialogic format, the search for contradictions, the analysis of codes. The teacher must display neither complete passivity nor complete dominance in discussion. From my experience in such classrooms, I know that the successful use of the problem posing and dialogic method usually leads to increasing participation by students. By the middle of the course, students are often themselves problematizing the assertions of their peers, the teacher becoming only one of many problem posers in the classroom.

I will not deny that my students have demonstrated resistance of various kinds, particularly in introductory composition classes. C. H. Knoblauch (1991, "Critical Teaching and Dominant Culture"), Cecilia Rodriguez Milanes (1991), and Dale Bauer (1990), among others, have reported similar experiences. What Ira Shor calls "desocializing students," that is, making them conscious of the concealed conflicts in their language, thought, and behavior, is never pursued without some discomfort. This resistance has as often taken the form of passivity as it has active and open opposition to locating dissonance in our coded responses to such areas of discussion as schooling, work, play, individuality, and their relation to class, race, and gender formations. Working together, my colleagues (primarily graduate students) and I have developed devices for dealing with this resistance. One of the most effective in the first-year composition course is to explain at the outset that the class will involve writing about the contradictions in our cultural codes. Since this will require that students participate in disagreement and conflict in open, free, and democratic dialogue, the students are asked to draw up a set of rules to govern members in their relations to each other. These rules are then published. The device has had the salutary effect of including students in the operation of the class from the start, thus averting passivity as well as inappropriate reactions. It also acts as a statement of rights to protect minority positions.

The success of the kind of classroom I am recommending depends on teachers knowing their students. The teacher must understand the unique economic, social, and cultural conditions of his or her students to arrive at the appropriate forms and contents that dialogue can assume. Extensive knowledge about the students' backgrounds enables sound planning about the topics, questions, and comments that are most likely to set a meaningful encounter in motion. Teachers must also be keenly aware of their own positions in the social relations of the classroom. The twenty-five-year-old African American female graduate student will have to develop strategies for interacting with students different from those needed by the fifty-year-old white female full professor. Indeed, if either attempts to emulate the other, failed classroom relations and an unsuccessful learning experience are almost certain to follow. The aim of the course remains the same in all situations: to enable students to become active, critical agents of their experience rather than passive victims of cultural codes. The "tactics," to use Freire's term, are always open to change. The final purpose of the course is to encourage citizens who are actively literate, that is, critical agents of change who are socially and politically engaged—in this way realizing some of the highest democratic ideals.

Reading and Writing for Critical Literacy

English studies refigured along the postmodern lines of social-epistemic rhetoric in the service of critical literacy would take the examination and teaching of reading and writing practices as its province. Rather than organizing its activities around the preservation and maintenance of a sacred canon of literary texts, it would focus on the production, distribution, exchange, and reception of textuality, in general and in specific cases, both in the past and present. English studies would thus explore the role of signifying practices in the ongoing life of societies—stated more specifically, in their relations to economic, social, political, and cultural arrangements. These signifying practices would be regarded in their concrete relations to subject formation, to the shaping of consciousness in lived experience. Here, once again, the subject is not the sovereign and free agent of traditional literary studies. Instead, the subject is the point of convergence of conflicted discourses—the product of discourse rather than the unencumbered initiator of it. English studies would thus examine the textual practices of reading and writing to explore their roles in consciousness formation within concrete historical conditions. Signifying practices serve as the mediator between these larger historical conditions and the formation of historical agents. Furthermore, the entire process is historical, in flux over time. Finally, the response of the agent to these signifying practices is at least partly unpredictable, involving a process of accommodation, negotiation, and resistance. The individual is neither altogether determined nor altogether free.

English courses must become self-consciously committed to the study of divergent reading and writing practices. Whatever literary and rhetorical texts are chosen, all must be considered in relation to their conditions of production, distribution, exchange, and reception. Students should examine both the variety of audiences for these texts and the variety of ways the texts were received in their own time as well as corresponding audiences and reception strategies across time. This would involve a selection of texts—including cross-cultural texts—and responses to them that demonstrate a wide range of interpretive reading practices. Historical interpretations that are different from our own, however, are accessible only to readers who understand the economic, social, political, and cultural stakes involved in different strategies. Different readings usually carry with them different assumptions about the relative distribution of wealth and power within a society. The conflicting receptions of the poetry and criticism of Matthew Arnold in his own time, for example, were often the result of the conflicting political loyalties of the periodicals considering his work, loyalties thoroughly enmeshed in questions of class and religion.

Students can learn to locate these ideological predispositions by considering rhetorical texts produced and read as part of the discursive network of the historical moment. In considering literary texts, they can study firsthand the intersections of aesthetic codes—certain formal and thematic elements, for example—with the economic and political. They can then undertake an analysis of changing responses to these various texts as successive generations of critics treat them—or, just as often, fail to treat them. In other words, examining the creation of a literary or rhetorical canon, with its inclusions and exclusions, becomes a part of this study. In examining the literary or rhetorical text, the concern, once again, is to look at the work in its generating generic environment, the generic environment in the generating ideological environment, and the ideological environment in the generating socioeconomic environment. This method of reading across three interacting registers of meaning merits closer examination.

Understanding the generic forms that texts assume requires an understanding of the textual environment that produced them. Writers of a political tract or a sonnet do not invent their discourses anew. Instead, they rely on certain features of texts that seem normal and natural to them. The "normal" and "natural," however, are always historically constituted. Thus, in examining the political pamphlet in England at the end of the eighteenth century, for example, we must locate the genre that guided the production of such texts, a genre that was in many respects invented only at that moment. The same inventiveness, however, characterized attempts to emulate the satirical poem or the pastoral. However much writers of these forms felt they were observing ancient principles of composition in shaping their efforts, they were in fact producing historically specific discourses, constructing variations rather than simple reproductions. This historical specificity applies to the readers of these productions as well. Discussions of the genres can be found in the literary and rhetorical commentary of the time, and students should of course explore these to arrive at some conception of the conflicts among different explanations. They must also, however, be aware of the contradictions and conflicts they will discover in comparing these comments on principles with texts said to demonstrate these principles, as well as the imputed relation to previous textual practices. In other words, the generating environment of texts will be marked by inconsistency and contention, and it is the work of the English studies class to locate these elements whenever possible.

Disagreements about literary and rhetorical genres are often the result of ideological disputes. Differences about what exists, what is good, what is possible, and the power arrangements among the three are frequently at issue in conflicting conceptions of the most appropriate rhetorical strategies or the best poetic forms and devices. These conflicts frequently grow out of divisions in class, race, gender, and related designations. Sometimes unexpected divisions are involved. An emergent group commonly forwards its own rhetorical and poetic forms to further its claim to power, denouncing those it strives to replace as pronouncements of the old order. It may also, however, appropriate existing forms while subverting their expected effects. An obvious example is Swift's "Modest Proposal." While this essay rigorously employs the strategies and formal patterns of Ciceronian rhetoric, it exposes the cruel ideological purposes this rational genre can be made to serve. Students must thus be encouraged to explore the complicated ways in which literary and rhetorical forms and genres are involved in ideological conflict.

Finally, ideological disputes about class, race, and gender are situated within larger conflicts about the economic, social, and political. Convictions about the existent, the good, and the possible are premises based on conceptions of the economic—the production, distribution, exchange, and consumption of wealth—and of political power—the distribution of authority in decision making. During the late eighteenth century, for example, disagreements in England about the colonies usually involved the place of the New World in the economic pursuits that England was encouraging for its own profit. Yet the arguments that disputants offered frequently underplayed the economic interests of an emergent merchant class and the compromise it had reached with the old aristocratic class in favor of religious or patriarchal concerns—the moral responsibilities of the governed to their government or the natural duties of a child to a parent. The emergence of a new ruling group in economics and politics was thus at the heart of the dispute, but the ideological terms of the issue often assumed the language of the old order. Arguments about taste in literature likewise usually involved class conflicts created by the economic ascendancy of the capitalist class.

While this three-tiered method is derived from a proposal by Bakhtin and Medvedev (1985), it also bears a strong relation to the recommendation of Fredric Jameson in *The Political Unconscious* (1981). Jameson offers a method of reading that involves "three concentric frameworks" (75), each of which he refers to as "semantic or interpretive horizons" (76). The first refers to "political history, in the narrow sense of punctual event and a chroniclelike sequence of happenings in time" (75). Here the text is considered within the concrete conditions of its historical production as they are presented in the text. The purpose is to discover the way in which the text—a novel, for instance—offers an "imaginary resolution of a real contradiction" (77), or, stated somewhat differently, "the function of inventing imaginary or formal 'solutions' to unresolvable social contradictions" (79). In the eighteenth century, for example, an obvious example of this sort of recognition of a genuine social conflict resolved imaginatively by a work of art is found in the classical realist novel in which class conflicts are erased through marriage. In this way, the genuine social conflicts are imaginatively dealt with and rendered harmless through their resolution at the level of private experience. The real battles of the public and social are privatized in order to be imaginatively resolved in the form of the work of art.

Jameson's second interpretive horizon is closely related to this but larger in scope. This is the level of "society, in the now already less diachronic and time-bound sense of a constitutive tension and struggle between social classes" (75). While the first concentric framework operated primarily at the level of historical genre, this horizon includes a larger historical version of the ideological conflicts that are a part of the text's historical production. Here the analysis extends to the historical conditions of the text to discover the class conflicts at work in the society. Calling on Bakhtin and Gramsci, Jameson indicates that the critic must here look for historical hegemonic formations and the ideological voices silenced to discover the ways these are dealt with textually. He gives as an example the use of religious codes in the seventeenth century to articulate the class conflicts involved in the English revolution. Religious discourse here becomes a surrogate for economic and political struggles.

The final concentric horizon, Jameson explains, is "history now conceived in its vastest sense of the sequence of modes of production and the succession and destiny of the various human social formations, from prehistoric life to whatever far future history has in store for us" (75). Here the text is situated within a larger economic and political framework as it is unfolding at the text's historical moment. The larger structures of history figured as comprehensive narratives are taken into account in considering the text. As Jameson explains, "within this final horizon the individual text or cultural artifact (with its appearance of autonomy which was dissolved in specific and original ways within the first two horizons as well) is here restructured as a field of force in which the dynamics of sign systems of several distinct modes of production can be registered and apprehended" (98). Taking the case of the eighteenth-century novel, attention is now given to the historical conflict among dominant, emergent, and residual economic systems—modes of production—and their effects on the political and social behavior of the time. At this level, as Jameson explains in a way that recalls Bakhtin and Medvedev, "'form' is apprehended as content" (99) so that the larger economic and political significances of genres can be discovered in all their complexity.

English studies thus occupies an unusual position in the investigation of past and present cultures. If signifying practices are central to the formation of subjects and society, then English studies must examine the ways conceptions of rhetorics and poetics codified signifying practices for particular groups at a particular historical moment. Rhetorics and poetics and their production and consumption provide directives about the relation of language and power, directives that change over time. They indicate who may speak and write, who may serve as auditors and how their interpretive strategies are constrained, what can and cannot be produced and interpreted, and what role language plays in enforcing all of these strictures.

Furthermore, conflict always exists among competing conceptions of rhetorics and poetics. Regardless of the dominance of any system, it never includes the entire range of practices of a historical period. There are always a multiplicity of formulations competing for hegemony. Usually this competition takes the form of a battle among the factions of a ruling class—for example, between Yale's proponents of liberal culture and Harvard's advocates of philological study after the turn of the century as their respective curricula moved closer together. At other times, the battles are between emergent and established ruling groups. For instance, arguments in the United States in the nineteenth century about the value of Whitman's poetry or Twain's fiction often represented a dispute between Jacksonian democrats interested in expanding access to power and an elite group of New England intellectuals who spoke for an old and established ruling class. A similar conflict in rhetoric took place at the same time between supporters of Emerson and Henry Day (see Berlin 1984). In short, competing conceptions of rhetorics and poetics are often indicators of competing power formations, of opposing groups forwarding different economic and political agendas. Language is always a major arena of contention, with opposing groups attempting to claim ownership of the "true" methods of writing and reading, speaking and listening. It is the business of English studies to study these conflicts in the past and the present. This involves a study of politics and power that moves English studies far away from Graff's recommendation for studying narrow departmental and disciplinary conflicts.

Conceptions of rhetorics and poetics thus inscribe a daunting array of detailed instructions about the subject who speaks and writes, the subjects who constitute the audience, the material and social conditions to which these subjects are responding, and the character of the signifying practices to be employed. Rhetorics and poetics and rhetorical and poetical texts can be regarded as a technology for producing consciousness, social and material conditions, and discourse activities that will ensure their continuance. The English classroom should enable students to locate these conflicting signifying practices in texts that demonstrate them at work, as well as in statements about these texts. It is also necessary to emphasize the inevitability of the negotiated character of all interpretations as readers construct the texts they encounter. This is a complicated matter that takes place at the historical level as students discover diverse interpretations of texts at the time of their construction as well as in successive ages. It also, however, involves the students' own reading of texts, their preference for one set of reading practices over others. This is likewise a concern in the students' production of texts in the class. The diversity of reading and writing practices must thus be taken into account. Of equal importance, the relations of these different practices to economic and political power must be investigated. Here questions of class, gender, race, age, ethnicity, and the like are crucial as students explore the webs of power in which texts appear. Thus, once again, the choice of a particular literary or rhetorical genre is related to the discursive environment, but this also has significance in relation to the ideological environment and the larger socioeconomic context. The guide of provisional conceptions of larger narratives within a context of overdetermined differences always remains paramount.

This classroom should not be a stage for the virtuoso performance of the teacher. The teacher has much to do and is never simply another member of the class; institutional power cannot be redistributed that easily. The teacher should, however, attempt at every turn to share authority in the selection of materials and activities. This means the student-teacher relation will be marked by a democratic dialogue that is by moments both collaborative and disputatious. The objectives of English studies are many. The most significant of these is developing a measure of facility in reading and writing practices so as to prepare students for public discourse in a democratic political community. Yet students should also learn to read and write for personal and private pleasure. Of course, reading and writing in the diverse methods advocated here will also prepare students for communication in their careers. These objectives can be achieved, however, only by sharing authority in the classroom, by allowing students to make choices, encouraging them to take part in the selection and evaluation of materials. Students should have choices that for once extend beyond commodity consumption.

The teacher should also share with the class the responsibility for the presentation of materials, arranging for students to work together in groups in investigating selected texts, texts they will then share in written and oral reports with other class members. At the beginning course level, the teacher will assign most of these materials, although the students can still choose the parts of them for which they will bear special responsibility. At the upper levels, it is often enough to identify texts and dates and periodicals, allowing students to fashion their own course materials. These materials and their presentation will involve students in a variety of reading and writing practices, cutting across textual genres in both interpretation and production, the students becoming composers as well as cultural critics.

The teacher's most demanding, engaging, and creative acts, then, are the encouraging of complex reading and writing strategies and practices. As we have seen, students must learn the signifying practices of text production—academic discourse, political discourse, poetic discourse, scientific discourse, media discourse—as well as the signifying practices of text reception. And both must be considered in their historical. and ideological context. Writing or reading the academic essay today, for example, is not an innocent act.

The first difficulty in addressing this responsibility is that no comprehensive set of terms exists for describing these activities. Prior to the triumph of the middle class in the nineteenth century, rhetoric provided this language. Consider, for example, the method of Aristotle, a method that influenced discourse production and reception for centuries. In the *Rhetoric* and *Poetics,* Aristotle presented a set of strategies and terms for generating and interpreting both rhetorical and poetic texts. Aristotle's terms are no longer adequate to the theory informing our understanding of language, although there are those who have attempted a revival of them in rhetoric and poetic. Even if this were not the case, the triumph of the professional middle class in discourse studies has been to naturalize its own rhetorical practices, concealing ideology by denying the role of language in structuring experience. The impulse to universalize its own conception of what is "natural" in economics, politics, sociology, and psychology was thus successfully extended to signifying practices. This is why teachers can ask students to write an essay about a literary text without saying anything about the methods of reading the student is to prefer or the production process to be followed in preparing the essay. Both text interpretation and production are effaced, made invisible, their procedures readily accessible to those of the right class, gender, and racial background, while remaining inaccessible to those whose class, gender, or racial backgrounds are "wrong." In this scheme, rhetoric becomes synonymous with falsity and distortion, opposed to scientific truth (language as transparent sign system) in one moment, to poetic truth (language as free play) in the next. There is no space for political discourse here. Public debate is silenced in the acquiescence to "what everybody knows."

The work of English studies is to reassess the place of discourse in shaping knowledge and consciousness, doing so within the contemporary context of theory in language, literature, and rhetoric. The teacher must call on recent discussions of discourse analysis to develop a terminology adequate to the complexity of signifying systems. While the various uses of semiotic theory in the work of Barthes, Eco, Hall, Fiske, Hodge and Kress, and others have begun this work, it remains the central task of teachers to rethink theory through classroom practice and classroom practice through theory. The result will be methods of locating and naming the discursive acts that encourage unjust class, race, gender, and other power relations through the tacit endorsement of certain economic, social, and political arrangements. Attempts to negotiate and resist semiotically enforced cultural codes can take place only when these codes can be named and interrogated in reading and writing, and this is a central role of the teacher in the literacy classroom.

One of the most effective ways of tackling the difficult job of identifying culturally determined textual codes is to examine the contrasting semiotics of different media. Indeed, critical pedagogy must insist that students be given devices to interpret and critique the signifying practices that schools have typically refused to take seriously: the discourse of radio and television and film. Studying the manner in which meaning is constructed in these media works to demystify their characteristic textual practices and inevitable ideological inscriptions. It also illuminates the textual practices of print, indicating through contrast the diverse semiotic strategies of the differing forms of communication. This multimedia study is especially effective when students are encouraged to engage in the production as well as the interpretation of various kinds of texts. Students ought to write as well as read poetry and fiction, create as well as interpret magazine ads, produce as well as critique television situation comedies and newscasts. In this way, the inevitable commitment of all of these textual forms to culturally coded ideological notions of race, class, age, ethnicity, sexual orientation, and gender in the service of economic and political projects becomes accessible. In learning to gain at least some control over these forms, students become active agents of social and political change, learning that the world has been made and can thus be remade to serve more justly the interests of a democratic society.

Of course, in this formulation, the classroom becomes a site of political activity and struggle, key features of democratic education in a free society. If the genuinely utopian and critical possibilities of art and rhetoric—whether in print, oral, or visual form—are to be realized, the student's position as a political agent in a democratic society must be foregrounded. The teacher must thus serve as a transformative intellectual—as Shor (1987) and Aronowitz and Giroux (1985) have shown us—concerned with improving economic and social conditions in the larger society. The teacher must realize that his or her students are the products of concrete histories that have brought them to their present political positions, positions that are often committed to denying the conflicts and contradictions in the signifying practices they daily encounter. More appropriate responses can come only in acknowledging and confronting this denial and in examining its material and social sources. Students who on one day rejoice over their country's magnificence because its billion-dollar-a-day military budget enables it to crush small third world nations at will and then on the next admit that they, like their parents, are painfully insecure about their job prospects need to come to terms with the contradictions of their experience, contradictions obviously not of their own making. The teacher's role within the classroom thus becomes an extension of his or her role as a force for progressive change everywhere in society.

7
Into the Classroom

I would now like to turn to concrete descriptions of the kind of classroom activities I am recommending. I want to outline two courses: a lower division offering entitled "Codes and Critiques" and an upper division class called "The Discourse of Revolution." Both are designed to involve students in an equal share of writing and reading, with student responses at the center of classroom activity. The two courses also insist on a balanced inclusion of poetical and rhetorical texts. In short, they are intended to challenge the old disciplinary binaries that privilege consumption over production and the aesthetic over the rhetorical. Both sets of concerns should be at the center of critique. I am, of course, especially interested in resisting the hierarchy of specialization that has separated the teaching of writing from the teaching of reading. My proposals for English studies thus encourage a professoriate as confident in teaching the ways of text production as it now is in dealing with certain forms of textual interpretation.

There are a number of qualifications I want to make in offering these course outlines. Most important, I do not wish to present them as anything more than possibilities. Their purpose is finally illustrative rather than prescriptive. I hope that teachers will find in them suggestions for developing course materials and activities appropriate to their own situations. These descriptions accordingly include considerable summary of course materials and their methods of presentation. I do want to emphasize, however, that the center of each course is the response of students to the materials and methods considered. Since this response varies dramatically from group to group and instructor to instructor, I will not try to capture the exact dimensions of any one classroom. Instead, I will simply sketch some of the conflicting reactions I have encountered. I should also note that the range of activities recommended for a refigured English studies can best be seen by considering both course descriptions. In other words, neither should be considered by itself a comprehensive suggestion of classroom possibilities for instruction in critical literacy.

Course One: Codes and Critiques

This course focuses on reading and writing the daily experiences of culture, with culture considered in its broadest formulation. It thus involves encounters with a wide variety of texts, including advertising, television, and film. The course is organized around an examination of the cultural codes—the social semiotics—that work themselves out in shaping consciousness in our students and ourselves. Since I devised the syllabus for this course to be shared with teaching assistants in my mentor groups at Purdue, and since my report here is based on our shared experience over the past four years, I will use the first-person plural in referring to the effort. I would also like to thank those teaching assistants for their generous cooperation.

We start with the personal experience of the students, with emphasis on the position of this experience within its formative context. Our main concern is the relation of current signifying practices to the structuring of subjectivities—of race, class, sexual orientation, age, ethnic, and gender formations, for example—in our students and ourselves. The effort is to make students aware of cultural codes, the competing discourses that influence their positioning as subjects of experience. Our larger purpose is to encourage students to negotiate and resist these codes—these hegemonic discourses—to bring about more democratic and personally humane economic, social, and political arrangements. From our perspective, only in this way can students become genuinely competent writers and readers.

We thus guide students to locate in their experience the points at which they are now engaging in negotiation and resistance with the cultural codes they daily encounter. These are then used as avenues of departure for a dialogue. The course consists of six units: advertising, work, play, education, gender, and individuality. Each unit begins by examining a variety of texts that feature competing representations of and orientations toward the topic of the unit. Here I will describe some of the main features of the unit on work. The unit provides a sampling of attitudes toward work from a broad range of perspectives. These include selections from Benjamin Franklin's "The Way to Wealth," Studs Terkel's *Working* (1985), Richard Selzer's *Mortal Lessons* (1976), William Ouchi's *Theory Z: How American Business Can Meet the Japanese Challenge* (1981), Adrienne Rich's poetry and her "Conditions for Work: The Common World of Women," and Toni Cade Bambara's fiction and her "What It Is I Think I'm Doing Now." The unit also includes films and videotapes of television programs that are useful treatments of work in the United States. The important consideration here is not only the texts in themselves, but the texts in relation to certain methods of interpreting them.

The course provides students with a set of heuristics—invention strategies—that grow out of the interaction of rhetoric, structuralism, poststructuralism, semiotics, and cultural studies. While those outlined here have been developed as a result of reading in Saussure, Pierce, Levi-Strauss, Barthes, Gramsci, Raymond Williams, Stuart Hall, and others, an excellent introduction for teachers and students can be found in John Fiske's *Introduction to Communication Studies* (1990) and Diana George and John Trimbur 's *Reading Culture* (1992). In examining any text—print, film, television—students must locate the key terms in the discourse and situate these terms within the structure of meaning of which they form a part. These terms, of course, derive from the central preoccupations of the text, but to determine how they work to constitute experience, students must examine their functions as parts of coded structures—a semiotic system. The terms are first set in relation to their binary opposites as suggested by the text itself. (This follows Saussure's description of the central place of contrast in signification and Levi-Strauss's application of it.) Sometimes these oppositions are indicated explicitly in the text, but more often they are not. Students must also learn that a term commonly occupies a position in opposition to more than one other term.

For example, we sometimes begin with an essay from the *Wall Street Journal* entitled "The Days of a Cowboy Are Marked by Danger, Drudgery, and Low Pay," by William Blundell (10 June 1981, A1+). This essay is most appropriate for the unit on work, but its codes are at once so varied and so accessible to students that it is a useful introduction to any unit. The reading strategy employed once again involves looking at the text successively within its generic, ideological, and socioeconomic environment.

Students first consider the context of the piece, exploring the characteristics of the readership of the newspaper and the historical events surrounding the essay's production, particularly as indicated within the text. The purpose of this analysis is to decide which terms probably acted as key signifiers for the original readers. The essay focuses on the cowboss, the ranch foreman who runs the cattle operation. The meaning of *cowboss* is established by seeing it in binary opposition both to the cowboys who work for him and the owners who work away from the ranch in cities. At other times in the essay, the cowboss is grouped together with the cowboys in opposition to office workers. Through the description of labor relations on the ranch, the cowboys are also situated in contrast to urban union workers, though the latter are never explicitly mentioned. Finally, the exclusively masculine nature of ranching is suggested only at the end of the essay, when the cowboss's wife is described in passing as living apart from the ranch on the cowboss's own small spread, creating a male-female domain binary. All of these binaries suggest others, such as the opposition of nature-civilization, country-city, and cowboy-urban cowboy. Students begin to see that these binaries are arranged hierarchically, with one term privileged over the other. They also see how unstable these hierarchies can be, with a term frequently shifting valences as it moves from one binary to another—for example, cowboy-union worker but cowboss-cowboy. It is also important to point out that this location of binaries is not an exact operation and that great diversity appears as students negotiate the text differently. Their reasons for doing so become clear at the next phase of analysis.

In this phase, students place these terms within the narrative structural forms suggested by the text, the culturally coded stories about patterns of behavior appropriate for people within certain situations. These codes deal with such social designations as race, class, gender, sexual orientation, age, ethnicity, and the like. Students analyze, discuss, and write about the position of the key terms within these socially constructed narrative codes. It is not too difficult to imagine how these narrative codes are at work in the binaries indicated above. Students can quickly detect the narratives that cluster around the figure of the cowboy in our culture in this essay—for example, patterns of behavior involving individuality, freedom, and independence. These narratives, however, are simultaneously coupled with self-discipline, respect for authority (good cowboys never complain), and submission to the will of the cowboss. Students usually point out the ways these narratives are conflicted while concurrently reinforcing differences in class and gender role expectations. Of particular value is to see the way the essay employs narratives that at once disparage *Wall Street Journal* readers because they are urban office workers while simultaneously enabling them to identify with the rugged freedom and adventure of the cowboys, seeing themselves as metaphorically enacting the masculine narrative of the cowboss in their separate domains. In other words, students discover that the essay attempts to position the reader in the role of a certain kind of masculine subject. They can then explore their own complicity and resistance in responding to this role.

In doing so, students situate these narrative patterns within larger narrative structures that have to do with economic, political, and cultural formulations. Here students examine capitalist economic narratives as demonstrated in the essay and their consequences for class, gender, and race relations and roles both in the workplace and elsewhere. They look, for example, at the distribution of work in beef production, with its divisions between managers and workers, thinkers and doers, producers and consumers. They also consider the place of narratives of democracy in the essay, discussing the nature of the political relations implied in the hierarchies of terms, persons, and social relations presented. It should be clear that at these two narrative levels considerable debate results, as students disagree about the narratives that ought to be invoked in interpreting the text, their relative worth as models for emulation, and the degree to which these narratives are conflicted. In other words, the discussion that emerges from the use of these heuristics is itself conflicted and unpredictable.

Thus, the term as it is designated within a hierarchical binary is situated within narratives of social roles. These roles are then located within more comprehensive narratives of economic and political formations in the larger society. The point of the interpretation is to see that texts—whether rhetorical or poetic—are ideologically invested in the construction of subjectivities within recommended economic, social, and political arrangements. Finally, this hermeneutic process is open-ended, leading in diverse and unpredictable directions in the classroom. This is one of its strengths, since it encourages open debate and wide-ranging speculation. Students arrive at widely variant readings, and these become the center of discussion.

The course is also designed to introduce students to methods for interpreting the cultural codes of television—methods based, in this case, on the work of John Fiske. In particular, we give students the first chapter of Fiske's *Television Culture* (1987), in which he offers a method for analyzing television codes closely related to the heuristic the students call upon in interpreting printed texts. This method involves three interconnected interpretive moments. As Fiske explains, the raw materials of television are always encoded by social codes that consist of "appearance, dress, make-up, environment, behavior, speech, gesture, expression, sound, etc." (5). These form the codes of what he labels "Level one: REALITY." These materials are in turn encoded electronically by technical codes that include "camera, lighting, editing, music, sound" (5). These technical codes "transmit the *conventional representational codes,* which shape the representations of, for example: narrative, conflict, character, action, dialogue, setting, casting, etc." (5). The technical and conventional representational codes form the codes of "Level two: REPRESENTATION." Both reality and representation are in turn "organized into coherence and social acceptability by the *ideological codes,* such as those of: individualism, patriarchy, race, class, materialism, capitalism, etc." (5).

In this segment of the course, then, we invoke Fiske's method as a guide to "reading" two situation comedies with which the students are usually familiar. *Family Ties* and *Roseanne,* for instance, have worked quite well. Students view selected episodes during the unit on work to learn to analyze television codes as well as to gather evidence for their essays on the cultural organization of work and its place in forming subjectivity in their lives. Students learn to see these domestic comedies not as simple presentations of reality but as re-presentations—that is, coded constructions—of an imagined reality. These two programs are especially useful in the work unit because they can be regarded as attempts to present family experience from the points of view of two different class positions.

Family Ties aired from 1982 to 1989, leaving at the peak of its popularity. The show centered around the Keatons, an upper-middle-class family of five living in an unnamed urban area in Ohio. The parents are successful professionals. Stephen, the father, is a manager at a PBS television station, and Elise, the mother, is an architect. The children are Alex, 17 when the show began, Mallory, 15, and Jennifer, 9. Over the course of the show's run, Alex and Mallory went on to college, but both continued to live at home. One of the recurring themes of the show was the conflict between the parents, who were 1960s political activists and Peace Corps members, and Alex, who is a political conservative motivated by the drive to be rich.

Roseanne began in 1989. The Connor family, the show's central focus, is lower middle class, living in a moderately priced neighborhood in a Chicago suburb. Both parents have experienced job disruptions. Dan, the father, was originally a self-employed building contractor taking on small jobs. He eventually realized his dream to own his own business by opening up a motorcycle shop. Later, the business went under. Early on in the series, Roseanne—the mother—worked as a waitress at a department store in a local shopping center, but she too loses her job. With the help of a gift from her mother, she opened up a sandwich shop with her sister. The business was eventually bought out, though she now works there as a waitress. The children are Becky, who eloped and moved to Wisconsin, but has recently moved back home with her husband; Darlene, away at college; and D.J., an early teenage son.

Students begin by writing descriptions of the physical settings of the homes and the characteristic dress of the characters depicted in the two programs. The point of this exercise is for students to recognize that the sets and costumes are created by the producers of the shows. They are not simply video copies of actual homes and people (except for the external shots of the neighborhood in *Roseanne).* The sharp contrasts in the two households lead to a discussion of social class and its relation to work, income, and ideology. Some of the differences between the attitudes and behavior found in the two households are the result of simple economics. For example, the action in the two dramas most commonly takes place in the kitchen, the center of domestic life in television sitcoms. The sizes of the two kitchens and the cost of the appliances obviously involve a disparity in income and expenditures. At the same time, the differences in the decor of the two houses are not exclusively a matter of money spent. Often, a sense of taste related to class affiliation rather than finance is at issue. For example, in one series of *Roseanne* episodes, the wife in an upper-middle-class family that moved in next door found the Connor family quite beneath her. The contrast between the decor of the two houses, identical twins architecturally in a tract-like neighborhood, became an issue, and the Connors clearly identified the taste of their neighbors with elitism and snobbery. In other words, the Connors decorated their house in a manner that simultaneously made them feel comfortable and asserted their class loyalty.

Problems the families in the two sitcoms encounter each week are often related to their incomes, job stability, and class. Both families, for instance, have faced decisions about college education for their children. The question for *Family Ties* revolved around finding colleges suitable to the interests and aptitudes of Alex and Mallory. Money was never a major concern, and in one episode Mrs. Keaton visited expensive private schools with her daughter. For the *Roseanne* household, Becky's hard-won success in high school and her plans to go away to college led to cruel disappointment when her parents lost their jobs. In fact, her eloping was a direct result of this turn of events. This contrast is especially worth considering because of its relation to gender codes across classes. Mallory is presented as a person more interested in clothes and dating than in school. Indeed, she is often made to appear shallow and thoughtless. Despite this, her parents are surprised when she indicates she does not want to go to college, planning instead to work in a women's clothing store in the hope that she will eventually have her own shop. Her parents applaud her entrepreneurial spirit, but finally convince her to try college for one year while using the clothing store dream as a back up. Becky, on the other hand, sees marriage as her only alternative to college. This class contrast is especially apparent when one is aware that in an earlier episode, Mallory also eloped with her inarticulate working-class boyfriend (who, for her parents, is redeemed because he is a talented artist), only to abruptly change her mind in the office of the justice of the peace. The differing gender codes that operate in the two social classes are clearly at issue here.

Students usually conclude that the two shows were the products of different economic times. *Family Ties* prospered during the 1980s, when economic success for those at the upper income levels was a reality. This program spoke for this successful group. *Roseanne is* a production for a time when the concentration of wealth depicted *in Family Ties* has reached such glaring disproportions that we now speak of the income of the "bottom ninety percent" of the population. This realization on the part of students, however, is an important discovery. They begin to understand that television's presentation of the family and the place of work in it are related to popular perceptions of "the real," "the normal," and "the everyday." In other words, the family the largest segment of the television audience chooses to watch is a function of its self-perception, and this in turn is as much related to its conception of what it would like to think is true as to what in fact exists. After all, the Keaton family in *Family Ties* in the mid-1980s represented a small proportion of families in the United States. Then, as now, less than 20 percent of the workforce consisted of college graduates, and much less than 10 percent enjoyed the apparent Keaton income. Indeed, *Roseanne* presents a family experience much closer to the daily lives of the overwhelming majority of Americans, past or present. In other words, most of those who viewed and enjoyed *Family Ties* were more like the Connors than the Keatons, yet they obviously derived pleasure from their weekly watch.

This leads to a discussion of subject formation, television, and cultural codes. As the students describe their responses to the two programs, explaining the pleasures of the text they experience in watching them, it becomes apparent that many women in the class do not enjoy watching *Roseanne.* While some men in the class find it entertaining, most women do not. As class members discuss their preference for *Family Ties,* they begin to consider the different subject positions the two shows attempt to create for the audience. The students obviously prefer the version of work and family life they are asked to endorse in viewing the Keatons. Moreover, they do so even after acknowledging that the genuine conflicts addressed in the program are usually avoided or ignored rather than resolved. Mallory offers challenges to her parents, but she always, often inexplicably, does what her parents think best. Alex rebels, but he does so in a socially approved manner, working hard to be rich. The adverse consequences of his extreme selfishness are never addressed; indeed, in the ingratiating actor Michael J. Fox's hands, ruthlessness is made charming. The students realize that neither the superficiality nor the dishonesty of *Family Ties* interferes with their pleasure in the half-hour presentation. Instead, they continue to find the characters attractive—a response to which I must also confess—since both parents and children display characteristics that the students admire in manners, dress, and general behavior. Stephen and Elise are professionals who approach work, parenting, and play in the successful manner that most beginning students at my institution find worthy of emulation. No problem is too hard for them to solve, even if the solutions cannot stand the light of close analysis. The program offers a fulfillment of most of my students' dreams for themselves as college graduates and professionals. Although the dreams may not be intellectually convincing, they offer an imaginary fulfillment of desire.

This realization leads, in turn, to a consideration of the ways conflicts in cultural codes are typically resolved in television programs, *Roseanne* included. *Family Ties* was indeed notable for addressing serious family problems, most obviously those that result from the clashes between parents and children on such issues as marriage, education, and careers. The program also considered crises at the workplace, with Elise being pursued by a young suitor and Stephen experiencing the difficulty of pleasing a demanding boss. Yet *Family Ties* was no less distinguished for its easy resolution of these difficulties. The lesson of most episodes was that there was no problem that could not be overcome by two or more family members simply sitting down at the kitchen table next to the Zinn range and talking it out. In other words, the program tended to present the upper-middle-class professional nuclear family as in itself the answer to all of life's problems—an extension, one student noted, of the Reagan administration's contention about the place of the family in resolving economic and social problems. Of course, *Roseanne* is not immune to this impulse. For example, the economic problems that the Connor family once faced were resolved by a sizeable financial gift from Roseanne's mother, a move made to punish Roseanne's father for his marital infidelity. The point of this discussion, then, is not to privilege one program over the other. Instead, its purpose is to understand the pleasures of television in their relation to the imaginary resolution of conflicts and the fulfillment of cultural expectations. To enjoy the artificial working out of genuinely serious economic, class, gender, and age conflicts within a thirty-minute television program is not a problem. To expect that these difficulties can be solved in the same manner in our own experience is quite another matter.

This segment on television most usefully ends with a final consideration of the medium's effects in shaping subjectivity among viewers. Students are encouraged to discuss the manner in which they negotiate and resist the cultural codes championed in the programs they watch. No one would argue that students are unwilling dupes of television. But they are not impervious to its seductions either. The larger question students are entertaining, of course, is the role of culture in shaping them as the subjects of their experience and their role as critical agents in a democratic society. Here they can explore their reasons for preferring the version of work and family found in one or the other program, investigating the class, gender, race, religious, and ethnic codes that they have been encouraged to enact. The purpose is neither to reject nor to celebrate their customary manner of responding to important experiences. The purpose is to become reflective agents actively involved in shaping their own consciousness as well as the democratic society of which they are an integral part. Unlike classrooms that insist that each student look within to discover a unique self, this course argues that only through understanding the workings of culture in shaping consciousness can students ever hope to achieve any degree of singularity. By exploring television programs and their dialectical relation to viewers in the operation of subject formation, students begin to come to terms with the apparatuses of culture as they create consciousness.

A final segment of the course as we have taught it has focused on film, calling in particular on the method offered in Graeme Turner's *Film as Social Practice* (1993). Like Fiske's method, it has considerable structural similarity with the heuristic the course teaches for decoding printed texts, combining a structuralist analysis of film as narrative with a poststructuralist ideological critique—a similarity that students readily recognize and find useful. Drawing upon Levi-Strauss's contention that cultural codes are based on a set of binary oppositions imaginatively resolved in their ruling mythologies, Turner argues that films too are organized around a set of binaries embodied in a narrative that attempts to reconcile them. Postructuralist ideological critique, however, goes beyond the analytical identification of binaries that narratives seek to reconcile—the characteristic strategy of Levi-Strauss's structuralism—by investigating the political and rhetorical effects of such narrative resolutions, what meanings they make available and what meanings they suppress. This is the move that distinguishes poststructuralism from structuralism, the move to problematize precisely those binary oppositions whose symbolic resolution gives narratives their sense of conventionalized closure.

Since the conflicts and contradictions a film addresses can never be totally resolved—or can be resolved imaginatively but not actually—the narrative will always result in some measure of ambiguity and ambivalence, some surplus of meaning that exceeds narrative resolution. In other words, the narrative will always carry within it traces of the conflicts and contradictions that resist the resolutions of the ruling mythologies. Moreover, since a film is located within a set of more or less determinable but changing historical influences, the ways in which its conflicts as well as their resolutions are read by viewers change over time. By way of example, Turner traces the changes the James Bond character underwent after 1960 in print and film in response to changing historical conditions (as discussed by Tony Bennett and Janet Woollacott 1987). Films are seen as responses to historical contexts, and the meanings that viewers find in them are a function of this context as much as the film itself. Thus, the binary conflicts that an audience discovers in a film as well as the resolution of these conflicts are as much a product of the historical conditions of the audience as of the elements of the film. Furthermore, the interpretive act is situated in ideological conditions, in representations of what really exists, what is good, and what is possible.

We thus ask students to locate the binary oppositions they see working in a film and to determine the kind of resolution of them the narrative movement of the film achieves. From this analysis, they can infer the ideological leaning of the film—that is, what they take to be its preferred reading. Here again, their responses are usually nowhere near unanimous. As Turner points out, films are texts that do not lend themselves to uniform readings. The divergences that do emerge, however, are not always as radically opposed to each other as they might at first appear. Still, these differences must be encouraged and entertained. I would like to outline the way this method can unfold in considering two recent films: *Other People's Money* and *Roger and Me.*

Other People's Money, released in 1991, is based on a mid-1980s off-Broadway play by Jerry Sterner. Students usually situate the film as a product of the late 1980s, when the merits of unbridled free enterprise were called into question by the consequences of the doings of Wall Street financial wizards. The plot involves an attempt to launch a corporate takeover by one Lawrence Garfield, the wealthy owner of an investment firm (played by Danny DeVito). The founding company of this diversified corporation, New England Wire and Cable, is losing money, while the corporation as a whole is solidly in the black. The result is that the corporation is worth much more than the face value of its stock. Garfield plans to win major control of the corporation, close down New England Wire and Cable, sell the land on which it is built, and clear a hefty profit as the stock then rises to its true value. He is opposed by the son of the late founder of the wire and cable company, Andrew Jorgensen (known as "Yorgy" and played by Gregory Peck), who runs his father's operation as a family business. Jorgensen is determined to fight Garfield, confident that eventually his company will once again make money. He is accordingly persuaded to request the assistance of Kate Sullivan, a partner in a prominent Wall Street legal firm and daughter of his longtime friend, fellow worker, and, perhaps, lover. Sullivan (played by Penelope Ann Miller) agrees to lead the effort to stop the takeover, even though she and Jorgensen clearly do not get along with each other. Meanwhile, Garfield falls in love with her, and there is some indication as the film unfolds that the feeling may be reciprocated.

The major issues at stake in the film's preferred narrative are articulated in the climactic scene in which Jorgensen and Garfield give stirring speeches defending their positions at a stockholders' meeting. Jorgensen stands for the corporation as paternal family, with managers industriously caring for the welfare of workers and the community as a whole. Closing down New England Wire and Cable would destroy the small Rhode Island town in which it is located, and Jorgensen would rather operate at a loss than do this, waiting for the day when the demand for his product will increase. Garfield stands for the corporation as generator of profits, concerned only with making sure that investors receive a maximum return on their investment. Only through constantly increasing profits can corporations truly serve the interests of the larger society, he argues. In the end, Garfield wins, as the stockholders vote with him and he assumes control of the corporation. In the closing scene of the film, however, negotiations between Sullivan and Japanese businessmen are presented in dumb show, and we finally learn that a Japanese corporation wants to hire the firm to build wire-constructed safety air bags for the auto industry. The workers will buy back the plant from Garfield, and Sullivan and Garfield will handle the negotiations, opening the possibility, of course, that they will get together romantically.

Students have little difficulty uncovering binary oppositions at play in the film. As they do so, however, they also discover that these binaries are both unstable and frequently contradictory. For instance, in the early part of the film, there is the constant juxtaposition of scenes between Manhattan and the plant in Rhode Island—the glamour, hard polish, and technology of the one against the mundane, quaint, and primitive charm of the other. These scenes seem to establish a city-country binary, and Jorgensen later reminds Sullivan of the clean air they enjoy as the two of them have a smoke on the spacious front porch of his quaint, hillside country home after Thanksgiving dinner. The shots of the plant, however, reveal a smoking industrial quagmire of pipes and tubes and dilapidated buildings. While the plant was shot in the most picturesque of manners, using color settings that cast it in nostalgic golds and browns, the facility was clearly an ancient, outdated steel foundry. One wonders just how clean the air can be. The country-city, nature-culture binary does not seem consistent.

This sort of visual binary that eventually results in contradiction is reproduced as the students consider gender and class codes. As is all too clear, both Jorgensen and Garfield are unapologetic sexists in their attitudes and behavior. Jorgensen must be tactfully persuaded to seek Sullivan's advice, and then he ignores it in forcing a stockholders' vote that she has insisted he will probably lose. Garfield's blatant sexual advances toward Sullivan are less offensive than they might be only because DeVito's impish charm is able to make them humorous in their unexpected bluntness and crude candor. (On their first meeting, he suddenly proposes they get together to sweat between satin sheets.) The film seems to ask us to see Sullivan as the feminist who reconciles the old capitalist order with the new, but she does so without influencing the blatant sexism that is at the heart of both. She is also the agent in saving the workers' jobs, but the sharp criticism of both Jorgensen and Garfield that this implies—if they're so smart, why didn't they think of this alternative?—is left unexplored. The conclusion even points to the conflicted response to the Japanese presented in a number of scenes; they are both admired for their success and resented for competing so effectively with the United States.

The film's treatment of social class is typical of most Hollywood productions of the 1980s in that workers are simply not allowed to speak for themselves. When asked to look for the workers' stance on the conflicts offered, students have no difficulty concluding that the company's employees are given no voice in the negotiations. Even worse, they are presented as totally dependent children who must be protected by the patriarch Jorgensen. They are center-screen only at the opening when they are shown entering the plant, a little later when a family-like photograph of all the employees is being taken, and again near the end when they are portrayed outside the hall where the stockholders' meeting is being held, listening intently to loudspeakers broadcasting the speeches of Jorgensen and Garfield. The only speaking part a worker is given involves a frightened man asking Jorgensen in a childlike manner to reassure him that everything will be all right despite the takeover bid. Jorgensen, of course, does so in the soothing tones a father uses with a frightened child. The patriarchy displayed in the gender relations in the film is thus extended to the treatment of workers. Garfield shares in this attitude, adding contempt to arrogance as he wonders aloud while entering the crowded plant site for the stockholders' meeting why the workers always bring their children to their demonstrations, doing so while he dismissively looks at them beating on his limousine windows.

This leads to *Roger and Me.* This 1989 film is on its face a documentary dealing with the lives of auto workers losing their jobs as a result of General Motors plant closings in Flint, Michigan. But this film speaks for workers and is finally a stinging and artfully presented denunciation of corporate capitalism. Indeed, the managerial class presented in relatively glowing terms in *Other People's Money is* here held up to vicious ridicule. The film thus serves a number of functions in the dialectical thinking students must undertake in addressing cultural codes. The film attempts to depict some of the grim realities of the capitalistic process that Garfield so blithely ignores. (Indeed, Garfield explicitly states that stockholders owe workers nothing, since workers have never done anything for stockholders except demand higher wages. For Garfield, as for Adam Smith, the system works best when each of us selfishly pursues our own individual interests.) In Flint, no Japanese firm miraculously appears to create new jobs for workers. Michael Moore, the film's creator and narrator, examines the catastrophic results of a corporation abandoning a city to seek higher profits elsewhere. Indeed, the recurring image in the film is the eviction of family after family from their homes by the county sheriff, their possessions ungraciously stacked up next to the street. At the same time, an analysis of the binary oppositions inscribed in the film reveals in them the same sort of instability and contradiction we saw in the other film. *Roger and Me* is as ideologically loaded as *Other People's Money,* and just as unsuccessful at resolving the conflicts and contradictions it presents as its counterpart.

The ideological reading of the narrative strategies of the two films, then, is designed to make students suspicious of easy resolutions of complex social, economic, and political problems. Texts should be understood in terms of what they omit as well as what they include, and they should be situated within their historical context. In a broader sense, motivating students to become critical readers and writers of film and television is meant to equip them to make more intelligent decisions in their public and private experience, particularly since they are encouraged to see the inescapable relation of the personal and the political. The two films offer comforting ideological narratives, but neither finally can be accepted at face value. Any successful response to the conflicts and contradictions they locate must include the dialectical interaction of both points of view.

I should also mention at this point that we have experimented with students producing their own short videotaped productions. The point of doing so is to enable them to see the immensely complex coding system involved in producing the effect found in even the most pedestrian television program. Students begin to discover firsthand how difficult it is to generate the effects of the real found in a professionally televised event. Perceiving television from the point of view of the producer encourages students to recognize the manufactured character of television programming, the manner in which it is constructed rather than simply recorded. Groups of three or four students who produce their own five-minute news program or an account of a sporting event come to view television from the point of view of production as well as consumption. Situated within a course emphasizing cultural critique, this effort makes students better readers of video texts.

After some experience with written and video texts, students apply these heuristics to their personal experiences to analyze in essay form the effect of an important cultural code on their lives. The students select the topic and content of the essay, but they do so within the context of the larger theme of each unit. Thus, in the unit on work, students choose some feature of their work experience or their observation of cultural codes regarding work—in the media, for example—that has been of particular personal significance. The students then locate points of conflict and dissonance in the cultural codes discovered, along with their ideological predispositions. They are not expected to attempt a resolution of these conflicts, a matter usually much more complex. Students commonly choose to write about their experiences in part-time jobs while in high school. For example, they have considered the differences in treatment accorded men and women or African American and white workers, discussing these disparities in terms of cultural codes regarding race and gender within a particular work context. A number of women who grew up in agricultural communities have discussed the unfair constraints imposed on them in performing farm work, prohibitions that seemed to them arbitrary and irrational. Many students have written about their experiences in fast-food restaurants, discussing the conflicting class, race, and gender codes that were subtly as well as overtly enforced. Most students have deplored the dissonance manifested in these codes, but others have attempted to justify them as economic or cultural expedients needed for a smoothly functioning social order. Since drafts of student essays are always shared with other class members, however, unreflective generalizations about the inevitability of class, race, gender, or age behavior never go unchallenged.

Students become accustomed to debate and disagreement in this course as they explore a diversity of cultural codes. The differences in their ways of negotiating and resisting these codes become quickly apparent, as when, for instance, they discuss both their direct subversions of work rules and their less confrontational avoidance of them. The important consideration is that the students situate the personal actions they invoke within race, class, gender, sexual orientation, ethnic, and age codes and then locate these codes within larger economic and social narratives. In this way, they begin to understand the coded nature of their daily behavior, and they begin to become active, critical subjects rather than passive objects of their experience.

As students develop material through the use of the heuristics and begin to write initial drafts of their essays, they discuss the culturally coded character of all parts of composing—from genre to patterns of organization to sentence structure. Students must learn to arrange their materials to conform to the genre codes of the form of the essay they are writing—the personal essay or the academic essay, for example. (The production of a video news story enables an encounter with still another kind of genre code, this one visual and aural.) These essay genres conform to socially indicated formal codes that students must identify and enact and of course carry great consequence for meaning. A given genre encourages certain kinds of messages while discouraging others. Next, at the level of the sentence, stylistic form comes into play, and the student must again learn to generate sentence structures and patterns of diction expected in the genre employed. Students must engage in sentence combining and sentence generating activities. It is important that students be made aware of the purposes of these codes, both practical and ideological. In other words, expecting certain formal and stylistic patterns is not simply a matter of securing "clear and effective communication." As most writing teachers realize, most errors in grammar and spelling do not in themselves interfere with the reader's understanding. The use of *who* for *whom,* for example, seldom creates any confusion in reference. These errors instead create interferences of a social and political nature.

Finally, I would like to restate a point on the interchangeability of reading and writing made earlier. In enacting the reading and writing process, students learn that all experience is situated within signifying practices and that learning to understand personal and social experience involves acts of discourse production and interpretation, the two acting reciprocally in reading and writing codes. Students discover that interpretation involves production as well as reproduction and is as constructive as composing itself. At the same time, they find out that the more one knows about a text—its author, place of publication, audience, historical context—the less indeterminate it becomes and the more confident the reader can be in interpreting and negotiating its preferred reading. Similarly, the more the writer understands the entire semiotic context in which he or she functions, the greater the likelihood that the text will serve as an effective intervention in an ongoing discussion. After all, despite the inevitable slippages that appear in the production and interpretation of codes, people do in fact regularly communicate with each other to get a great variety of work done successfully. At the same time, even these efficacious exchanges can harbor concealed or ignored contradictions. These contradictions are important for the reader and writer to discover, because they foreground the political unconscious of decision making, a level of unspoken assumptions often repressed in ordinary discourse.

Again, an important objective of this course is to prepare students for critical citizenship in a democracy. We want students to begin to understand that language is never innocent, that it instead constitutes a terrain for ideological battle. Language—textuality—is the terrain on which different conceptions of economic, social, and political conditions are contested, with consequences for the formation of the subjects of history, the consciousness of the historical agent. We are thus committed to teaching reading and writing as an inescapably political act, the working out of contested cultural codes affecting every feature of experience. This involves teachers in an effort to problematize students' experiences, requiring them to challenge the ideological codes students bring to college by placing their signifying practices against alternatives. Sometimes this can be done cooperatively, with teachers and students agreeing about the conflicts apparent in a particular cultural formation—for example, the elitist and often ruthlessly competitive organization of varsity sports in high schools. Students can thus locate points of personal resistance and negotiation in dealing with the injustices of this common social practice. At other times, students and teachers are at odds with each other or, just as often, the students are themselves divided about the operation and effects of conflicting codes. This often results in spirited exchange. The role of the teacher is to act as a mediator while ensuring that no code, including his or her own, goes unchallenged.

Course Two: The Discourse of Revolution

I would like now to describe a course for college juniors and seniors that might be called "The Discourse of Revolution." Once again, I describe one possibility, an example rather than a definitive model. As I indicated in the last chapter, the moments at which large changes in economic, social, political, and cultural conditions take place most clearly demonstrate the conflicts between different conceptions of reading and writing practices, of poetics and rhetorics. This course is organized around a consideration of signifying practices and their relation to subject formation within the contexts of power at one of these important moments in political and textual history, focusing on texts and their contexts in England during the time of the two revolutions at the end of the eighteenth century—roughly between 1775 and 1800. Once again, the heuristic to be employed in examining both rhetorical and poetical discourse requires looking at each text in its interacting generic, ideological, and socioeconomic environments. At each level, the reader attempts to locate the conflicts and contradictions addressed, resolved, ignored, or concealed with a view to considering their significance to the formation of subjects and to the larger culture. In the case of literary texts, the unique historical role of the aesthetic is a special concern. I should add that I have in mind a teacher who is familiar with, although not necessarily an expert in, the period under study.

The course begins with a consideration of the concrete economic, social, and political events of the period. Students read in the history of the time. The version I have found most useful is Michel Beaud's *A History of Capitalism* (1983), especially chapter three, "The Century of the Three Revolutions (Eighteenth Century)." Beaud establishes in clear detail the complex interactions of four major economic and political events of the century, events especially evident in the period being considered. These events are at the center of the development of mercantile capitalism and the beginnings of industrial capitalism.

The first of these events was the extension of England's colonial domination and worldwide trade through the development of merchant capitalism. The construction of a banking system that made possible the financing of commercial expansion was crucial. England began the export of coal and wheat, became a transport center for the traders of other countries, and established itself as a warehouse center for goods traveling through the Americas, the Indies, and Europe. The cultivation of international economic exchange led to an increasing supply of primary products—such as tea, sugar, and cotton—and a corresponding enlargement of manufacturing due to new market outlets for textiles and other manufactured products. Beaud is especially effective in tracing the role of slavery in the establishment of England's economic success. This trading cycle involved the selling of English guns in Africa that were used to kidnap and enslave Africans. The slaves were then sold to the colonies as cheap labor for the production of cotton, tobacco, and sugar. These materials were then returned to England for processing, manufacture, and export. Since England also built the ships involved in this trade and provided the seaports for warehousing and exchange, it is not difficult to see the reasons behind its great economic growth in the eighteenth century.

The second element in the rise of England as an economic and political power had to do with the enclosure acts and the modernization of agriculture. The enclosure acts appropriated land that had historically been used by the common people to supplement their meager wages. With the enclosure acts, the use of this land was restricted to the major land owners in a district. At the same time, landed gentry and aristocrats developed new farming techniques that increased yields and profits. These techniques improved efficiency and lessened the need for workers. The combination of the enclosure acts and the loss of work to new farming techniques created a surplus labor force that could be called upon by the newly developed manufacturing enterprises of the cities.

This availability of labor was central to the third major element in the development of England's economic growth. The scientific spirit and the techniques applied to production led to a series of inventions that grew upon one another. These inventions ranged from the development of machines for the rapid production of textiles to the introduction of steam power in mills. Such new manufacturing enterprises hired the workers who had been displaced from rural areas by the enclosure acts and scientific farming. Finally, the additional capital made available by commerce and agriculture paid for the construction of more mills.

All of this led to increased production and an extension of wage payment. Since worker struggles intensified, the state interceded on behalf of the monied interests in a series of protectionist measures, establishing policies designed to suppress worker revolts. In 1769, for example, to destroy machines or the building in which they were housed was designated a felony offense, punishable by death. Government troops were used to break up worker riots in Lancaster in 1779 and Yorkshire in 1796. By 1799, laws were enacted to prohibit workers' associations formed to press for better wages, reduced working days, and the improvement of working conditions. This suppression of the working class was undertaken by an emerging power bloc made up of the new bourgeoisie and the old aristocracy. Ultimately, these two groups called upon a shared version of culture and taste to provide a common ground for their economic and political alliance. In a nation of some 6,000,000 people, the electorate was made up of 450,000 men consisting of lawyers, local notables, well-to-do farmers, clergy, and university professors. Parliament thus represented the interests of these groups.

Once students have read and discussed Beaud, they move on to contrast his account of these events with the account offered in Linda Colley's *Britons: Forging the Nation, 1707-1837* (1992). While Colley details the interaction of the economic, social, and political developments found in Beaud's account, she places them within a different narrative frame. Rather than foregrounding economic activity as the most important influence in the events of the eighteenth century, Colley argues for the primacy of the political. For her, the story of this period is the reaction of the Britons to military threats from abroad, especially France. These threats, she argues, were most responsible for forming a national identity and encouraging a complex range of social and economic as well as military responses. She is especially interested in tracing the effects of these threats on forming a national identity. Thus, she places significant features of national behavior between 1707 and 1837 within a narrative organized around two major themes. Colley explains:

> What made these themes, mass allegiance on the one hand and the invention of Britishness on the other, so central during this 130-year long period was a succession of wars between Britain and France. Prime powers on sea and on land respectively, the whale and the elephant as Paul Kennedy styles them, they were at war between 1689 and 1697, and on a larger scale and for higher stakes between 1702 and 1713, 1743 and 1748, 1756 and 1763, 1778 and 1783, 1793 and 1802, and, finally, between 1803 and the Battle of Waterloo in 1815. And these were only the most violent expressions of a much longer and many-layered rivalry. (1)

Colley thus deals extensively with the two revolutions central to this course and in doing so presents an especially rich analysis of their consequences for gender, class, and race formations and relations. One purpose of studying her account next to Beaud's is to examine the effects of different narrative frames on the interpretation of specific historical events. This experience is also meant to encourage students to look for similar contrasts in the interpretation of rhetorical and poetic texts. Students thus arrive at conclusions about the place of narrative frames in understanding historical events and the role of writing and reading practices in influencing these frames.

Having looked at different narrative accounts of the larger historical events of the period, students go on to examine the changes in publication practices and the reading public that appeared in response to the emerging economic and political conditions. Although somewhat dated, Ian Watt's "The Reading Public and the Rise of the Novel" in *The Rise of the Novel* (1957) is still useful. This can be supplemented by student reports on J. Paul Hunter's *Before Novels* (1990), Isabel Rivers's collection *Books and their Readers in Eighteenth-Century England* (1982), and Bridget Hill's *Women, Work, and Sexual Politics in Eighteenth-Century England* (1989). These provide an overview of the production, distribution, and consumption of printed texts during this period. They are especially effective in charting transformations in the social structure, particularly in the formation of the new middle class. Reading and writing were being redefined along class lines, and the specialization of these activities for different groups became commonplace. Reading became an activity undertaken for pleasure, a pursuit of leisure, as well as for the purposes of knowledge and moral improvement. Written texts became commodities for entertainment, to be exchanged in the growing market economy. This encouraged a new group of writers, since it was possible for a select few to earn a living by the profits from their writing, even though wealthy patrons still bore the costs of publishing many books in the period. Changes in publishing were also related to transformations in the role of women in all classes at this time. Shifting economic and social conditions created new opportunities for women's independence as well as new forms of repression. Their role as producers and consumers in the expanding reading public was especially important.

Again, the purpose of asking students to undertake this work is to prepare them to consider the ways in which the signifying practices in texts were working to form subjects, to create particular kinds of consciousness, along the lines of gender, class, race, age, sexual orientation, and related categories. As students will quickly discover, the texts they encounter respond to these subject formations and the contradictions and conflicts they create, doing so both openly and in covert and unconscious ways. Students can thus examine the power conflicts and contradictions among classes and among individuals as they are revealed in the texts of this period. These conflicts can then form the basis for large and small group discussions as well as for individual and collaborative written responses, considerations that call for a comment on the pedagogical procedures to be followed in the classroom.

As I indicated earlier, authority should be shared as much as possible. While the teacher sets up the syllabus, maps out a diverse body of readings, and offers methods for responding to them, students should have a choice in activities, assume leadership roles in instruction, and participate in an ongoing dialogue on the issues explored. All texts cannot be read in their entirety. Thus, small groups of three or four students should present their interpretation of a particular text to the class, explaining such matters as the rhetorical patterns they see at work, the narratives inscribed in the text, and the ideological loyalties they discover. They will, of course, also seek the conflicts and contradictions these narratives ignore or resolve in unconvincing ways, paying particular attention to the class, race, and gender roles at issue and their relation to larger socioeconomic proposals. Such encounters commonly lead to disagreement as students arrive at different interpretations, often even as they use similar interpretive categories in reading. Here the productive nature of reading can be explored, particularly the possibilities for a variety of formulations of a common text. Disagreement is to be expected as the students observe the diverse ideological positions of the texts they read.

Class members should also, of course, be involved in text production. They should keep journals, prepare position papers for the class, and even imitate and parody the materials of the late eighteenth century in an attempt to understand the methods of signification called upon and their relationship to economic, social, political, and cultural constructions. They should self-consciously pursue particular rhetorical devices, devices chosen because of their effectiveness in making a case. In other words, the rhetorics and rhetorical texts of the late eighteenth century must be seen in terms of their differences from contemporary constructions as well as their similarities. Students will learn that producing different utterances about a single event commonly involves producing different meanings. On average, class members should thus prepare about five pages of typewritten text every three weeks or so and a larger term project on a problem of special personal interest. Meanwhile, their journals, written in three half-hour sittings weekly, can serve as commentary on the class's activities and the students' experience in developing new reading and writing strategies. Of course, the journal also acts as a private forum for considering issues raised in the class.

Students begin their encounter with primary texts by considering the rhetorical treatises that present in detail the conflicting norms for communication being debated during the time under study, beginning with John Ward's neoclassical Ciceronian rhetoric A *System of Oratory* (1759). Ward's book is important because it represents one of the more prominent discussions of the rhetorical forms preferred by ruling groups during most of the century. This book can be followed by the new rhetorics that articulate the signifying practices, subject formations, and economic and political conditions favored by the emerging bourgeoisie and their aristocratic allies, such as George Campbell's *The Philosophy of Rhetoric* (1776) and Hugh Blair's *Lectures on Rhetoric and Belles Lettres* (1783). Both Campbell and Blair were Scottish clerics and university professors, Campbell at Marischall College, Aberdeen, and Blair at Edinburgh, where he was Regius Professor of Rhetoric and Belles Lettres. The two rhetorics were extremely popular, with Blair's going through 130 editions in England and America, the last in 1911. Both are grounded in Scottish Common Sense Realism, and while Campbell's is the more rigorously philosophical of the two, Blair's is notable for its relation to Adam Smith's lectures on rhetoric delivered at the University of Glasgow when Blair was a student, as well as for its readable style.

These rhetorics of the emerging bourgeois order must be considered not only in relation to the positions they replaced, but also in relation to those competing with them for primacy. Two of these that are especially worth considering because they offer a rhetoric designed for the new gender designations of the period are Hannah More's *Strictures on the Modern System of Female Education* (1799) and Catherine Macaulay's *Letters on Education* (1790). While both are primarily concerned with the unique conditions of education for girls, both also consider rhetoric. More and Macaulay were themselves members of the new middle class of women writers, offering at once encouragement and implicit criticism of the patriarchal rhetorics of Blair and Campbell. Mary Wollstonecraft's *Vindication of the Rights of Woman* (1792), on the other hand, presents rhetorical principles designed to directly counter the patriarchal ideology of the emerging middle class.

In examining the sections of these rhetorics selected by the teacher—or, as often happens, by a student group working collaboratively—class members should interrogate the texts in a particular way. This does not mean, I should caution, that only one method of reading should be tolerated in the class. No one expects students to abandon their customary methods of interpreting texts. Indeed, old and new hermeneutic strategies should interact in the students' reaction to the text, and this interaction should become a part of the ongoing class discussion as well as written assignments.

Students should first determine the recommended subject position of the interlocutor portrayed in the rhetoric along with the corresponding subject position indicated for the audience. In other words, students must determine who is allowed to speak and who is allowed to listen and act on the message of the speaker. The object is to analyze the features of these two interacting subject formations. After all, a rhetoric is primarily a device to train producers of discourse. During the time under study, however, rhetorics became as interested in advising audiences as interlocutors. Indeed, Blair's text is the first I know that argues that it is also intended for people who will never have to speak or write but are interested in text interpretation. Blair may be referring to the new class of women readers who were a part of an identifiable reading public but whose access to textual production was limited—except, of course, for a few members who were engaged in certain literary genres. Indeed, women were attending classroom lectures at Edinburgh at this time, although they were not allowed formal matriculation. Once again, issues of class and gender emerge as the rhetorics define the characteristics of the expected interlocutor and audience.

Students should also examine the rules for evidence these rhetorics display, a concern that deals with questions of epistemology and ideology. In other words, they should locate principles for discovering the available means of persuasion, principles that distinguish true from untrue knowledge, indicating what counts as real and what is ephemeral, what is good, and what is possible. The inductive rhetorics of Campbell and Blair, authorizing certain bourgeois conceptions of nature and human behavior, can thus be distinguished from the deductive and vaguely aristocratic rhetoric of Ward, on the one hand, and the feminist, communal, and egalitarian rhetoric of Wollstonecraft, on the other.

Last, students should determine the manner in which language is conceived in each rhetoric, considering its relation to knowledge and its role in bringing about agreement and disagreement. As in their work on subject formations, students will see here the play of class, gender, race, sexual orientation, ethnicity, age, and similar designations in determining what can and cannot be communicated. Of course, the contrasting and contradictory recommendations of the varied rhetorics in all of these matters should constantly be studied in their differing relations to power formations.

Having considered these more or less theoretical treatises, students turn their attention to actual rhetorical texts that addressed the revolutions that were at the center of the period. (I want to thank Mark Gellis for the suggestions for this section provided in his doctoral dissertation "Burke, Campbell, Johnson, and Priestley: A Rhetorical Analysis of Four British Pamphlets of the American Revolution.") These texts represent various ideological positions, roughly corresponding to those in the rhetorical texts examined. The rhetorics taken up earlier were inspected for their presentation of the subject of the address, the subjects addressed, the rules of knowledge to be invoked, and the relation of language to all of these. Exploring rhetorical texts involves applying the differing formulations of these elements to the conflicting representations of revolution offered. The purpose is to relate the versions of subjects, communities (audiences), and language to actual narrative interpretations of experience. In other words, the ruling conceptions of each argument should be examined as they unfold in the narrative presentation of events and their principle actors in the portrayal of revolution. The genre of the text here becomes important, as students determine the formal patterns of the argument—inductive, deductive, emotional, ethical—and the way a particular rhetoric indicates they are to proceed. Style, of course, is also of concern here, as the characteristic choices in diction and syntax are related to rhetorical and ideological commitments.

One of the more accessible devices for enabling students to deal with narrative patterns is Kenneth Burke's dramatistic scheme (1966). It conceives of the formation of plot in terms of the relations among scene, act, agent, agency, and purpose. Students can with little difficulty locate the elements of the presentation that fall into each category and then determine their relative importance in the plot design of the text. In turn, the plot can be situated within ideological predispositions that Burke locates in certain configurations of the interacting elements. It can then be related to larger socioeconomic patterns.

A good first case to take up is George Campbell's pamphlet arguing against the American Revolution, *The Duty of Allegiance* (1777). This can be followed by Edmund Burke's contrary treatment of the American Revolution in *A Letter to the Sheriffs of Bristol* (1777). The contrast is intended to encourage an exploration of the different rhetorical devices used in the defense of different positions, but students should also pay careful attention to the conflicting representation of historical events both texts address. In other words, while Campbell and Burke often agree on the details of an important incident, they usually disagree about its causes and consequences. Next up might be Burke's *Reflections on the Revolution in France* (1790), along with Wollstonecraft's *A Vindication of the Rights of Men* (1790), a work written to rebut Burke, and *A Vindication of the Rights of Woman* (1792). These might be followed, in turn, by a discussion of Thomas Paine's *The Rights of Man* (1791-1792) and, finally, selections from Olaudah Equiano's *The Interesting Narrative of the Life of Olaudah Equiano or Gustavus Vassa, the African* (1789). The last is a memoir that reveals vividly the cruelties of slavery as related by one of its victims, a person stolen from Africa and enslaved in 1756, eventually to be located on a plantation in Virginia. After being sold to a Philadelphia businessman, Equiano was able to save enough money to buy his freedom and move to London in 1766. The book is a valuable firsthand account of a gifted writer's experience of the inhumanity of slavery, told in the style of high Augustan Humanism.

At this point, the class turns to a sharply contrasting set of signifying practices, practices themselves marked by difference. The second half of the course, that is, is devoted to sampling the variety of poetics and poetic texts that the period produced. Here the effort is to see the intense conflict over poetic forms that appeared at this time and the relation of these differences to economics and politics. It is common, for instance, for students in courses dealing with English Romantic poetry to be told about the instantaneous and extraordinary departure of the poetical methods of Wordsworth and Coleridge from the work of their predecessors. In this course, however, students are asked to read a variety of the texts appearing during the last quarter of the eighteenth century to test the adequacy of this proposition. In the process, they will arrive at—or at least have to consider—alternative formulations that certainly seem more attentive to the actual events and practices of the time. In other words, students will examine a range of poetic texts to realize the remarkable variety in the different forms appearing and to locate the relation of these varieties to literary, ideological, and socioeconomic developments.

This section of the course begins with readings in poetic theory and criticism. Samuel Johnson represents a useful starting point, since he is commonly thought of as the representative figure of the third quarter of the century—a proposition, incidentally, that will be challenged in this section of the course. Students should read *Rasselas* (1759) and selections from the "Preface to Shakespeare" (1765) to see a prominent conception of the nature of poetry and the role of the poet in the life of the society appearing at this time. (I realize these selections appear a bit before the period considered, but their contrastive value in these later discussions justify their selection.) Once again, students should read with a view to locating the rhetorical elements of the act of poetic production and reception, discovering the notion of the subject of creation and interpretation, the epistemological and ideological guides for determining the matter and method of poetic texts, and the signifying practices to be preferred. These texts will, of course, reinforce certain notions of economic, political, and cultural constraints encountered in the rhetorical texts read earlier, with the category of the aesthetic a key concern. Students must locate the preferred formal properties of the poetry encouraged, including diction, syntax, and metrical patterns as well as generic formulas. They will discover that certain kinds of subject matter, themes, and narrative paradigms are preferred as well.

Johnson can be followed by selections from Burke's *Philosophical Enquiry into the Origins of Our Ideas of the Sublime and the Beautiful* (1757) and Archibald Alison's *Essays on the Nature and Principles of Taste* (1790). While Burke's essay is years prior to the period considered here, it was continually influential, as evidenced by Alison's treatment of the beautiful and sublime. Students might also consider statements by Campbell on poetics, particularly the taxonomy in which he makes poetry a lower subdivision of persuasive oratory, and statements by Blair, who devotes the largest part of his *Lectures on Rhetoric and Belles Lettres* to poetic texts. Students should also read selections from Maria Edgeworth's *Letters for Literary Ladies* (1795). Although Edgeworth is concerned with novelists as well as poets, her perspective on the unique strengths and weaknesses of women artists is instructive. Finally, the class might read Wordsworth's "Preface to *Lyrical Ballads*" (1800).

The overall effect of examining these disparate comments is to familiarize students with the remarkably divergent statements on poetry offered at this time. Furthermore, when they turn to the poetry itself, students are likely to find diversity even greater than they had anticipated. They might best begin with the canonical texts, those most likely to display features considered in the most prominent critical statements, such as Johnson's *The Vanity of Human Wishes* (1749). This poem appeared long before 1775, but it once again enables discussion of some of the salient thematic, narrative, and formal features of a major strand of eighteenth-century verse. Students can readily locate the classical influences; the conventional devices favored, including the couplet; and the abstract, specialized poetic diction preferred in this genre. They should also consider the satiric intention and the devices used to achieve it. This poetry of the urbane and the urban might then be contrasted with the canonical poetry of the countryside. Particularly worth considering is George Crabbe's *The Village* (1783). This work depicts the dark side of rural life from the point of view of an unfriendly observer of the lower orders while following many of the expected conventions of the Augustan pastoral genre. Crabbe was encouraged by both Burke and Johnson, the latter offering revisions of portions of *The Village.* This can be followed very usefully by a selection from William Cowper's *The Task* (1785), an English Georgic poem with mock epic tones reflecting on the daily experience of country life before the French Revolution and including comments on such topics as the cruelty of war and slavery. *The Task is* especially noteworthy since by 1800 it had sealed its author's reputation as the most famous poet of England.

The next group of poems I recommend consists of works that were well regarded in their own day but which have failed to make it into the contemporary canon. The authors of these texts were self-consciously responding to the work of the canonical poets of the first group. The important difference is that they were writing from the unique perspective of women, sometimes in an attempt to align themselves with what they saw to be their male counterparts, sometimes in open opposition to them. Their readers, it should be noted, were often the same as those of the male poets of the age, a middle-class group that probably included at least as many women as men.

One of the most successful was Hannah More, a poet praised by Johnson but commonly denounced by Coleridge, Southey, and De-Quincey. More was conservative in art and politics while arguing for more equitable—but not equal—relations between women and men. She also included in certain poems attacks on the horrors of slavery. Anna Seward was considered in her own day one of the outstanding poets of the 1780s. She openly opposed Johnson's poetic and wrote verse that was praised by Wordsworth, but she remained politically conservative, eventually denouncing the French Revolution. Anna Leatitia Barbauld displayed a remarkable complexity in her poetics and politics. She was a part of the Johnson circle but a supporter of the French Revolution and a strong opponent of slavery. She was also an acquaintance of Wordsworth, Coleridge, and Southey, and her subject matter includes the ordinary concerns of common people—as in "Washing Day" and "To the Poor." She often cannot, however, escape the diction and syntax of an earlier time. Helen Maria Williams was also a part of the Johnson circle but Boswell dropped the "amiable" he had used to describe her in his *Life of Johnson* because of her support of the French Revolution. Williams represents a genuine departure in the form and themes of her poetry, so much so that Wordsworth dedicated his first published poem to her (Lonsdale 1989, 413-14). Mary Robinson was a successful actress and poet who, despite public censure for her personal life—at one point she was the contractual mistress of the Prince of Wales—was one of the most highly regarded and frequently published poets of her day. Her poetry displays the radical themes and, occasionally, the forms that were the counterparts of her politics and her defiance of conventional norms. She is an especially keen observer of the subtleties as well as obvious injustices of the class structure in the city Finally, Phyllis Wheatley, an American slave educated by her master, published *Poems on Various Subjects, Religious and Moral* in 1773 during a trip to London with her master's son. She was later freed, but died in poverty and obscurity in 1784. Wheatley's poetry offers the rich contrast of a slave's perspective couched in the form and language of neoclassic and eighteenth-century religious verse.

These poets can be followed by a set of writers representing the emergence of the working class in literary circles, a group sometimes referred to as the "plebeian poets" or "peasant poets." Gustav Klaus's *The Literature of Labour: Two Hundred Years of Working-Class Writing* (1985) and Donna Landry's *The Muses of Resistance: Laboring-Class Women's Poetry in Britain, 1739-1796* (1990) are good introductions to this topic. These poets' appearance is related to the increase in education among workers due to the Charity Schools and Sunday Schools, but their rise to prominence at this time is largely attributable to the support of patrons.

Anne Yearsley was among the best known of the peasant poets, and Elizabeth Hands among the most highly regarded. Yearsley was promoted in her career by Hannah More, although her patron never felt it appropriate that she attempt to make a living as an author. Yearsley's *Poems on Several Occasions* (1785) was published with the support of a subscription raised by More, but by its fourth edition in 1786 the poet found it necessary to append an "Autobiographical Narrative" defending herself from More's attempt to manage her finances. She also published "Poem on the Inhumanity of the Slave Trade" (1788) and collections entitled *Stanzas of Woe* (1790) and *The Rural Lyre* (1796) as well as a novel and a play and some political pamphlets. Yearsley's poetry examines the class and gender conflicts that marked her life, moving between conventional themes and techniques and political and formal boldness. As Landry (1990) notes, her later poetry places her somewhere "between civic poet and social dissident" (122). Elizabeth Hands's single volume of verse, *The Death of Amnon. A Poem. With an Appendix: Containing Pastorals, and Other Poetical Pieces,* was published in 1789. Its title piece is a skillful comic satire in the manner of Swift presented from the perspective of a feminist social critic. Hands is probably the most resourceful of the peasant poets, fluent, as Landry puts it, in "the English literary tradition yet bold enough to mock it, paying homage to the fathers yet reworking pastoral verse forms in a feminizing way" (186). Hands brilliantly turns the conventions of the genres she calls on against the themes they traditionally forwarded, using her class and gender position to challenge dominant conceptions—even if she cannot finally resist a conservative stance.

James Woodhouse and Robert Bloomfield were peasant poets who suffered under the burden of being thought of as the embodiment of the untutored, natural genius. Woodhouse's *The Life and Lucubrations of Crispinus Scriblerus* (written in 1795 but not published until 1896) provides an autobiographical account of the difficulties of the self-educated, working-class poet, a figure treated at once as a celebrity and a freak. Woodhouse's relationship to Elizabeth Montagu, his patron, parallels that of Yearsley in its bitter disputes. Robert Bloomfield's *The Farmer's Boy* (1800) was a critical success and widely read. It offers a personalized account of the social life of rural England, including a critique from the perspective of the loyal peasant. Bloomfield and Woodhouse both reveal in their poetry the clash of competing styles in form and theme, as the language and experience of the worker in the field contend with the conventions of the Georgic pastoral celebrated in the parlors of polite society.

Finally, I like to have the class turn to selections from Wordsworth and Coleridge's *Lyrical Ballads* (1798 and 1800), especially the preface from the 1800 edition. This collection and the statement of its principles of composition, of course, have long been considered revolutionary departures in the history of English letters—a status most often grounded in the language of binary opposition, with a coherent version of Romanticism put up against a coherent version of Neoclassicism. The introductory remarks on the Romantic period in *The Norton Anthology of English Literature,* for example, are not unusual. Here the romantics are at every turn praised for their departures from their benighted predecessors. While the last age of poets looked to the outer world and favored the epic and drama, we are told, the new poetry looked to the inner world in a celebration of the lyric. Against the ordinary experience of daily public life, the Romantics offered imaginative vision and the autobiographical. The poet as the observer of public manners is replaced by the poet as prophet. Rules and decorum are supplanted by feeling and spontaneity and original and organic forms. A mechanistic conception of nature is challenged by a natural world of divine force. Rural scenes are now to be frequented for their spiritual character, and the rustic and the commonplace are preferred to the city and its quest for novelty. In place of the common sense, order, and middle path of the neoclassical is proffered the radically individual, the creative, the imaginative, the infinite. Finally, the apocalyptic vision of the Bible is extended to history as the French Revolution is seen by some to be the fulfillment of human destiny in the establishment of a perfect order on earth.

It will require little effort on the part of students to see that these generalizations do not always square with their experience of the texts of this period. The students' final project might thus be to critique these simple binaries, testing the adequacy of them when measured against their own estimates. For instance, Margaret Anne Doody's *The Daring Muse: Augustan Poetry Reconsidered* (1985) challenges the accuracy of these generalizations for even the earliest Augustans. Students can thus try to account for the valorizing of a certain set of writing and reading practices as the basis of a literary canon and the attendant attribution of these characteristics almost exclusively to Wordsworth and Coleridge. *The Norton Anthology,* for example, claims that in "his democratization of poetry," Wordsworth was "more radical than any of his contemporaries. He effected an immense enlargement of our imaginative sympathies and brought into the province of serious literature a range of materials and interests which are still being explored by writers of the present day" (10). This passage will not ring true to students who have read noncanonical texts of the era.

This critique also encourages an equally significant observation: canon formation involves a discussion of our own discursive practices, our own loyalties in rhetoric and poetic. Indeed, the Preface to the *Lyrical Ballads* can be read as a rhetoric, a statement about signification in its broadest sense that forwards certain arguments for the character of discourse in politics and economics as well as poetry. As students examine it from this perspective, the central place of Wordsworth and Coleridge in the Romantic literary canon may suggest an attempt to recuperate in them certain kinds of ideological assertions. The poetry and criticism of *Lyrical Ballads* can be placed in relation to many of the most fundamental convictions of today's professional middle class about the existent, the good, and the possible, particularly in its insistence on the efficacy of the sovereign subject in economic and political action.

By the end of the course, students will have examined in detail the role of signification in forming our understanding of events. In considering the competing representations of the two revolutions, they will have explored the varied formulations that differing generic, ideological, and socioeconomic frames encourage. The case of the American Revolution is especially useful, since it offers interpretations widely at odds with those students customarily encounter this side of the Atlantic. The rhetorical analysis encouraged in the class assists students in arriving at judgments about the relative value of each. They also should at least begin to realize the role of the reading and writing practices of a particular moment in influencing decision making and action, including their own. This realization will be most potent, perhaps, for poetic texts, which the course seeks to present as important historical forces in consciousness formation, addressing significant personal and political issues, a central part of the play of power in historical conflicts. Students should come to see, in other words, that those texts that continue to be read are chosen as much for their uses to the disputants in these conflicts as for their reputed aesthetic value. The qualities of the aesthetic are variously defined across time, and they always appear in relation to other valued cultural codes.

Finally, I would again emphasize that the course described here is meant to be open-ended. Students should be encouraged to come to their own conclusions, the only provision being that they be prepared to support them and have them challenged. As I emphasized in the last chapter, students should be regarded as subjects of their experience, not empty receptacles to be filled with teacher-originated knowledge. This will make for a diversity of discoveries and for disagreement in discussion. Such activity, however, is to be expected and even fostered. It is a part of students actively becoming agents of change in a democratic society. Students in this kind of course are at every turn asked to challenge accepted wisdom and to come to their own positions about the issues under consideration. In addition, the reading and writing practices that the course encourages will further their ability to enter public dialogue, to master the operations of signification in the distribution of power. Students in such a course should thus become better writers and readers as citizens, workers, and critics of their cultures.

IV Department Directions

8
Sample Programs and Research

I have so far outlined the history of the formation of English studies, explained the inadequacy of an older model for the present, proposed a revised version, and offered examples of the way this alternative model might manifest itself in the classroom. I would now like to consider three English departments that have introduced exemplary new curricula for undergraduate and graduate instruction in English studies. I should say at the outset that I am not claiming that these departments would agree with my recommendations. Instead, I am simply pointing to them as useful efforts to address the crisis in English studies as I have described it. I should add, however, that despite their important differences, each has included elements recommended in this study in a manner that I cannot help but endorse. At the same time, all demonstrate shortcomings that I will consider briefly, albeit by way of offering suggestions for improvement. After considering these three departments, I want to comment briefly on recent efforts in creative writing instruction that reflect thinking similar to my own. The chapter will close with a survey of the kinds of research projects in graduate study that I would hope the proposals I have offered would encourage.

The three departments I will describe are located at Carnage Mellow University, the University of Pittsburgh, and the State University of New York at Albany. Each has self-consciously responded to conditions peculiar to itself, including its unique historical narrative and the needs of its student population. All are committed, however, to disrupting the old. hierarchical binaries of the discipline and to reformulating them in the light of postmodern theory. In discussing the three programs, I will rely on published descriptions prepared by supportive members of their faculties, hoping in this way to avoid misrepresenting them.

The Three Programs

Carnegie Mellon's English department offers undergraduate majors in creative writing, professional writing, and cultural studies. Of these, creative writing is the oldest, having been established in 1969. The professional writing major was a part of the newly installed program in rhetoric, set up by Richard Young in the 1979-80 school year. After having established the Ph.D. program in rhetoric, the department moved in 1982 to establish a Ph.D. program in cultural studies. The undergraduate program, for its part, is attempting to integrate the three elements of the department, an effort that is constantly being revised.

Alan Kennedy (1993), a literary theorist who served as the department's head during the later changes, has described the department's creation of a rhetoric program as "a much more radical possible transformation of our discipline than . . . the much contested [and later] appearance of cultural studies in our midst" (26). The rhetoric program, he explains, "mandated a theoretical concern with reading and writing processes, and with the social function of speech acts (production and reception of discourse) as a defining element of an English department" (26). Here the department attempted to disrupt the poetic-rhetoric binary, "the split between the elite study of literature (or the elite version of cultural studies, which stands to inherit much of the unpleasant side of the elitism of the old canon) on the one hand, and the underclass work of teaching writing on the other" (26).

Kennedy makes clear that every effort is made to resist privileging any one of the three programs. Instead, the objective is to provide "a congenial space for creative writers, rhetorical theorists, and people in literary and cultural theory" (37). The department works to decenter its curriculum, both in the theory that goes into its construction and in the non-hierarchical arrangement of its elements. Kennedy explains, "That lack of a center makes it possible for us to have an extremely wide range of options for our students. They can do a degree in creative writing while taking classes in cultural studies, feminist studies, film studies and professional writing. They can take a class in journalism, while doing one in Shakespeare, another in advertising, and another dealing with the way in which the portrayal of the erotic in film has been influenced by the discourse on AIDS" (37). The usual "hierarchy of privilege" in which canonical literary texts are at the center of the department's concern is thus disrupted. The governing conception instead becomes the utility of the curriculum in serving the needs and interests of students and their society.

This curriculum challenges at every turn the old notion of coverage and its insistence on the aesthetic focus of a literary education. Carnegie Mellon instead sees its English department as socially and politically useful. This does not mean, Kennedy hastens to add, a dedication to serving the market interests of multinational corporations. It does, however, recognize that English departments ought "to work in such a way as to help our students get jobs" (30-31). English classes must be as useful to students as they are to their teachers, who, after all, make a living teaching them. This is accomplished through offering courses and teaching them in a way that works for the shaping and reshaping of human values. Such an effort deals with difference and in this way arrives at politics. The point, Kennedy explains, is that committing to this curriculum means "producing the contradictions inherent in ideas like culture, self, and so on" (31). This is not the "difference" of bourgeois individualism. It is instead a concern for "real differences—that is, differences that occupy material positions, that inhabit political and economic boundaries" (32). These are the differences that "need to be made visible" (32).

Kennedy's argument for a curriculum grounded in a cultural and economic materialism is closely allied with deconstruction theory. Here he finds two important lessons: that "history is what there is, and that ethics is a fundamental concern of theory" (32). In considering history, deconstruction presents the rule of perpetual change:

> Forms, structures, systems, are constructed in time, they change in time and evolve into other forms, systems and structures. If we can not engage our students in the lifelong process of beginning to understand change and difference, we will do nothing of significance in our curricula. When we come to see that judgments about forms, values, and structures, are not timeless, are not the acts of gods, but are rather time-bound, historically positioned, we become capable not only of studying cultural objects from inside, but also of considering the history of the ways in which we study such things. (32)

Deconstruction, then, teaches us to locate temporal difference. The ethical lesson of deconstruction is functionally related: "If there were no differing value systems, there would be no basis for evaluating at all. With the disappearance of difference, we would witness the disappearance of value" (33). In recognizing the inevitability of difference in values, students will have a heuristic for arriving at value judgments: "They will not be victims of indoctrination, nor will they be subject to a curriculum that is inherently nihilistic. They will learn that there are different, and often contradictory, value systems in the world. But they will not necessarily learn therefore that all values are worthless" (33). In other words, differences in values are unavoidable because of the necessity to continually make judgments about human value. Existence without value construction is simply unimaginable.

In this scheme of study, all cultural texts are placed within the historical context that has given them meaning. Here the cultural concerns of the curriculum converge with the rhetorical, as Kennedy insists that all texts are finally rhetorical, that is, designed to bring about effects in the material world. The new English curriculum teaches students to become aware of the rhetorical effects of their own texts, literary and otherwise, to be "the producers as well as consumers of culture (33). Once again, this teaching and learning must take place within a context of values, and the English department must do more than simply "teach the conflicts" and encourage a "liberal polylogue." Forwarding such objectives unreflectively as ends in themselves, after all, usually obscures the power relations they encourage, and the purpose of English studies is to reveal, not conceal, commitments.

Pedagogy is thus a central concern of this department. Indeed, in describing this commitment, Kennedy focuses on the first-year writing course to demonstrate his claims. Of course, this focus is in itself a political statement about the power relations in this English department, since this course is ordinarily not the one advertised by department heads in recommending their programs to others. The first-year writing experience, Kennedy explains, is crucial, since it serves as an introduction to the department's offerings as well as to the uses of language in students' other courses. This classroom must be compatible with the larger purposes of the department and its conception of the humanities; that is, it must be useful to the student and society.

Its first objective, then, is to understand positionality and politics: "We want our students to be able to understand the idea of position. . . . We want them to be capable of occupying responsible and demanding positions. We want them to understand competing positions in world affairs. We want them to recognize their own positions, and be able to compare their positioning to that of others perhaps more or less fortunate" (37). Students learn that all reading is interpretive and representative; there are no simple summaries of material. They learn to look for absences in texts, the unstated margins of discourse. They learn that all issues are located at the center of multiple disputes. They learn the elements that go into forming an argument through reading and writing arguments. This material, however, is always related to the student's own experience. The purpose is not "to bare their souls" but to make their "own contribution," to establish their own agency in ongoing issues of public discourse. Students are not simply to choose the expert they find most understandable or compelling, but to engage the experts in debate to offer their own position, from their own perspective.

The reading and writing methods mutually encouraged by cultural studies and rhetoric come into play as students explore the texts of film, television, radio, and advertising in all its forms. These are examined in their economic, social, and political positionality, considering the ways "they persuade us, cajole us, deter us, exhort us, encourage, calm, and recompense us. All of the things traditionally claimed, in fact, for art" (39). The texts of high culture and everyday life are seen as rhetorical objects that "make claims on us" (39). They must be considered as arguments that are a part of an ongoing debate about important issues regarding how we live our lives and the structures of the institutions that shape us. The result is that cultural studies and rhetorical studies intersect, "extending rhetorical principles to cover writing on the one hand, and the study of culture on the other" (40).

Carnegie Mellon's effort is formidable. At the same time, though—the shortcomings I promised to raise—claims for the integration of rhetoric, literature, and creative writing are not always convincing. While the three may appear together in the first-year writing course, the curriculum as a whole is still divided along the lines of specialization, with clearly demarcated courses in literature, rhetoric, cultural studies, and creative writing. In other words, the commitment to integration has still not been worked out in the entire curriculum, as old disciplinary divisions continue to assert themselves. The potential contradictions between the uses of English studies to students, on the one hand, and to their employers, on the other, is likewise ignored. I readily acknowledge that the relation between the course described by Kennedy and the students' efforts as critical citizens is solidly established. The potential difficulties that this contestatory stance may cause in the workplace, however, are not addressed, even though the roles of the citizen and the worker are not always on this score compatible. Finally, despite the claims made for the accommodation of creative writing in the curriculum, there is little evidence of it in the course described. Creative writing offers special challenges to any integrated curriculum, and one wonders why Kennedy so scrupulously avoided any mention of them. In short, the program Kennedy describes is admirable, but the inevitable difficulties any effort of this scope will encounter are given short shrift. Kennedy, however, ends his description on a more convincing note, asserting that "curricular planning, a theory in practice, will always have local material determinants, and that there are no longer any readily exportable models for core curricula" (41).

This lesson is echoed by Philip E. Smith II, writing as chair of the English department at the University of Pittsburgh in "Composing a Cultural Studies Curriculum at Pitt" (1993). He explains that in 1977, his English department began to discuss the "distinction between a static, canon-based curriculum that certifies revealed cultural truths and a dynamic, postmodern curriculum that interrogates knowledge and ways of knowing" (46). The result has been the development of an undergraduate and graduate program in cultural studies, culminating in 1986 in a new Ph.D. program called "Cultural and Critical Studies." Smith describes the process in now familiar terms: "We re-defined the 'coverage' model of aestheticized literary study by confronting it with recent developments in canon revision and in theory (literary, cultural, and feminist), pedagogy, film, media, and popular culture, by including the global dispersion of literatures in English as well as the special discourses of gender, race, and class, and by developing the graduate study of composition, literacy, and instructional history" (47). This curriculum combined new literary and pedagogical theory and praxis with new textual objects of study. The texts to be considered changed, resulting in "courses in working-class, African-American, ethnic, women's, immigrants', popular, and other non-standard literatures and in presentation modes such as melodrama, television, and film" (47). A revised commitment to teaching led to the placing of student writing at the center of all courses, not just those in composition. Furthermore, all courses "adopted a pedagogy of problem-posing [as a] principle of internal guidance" (47). Of course, the development of the curriculum is in no sense finished, since it is in its very formulation continually under revision.

Pittsburgh is a large program, consisting of 52 full-time faculty, 83 part-time faculty, and 80 graduate teaching assistants serving some 13,300 students. Nevertheless, changes in the program have always been "bottom-up," including representatives of faculty and graduate students. This has made for gradual but relatively harmonious change.

One conspicuous feature of this change has been the integration of department activities: "of composition with literature and film, graduate study with undergraduate." The lines of disciplinary study have also been blurred: "more reading in composition courses, more writing in literature courses, more theory in literature and composition courses, more teaching of both kinds of courses by faculty and graduates from literature, film, composition, and creative writing programs" (49).

Smith describes a number of courses that demonstrate the new direction of the curriculum. "Introduction to Critical Reading" is a sophomore-level general education course that also serves as a required introduction to English studies for majors. This course, designed by Mariolina Salvatori, involves the "in-depth and recursive readings of three classic (canonical) texts—*King Lear, Madame Bovary,* and 'The Waste Land'—and a set of professional critics' readings of these texts" (50). The course is pedagogically organized around the distinction between *pedagogy* and *didactics.* Didactics resists "the teacher's and the student's critical reflexivity on the act of knowing and promotes the reduction of somebody else's way of knowing into a schematization of that method" (50). This is the traditional pursuit of emulating models of reading without considering the conditions of the production of the models. Pedagogy, in contrast, "inquires into the prehistory of those models, and analyzes and assesses their formation" (50). As Salvatori explains, "Our pedagogical imperative should be consciously and consistently to make *manifest* the rules and practices of interpretation we have acquired from institutional training, and to teach all students—remedial as well as mainstream, undergraduate as well as graduate—the very methods we practice in the classroom and use to produce the texts that grant us professional status" (quoted in Smith 1993, 50). In Salvatori's course, then, students read professional critics to critique them. The larger purpose is for students to arrive at their own understandings and self-conscious reflections on these understandings. The student text becomes the center of the classroom—not the canonical literary text or its institutionally sanctioned critical interpretations. This effort, Smith explains, is encouraged in all course offerings in the program.

The problem-posing method that Smith describes as central to pedagogy in the department is based on the work of Paulo Freire, where it is offered in opposition to the banking method of education. In the latter, knowledge is a valuable commodity passively transferred from teacher to student. As Smith explains, "It says to a student, learn the immutable ways of the world, be satisfied in your place, don't try to change things" (52). Problem posing, by contrast, asks students to look at all knowledge as a historical construction that must be critically examined for its adequacy to present circumstances. It involves creativity, reflection, and action for change. Freire reinforced the program's commitment to historicity and, coupled with Salvatori's notion of pedagogy, influenced the curricular model now in place.

Smith's essay describes other courses that appeared as the curriculum developed. For example, an upper-level literature survey course titled "The Medieval Imagination" modeled "the department's concern to shift its attention from literature as artifact of aesthetic form (in the older version of the course, called 'Epic and Romance') to literature as a product of culture and history" (53). This course became the first of a core of seven period survey courses required of majors, including early British literature, American literature to 1860, and late nineteenth and early twentieth century literature written in English. In these courses, the effort is "to counter our profession's tendency to reproduce an uncriticized, 'natural' history of literature or culture" (54). Thus, students "study not only the texts and their place in contextual discourse, but also the problems of accounting for them in a historical narrative that [has] meaning for a student in the 'here and now'" (54). Smith also describes in detail a new set of general education courses introduced in 1982 to carry out the reading and writing commitments of the new curriculum. These courses emphasized the historical conflict surrounding the production and reception of literary texts. Once again, the center of these courses is student writing and revision within the context of problem posing and pedagogy.

Smith provides a detailed description of a first-year "General Writing" course designed by David Bartholomae and Anthony Petrosky. It features composing as an act of negotiating multiple perspectives. Students pursue a sequenced set of writing topics that encourage, as the designers explain, "pushing against habitual ways of thinking, learning to examine an issue from different angles, rejecting quick conclusions, seeing the power of understanding that comes from repeated effort, and feeling the pleasure writers take when they find their own place in the context of others whose work they admire" (quoted in Smith 1993, 57). This course is especially important in Smith's narrative, since it is the one most commonly taught by graduate teaching assistants. This group, Smith notes, undergoes an unusually thoughtful and rigorous training program.

Each fall, the entering twenty-five students—divided equally among the M.A., M.F.A., and Ph.D. programs—are required to enroll in a two-semester graduate seminar designed to assist them in their first year of teaching. The course, however, does much more. Most important, it serves as an orientation to the principles involved in the department's curriculum. Rather than simple recipes for teaching first-year composition, "graduate students investigate the intellectual assumptions behind the course they teach as well as their own location within the institutional structure of the department, the university, and the history of English studies" (59). The course deals with pedagogy, but it does so within the larger context of "the history of the profession, literary and composition theory, and cultural criticism" (59). In short, graduate students entertain the issues at the center of debates about the nature of English studies today and actively engage in reading and writing activities that allow them to situate themselves within the larger professional discussion. Teaching first-year composition thus becomes the occasion for examining the historical role of the English department within the democratic society it serves. Smith offers samples of written statements from graduate students in this course; clearly important questions about signifying practices, subject formation, and democratic political power in the lives of undergraduate and graduate students are continually engaged. Contesting theories of rhetoric, literature, and culture are related to the practices of writing, problem posing, and pedagogy in the life of school and society. These graduate students receive a uniquely valuable introduction to the profession.

Still, while there is clearly much to admire in the Pittsburgh plan, it is not always as loyal to its own curricular agenda as it might be. Given the program's commitment to disrupting traditional hierarchies, the exclusive focus on canonical texts in the "Introduction to Critical Reading" course appears somewhat retrograde. There is also no mention of the historical contexts in which these works and their commentators were situated. This limitation on the scope of the critique to be pursued is also apparent in the first-year "General Writing" course designed by Bartholomae and Petrosky. Its attention to multiple perspectives is conspicuously lacking in mention of the political conflict that usually accompanies "pushing against habitual ways of thinking" and examining "an issue from different angles" (57). While it is important for students to feel "the pleasure writers take when they find their own place in the context of others whose work they admire"

(57), they should also attempt the critical interrogation of these authors as well as the investigation of authors whom they find less than admirable. The focus on problem posing and student response as the center of coursework also seems to be compromised in a major that requires students to enroll in seven separate courses. This is an especially important consideration given that the courses described so often fail to break the boundaries between domains of specialization. In other words, it is surprising to find so little rhetoric in the literature courses and so little noncanonical literature in the writing classes. Creative writing, meanwhile, is simply not described. Of course, one wonders how widespread the effort to disrupt the barriers between these areas can be in a program that involves no less than 83 part-time faculty. Finally, one wishes that the problems encountered in implementing Pittsburgh's commendable curriculum had been more candidly addressed.

The last innovative program in English studies I want to consider is the new Ph.D. program at the State University of New York at Albany. Called "Writing, Teaching, and Criticism," the course of study is meant to integrate the historical concerns of the English department, that is, the work of creative writers, critics, and theorists of rhetoric and composition. The program attempts to achieve this synthesis within the framework of the classroom.

Once again, this program has its unique history. The traditional Ph.D. program in literature at Albany was deregistered by the state in response to financial exigencies in 1975. After this, graduate work in English was organized around the Doctor of Arts degree. As Warren Ginsberg (1994), chair of the department when the new Ph.D. was officially approved, explains, "by affirming the DA's emphasis on pedagogy, and by combining it with the department's strong interest in creative writing and rhetoric and composition, the Albany D.A. developed a national reputation for producing students with strong credentials in writing and teaching" (2). In addition, during the late 1970s and 1980s, the program "increasingly examined the intersection of literary theory and pedagogy" (2). By 1987, the department concluded that the attention to integrating pedagogy in graduate work in English had become so common in other programs that it was time to reconsider the Doctor of Arts program. After a year's consulting with David Simpson (known for his unsuccessful championing of "Raymond Williams's English" at Cambridge and now chair of English at the University of Colorado at Boulder), the present graduate curriculum was formulated and finally put in place in 1990. This Ph.D. in Writing, Teaching, and Criticism was formally approved by the state in 1992.

As Ginsberg explains, no one concern of English studies is privileged at Albany. Instead, "writing, rhetoric, criticism, pedagogy, language study, and literary history constantly intersect and are called into question" (4). Most important, this broad mutual interrogation forms the center of each of the program's courses. Ginsberg explains by quoting from the program proposal: "Every course, whatever its focus, explores its subject from the perspectives which creative writers, students of rhetoric and composition, and literary critics bring to bear on it" (4). The purpose is to break down the historical hierarchical divisions in English studies, situating the interactions of composition, creative writing, literary criticism, and pedagogy within the "theory, ideology and institutionality that underwrite the methods by which they are investigated" (5). In other words, the enabling historical conditions underwriting claims to primacy of any one of these areas will constantly be examined, employing the interacting perspectives of all of them. In the words of the proposal, "Writers, rhetoricians and literary critics will find the assumptions and practices of their discourses in turn privileged and placed in unfamiliar contexts. Thus they will gain a better understanding of their own practices by seeing the extent to which each writer is also a literary critic and rhetorician, every rhetorician both writer and reader of literature, all literary critics rhetoricians and writers as well" (5). Since this interchange forms the center of all courses in the program, Ginsberg explains, "we fully intended to stake our cohesiveness" in committing to pedagogy (7). The classroom thus becomes the main arena for working out the new curriculum.

In "The Albany Graduate English Curriculum," C. H. Knoblauch (1991) has offered additional materials on the program and its creation. Its larger purpose, he explains, was to promote the critical investigation of school and society, to write "a curriculum that intends to develop politically reflective scholar-teachers while establishing graduate instruction in English as an appropriate site for the scrutiny of educational life" (19). While ideological critique was a central concern, the commitment to any single position—such as "Marxism, feminism, poststructuralism, 'philosophy of composition'"—was not. Instead, Knoblauch explains, department members were "motivated by convictions that might be upheld, or not, in all of them: that the practices of reading, writing, and teaching are never ideologically innocent; that those activities entail theoretical rationales and commitments about which practitioners ought to remain reflective; and that the discourses of rhetoric, poetic, and pedagogy are impoverished when they are isolated from one another" (19).

Reinforcing Ginsberg's assertions, Knoblauch argues that the program is a move "away from scholastic or dilettantish notions of 'literature' and textual study, toward a concern for the cultural practices of writing and reading; away from unreflective, unproblematic teaching (typically framed as the transmitting of information to passive student consumers), towards a concern for the politics of education" (19). The echoes of Freire are intentional, as Knoblauch later describes the encouragement of critical investigators of knowledge rather than passive consumers—the student as producer of cultural experience rather than mere recipient. Courses are thus organized around "problem posing rather than the disseminating of old or even new information" (20). Authoritarian classroom models are abandoned: "Students and teachers will have to cooperate in producing the knowledge that our curriculum can only make promises about" (20). Classrooms become sites of discovery, not simply of recapitulation and transmission: "The measure of success for our curriculum will be students who leave it knowing more than their teachers about what it had tried, haltingly, to articulate" (20).

Knoblauch goes on to describe in some detail the aims of the program. We have already considered its intention to integrate writing, teaching, and criticism in defiance of the traditional hierarchical department divisions and to situate these practices within the historical and ideological social contexts that produced them. The program also explores in these three domains "the dialectical relation between theory and practice, reflection and action" (19). Furthermore, the historical concerns of English studies, particularly its creation of a canon, are situated historically, with a view to locating the interests influencing the production and reception of these concerns. The program should self-consciously critique its own history and the interests it has served. This must include "issues of gender, race, ethnicity, and class as essential themes in any narrative of English studies in particular or American education in general" (19-20). Finally, the most important of the program's aims is to continually interrogate itself, "to destabilize our 'new' curriculum through self-critique in order to prevent its becoming the latest version of everything we have tried to avoid" (20).

Doctoral students are required to complete seventy-two hours of coursework and a comprehensive examination designed, as Ginsberg explains, "to demonstrate their growing mastery of a variety of perspectives and critical strategies about a particular subject" (21-22). The exam involves a written part and two orals based on papers the students have submitted, one of which is to serve as an exploratory prospectus for a dissertation. Coursework is to be selected from offerings organized into seven interdependent areas of study. Each area is organized around a core course "designed to introduce the questions posed in that area" (Knoblauch 1991, 20). These areas are (1) Writing in History, considering the historical contexts involved in influencing the conceptions of creative writing, rhetoric, and literary criticism and theory; (2) Writing Theory and Practice, the investigation of the relations between text construction and poetics; (3) Rhetoric and Composition, studying rhetorical history and theory; (4) Critical Theory and Practice, examining literary criticism and theory historically; (5) Teaching Theory and Practice, focusing on pedagogy within historical contexts; (6) Language and Language Theory, introducing historical conceptions of language and their relations to writing, teaching, and criticism; (7) Literary History, reading literature and its various constructions within historical contexts. Students are required to enroll in four core courses, two of which are chosen by them. The other two are "The History of English Studies, 1880 to the Present" (from Literary History) and "Teaching Writing and Literature" (from Teaching Theory and Practice). Students choose their other courses on the basis of their interests and larger career purposes. As Knoblauch explains, "Coherence rather than coverage is the goal" (20).

Two other features of the graduate program are worth mentioning. All students are required to take part in a practicum in teaching and an internship. The practicum is offered in connection with the required "Teaching Writing and Literature" course. It provides guidance for the first-year teaching experience as well as an opportunity for the student to see these practices within institutional and social contexts. Once again, teaching, writing, and criticism are integrated. The internship involves the student in a project related to the program of study he or she has devised and is undertaken in a semester-long consultation with a faculty member. This may include team-teaching with a faculty member, work in the University Writing Center, or even a period of work in a state agency or private corporation. The internship is meant to provide the student with an opportunity to further explore the theory-practice interconnections at the center of the program.

The SUNY at Albany program is especially admirable for its attention to the disciplinary and theoretical divisions that currently mark English studies and for its determination to address them. In reading the published materials on this program, one gets the impression that no voice has been silenced in the forging of the new degree. Devising courses that present these diverse positions, however, will not be an easy matter. For example, Ginsberg describes a course he designed for the Language and Language Theory branch of study, an offering called "Problems in the Development of Literary Language." While it is an admirable treatment of the historical constitution of the aesthetic and its relation to political formations, the course says nothing of the rhetorical practices of the periods considered, even though these are central to the issues addressed. I should quickly add that I mention this not to argue that either the course or the program is doomed to fail. Indeed, I would argue that both, given the current practices in most graduate programs, are resounding successes. I simply want to indicate the difficulty of offering students the integrated perspective called for here in a discipline that has forced its members into the straightjackets of specialization. Obviously, the SUNY at Albany program has gone a long way toward escaping these confines.

Actually, I expect it will be the students now working in this program and others like it who will more fully demonstrate what rethinking the discipline along integrated lines means for pedagogy and research. I also anticipate that their contribution will include a candid account of the conflicts that such an effort uncovers, conflicts in the historical disputes of the past and in the disciplinary struggles of the present. In other words, changes in our discipline will be no smoother than the changes we see in our investigations of past debates on the role of discourse in power and politics. As I said at the very start of this study, cultural capital in the academy is no more generously shared than financial capital in the marketplace.

As should now be clear, I have not dwelt on the specific features of these three programs because I think they are, in some easily generalizable way, perfect models for other programs to follow, but because they are usefully suggestive, helping us imagine some of the possibilities of reforming English studies along the comprehensive theoretical and practical lines forwarded in this book. Indeed, I might well have included other programs to the same end. The University of Oklahoma, for example, offers an undergraduate major within which students can choose a track in literature, writing, or critical theory/cultural texts. Illinois State University has similarly amended its major to include the concerns of literary theory and rhetoric. At the graduate level, George Mason University features a program in cultural studies designed in part to provide cultural workers for government agencies—such as, say, the National Endowment for the Humanities. And the much-discussed Syracuse University program, for all its difficulties—rhetoric and composition now function outside the confines of the English department—still has much to teach us about the whole process of refiguring the discipline.

Surely the most crucial lesson to be learned from any of these institutional efforts is that undergraduate and graduate programs in English should be the products of their unique situations, taking into account their students, faculties, larger communities, and their broader purposes—all of which should be considered within the theories and practices of the historical moment. English departments must consider their missions as organized around the most worthy objectives of a democratic society in its economic, political, and cultural behavior. This involves responding to local as well as national and international conditions. The decisions for the English curriculum will thus arise out of faculties and students hammering out arrangements that address their actual situations. Imitating Yale or Hopkins or Wisconsin or Berkeley will simply no longer be the first and last consideration.

The Creative Writing Classroom

A number of current efforts in creative writing attempt to integrate literary theory, rhetoric, and the production of aesthetic texts in the classroom. This effort is reflected most vividly in a recent discussion in the *AWP Chronicle*. D. W. Fenza (1992), publications editor, offered a long essay on the dangers literary theory posed to creative writers and their teaching, ending with a plea for responses. The piece is both entertaining and provocative, particularly in its conclusion.

Speaking as a participant in "the twelve-step recovery program of the DDDD (Detoxified, Disbarred, Defrocked Deconstructionists)" (16), Fenza lists twelve objections to introducing theory into English departments. These "specialized literary enterprises (New Historicism, deconstruction, etc.)" (16) are dangerous, he explains, because they offer students bad models of prose. In addition, "they teach students the faults of literature rather than the virtues, meanings, and pleasures of literature" (16). They use political criteria rather than aesthetic criteria to evaluate literary texts, disposing of authors by making them unwitting mouthpieces of oppressive forces. Furthermore, literary theory displaces textual hierarchies by emphasizing political values, thereby "creating a recommended reading list so vast that only an immortal, professional reader could make use of it" (16). English departments have thus become "so highly specialized that they can only be understood by other specialists, thwarting possibilities for public debate, estranging the general reader, and further constricting literature's already limited audience" (16). The quest for theory has reversed the traditional order of values in the department "by upholding the apotheosis of subjectivity over objectivity, intuition over reason, attitudes over logic, impressions over research, and style over content" (16). Sex is so central to the new theory that literature is seen "through the mind's crotch" (16). Finally, the new theories are fascistic: in creating "separatism and resentment, . . . they are dangerously subversive—cultural sabotage perpetrated by the radical Left" (16). Those who subscribe to these theories end by becoming "ludicrous social and political failures, unable to subvert or teach due to an inclination to preach to like-minded colleagues" (20).

Readers of earlier chapters in this study will recognize in this list an outline of the binary oppositions I have located in the distinction between poetic and rhetoric in English studies as well as an assault on poststructuralist claims regarding signification, subjectivity, and metanarratives. There is a curious inversion in Fenza's making literary theory the counterpart of poetic in its preference for the subjective, intuitive, illogical, impressionistic, and stylistic—all of which would seem to make it an ally of the poetic rather than an enemy. On the other hand, Fenza's move is designed to point to the dangerously transgressive impulse of theory, trying to reproduce the methods of what it has no right to imitate. Thus, Fenza finally upholds the rhetoric-poetic binary by reinscribing scholarship—the larger category for theory—in the rhetorical camp.

As is clear even from my somewhat toned-down summary, Fenza was trying to pick a fight, and in his conclusion he invited reactions, particularly oppositional ones, promising to publish the best. True to his word, the following four issues contained a number of them, more or less equally distributed among those who supported and those who opposed his stance. Three of the rebuttals are especially useful to my purposes here in that they indicate support for the argument of this book.

The first of these was offered by Carolyn Forche, poet and creative writing teacher at George Mason University. Entitled "Literary Acts of Resistance" (1992), the essay calls on feminist and historicist categories of thought in answering Fenza's assault on theory. It first accounts for creative writing in the academy by locating it within its historical moment and contrasting this position to that of the last century. Nineteenth-century England, she explains, supported a few star poets widely admired and studied by a class of readers who used their knowledge as cultural capital in "a very complicated form of class negotiation" (2). In the United States today, on the other hand, democracy has led to the diffusion of poetry over a much more diverse group of readers. As Forche explains, "a country that produces more than 1,000 books of poetry a year, and has over 20,000 students involved in accredited writing programs is not a country that lacks an audience for poetry" (2). Her point is that the historicist perspective enables the analyst to see that literature is a category constructed through the negotiation of artists, critics, theorists, and teachers within concrete historical conditions. The most significant lesson history offers in this matter is the democratization of poetry to include groups previously excluded from the pantheon of poetic creation. This, she insists, is to be applauded rather than regarded as a fall from poetic grace.

This consideration of social class leads Forche to a discussion of the working conditions of creative writing teachers in the English department. Since English studies as a whole is situated within a specific institutional context as well as a larger historical context, it can ill afford to succumb to the impulse of individual divisions to go it alone. Pointing to the large group of poorly compensated and insecure part-time writing teachers created as a money-saving move, she calls for the partnership of creative writing, literary study, and theory as a practical political device for survival. The institutional strategy of divide and conquer in the current economic climate in the university could easily lead to the drastic diminishing of all branches of English studies.

Of equal importance, Forche sees theory as a natural ally of poetry in its responses to changing historical conditions. Poets and philosophers have historically been closely affiliated, particularly in the twentieth century. Furthermore, she notes, "in the days of high modernism, poets founded and developed the New Criticism" (4). The historical relation of poetry and theory is indisputable. Far from ignoring postmodern perspectives on language, creative writers must recognize the central place of signification in human experience: "rather than considering such [theoretical] language an elitist form of obscurantism, we should acknowledge that when the problems under examination are hidden within the language itself, the invention of a new critical language is necessary (4). The new theory, Forche argues, is often part and parcel of new forms of art—for example, "cultural and utopian studies, subaltern and feminist criticism" (4). Theory can thus become "a provocation for poetry and can broaden the notion of experience so we are not confined to writing out of the singularity of our remembered pasts" (4).

Thus, for Forche, theory, teaching, and poetic production must remain together, acting as complementary elements of a single whole. Just as the institution of English studies and the workers in it are always situated within an economic and political context, our understanding of the work of the individual poet must likewise be contextually located. In the last part of her essay, Forche makes an eloquent plea for the dialectical interaction of the personal and the political and warns of the dangers of neglecting the one for the other. As she explains, poets, critics, and teachers "need a third term, one that can describe the space between the institutions of political reproduction and the safe havens of the personal" (6). In making her case, Forche calls upon what she calls "the poetry of witness," poems dealing with direct political protest and affirmation, to argue for the political involvement of all poetic texts. To use my own terms, hers is a compelling plea for situating the production and reception of texts within their generating literary and rhetorical environment, this environment within the converging ideological context, and the ideological within the larger economic, social, and political conditions of the moment. As Forche demonstrates, this sort of investigation breaks down the false divisions of "the individual against the communal, alterity against universality" (8), locates the dialectical interplay of the two, and works for the amelioration of both the personal and the political.

In "Writing after Theory" (1992), Tom Andrews, poet and assistant professor of English at Ohio University, takes a somewhat different but related tack in responding to Fenza. Calling on Gerald Graff's history of the English department, Andrews reminds us that Douglas Bush's 1948 characterization of the evils of New Criticism was made in terms strongly reminiscent of Fenza's own. This earlier list of vices included intellectuality, amorality, self-centeredness, and the dismissal of the ordinary reader in favor of the expert. As Graff has demonstrated, this form of attack was a recurrent feature in department disputes of the past. Andrews next defends the poststructuralist critique of authorial intention. Invoking the commonplace that writers often lose control of their own creations, he points to moments when "the material talks back, making its own strange demands and asking one to let go of one's intentions—a moment many believe crucial to the creative act" (13-14). In other words, poststructuralist descriptions of text production more accurately describe the actual experience of the writing act, accounting for the "'luck' involved in any piece of writing—the disruptions and stray impulses that work out, the bonuses that come from play and random associations" (14). In short, poststructuralism helps explain the "indeterminacy" of the creative act.

For Andrews, the new theory also reminds authors of their situation within influencing contexts: "to what extent are we 'written' by language when we do our work? How is meaning constituted in our work? What social structures are we privileging, unwittingly or intentionally?" (14). Writers never act in total isolation, and their connectedness must be taken into account in their creative acts. Andrews likewise asserts the inevitable relation of theory to poetic production, citing John Crowe Ransom's insistence that all criticism is grounded in theory. He even points to the self-conscious attempts to integrate the personal and the theoretical in such experimental works as Nancy K. Miller's *Getting Personal: Feminist Occasions and Other Autobiographical Acts* (1991) and Rachel Blau DuPlessis's *The Pink Guitar: Writing as Feminist Practice* (1990). Finally, Andrews insists that the conflicts between the new and the old theories of text production must be examined within the classroom. Following Graff, he argues that the responsibility of English courses is to study the conflicts, not to resolve them once and for all.

Martin Schecter, a novelist and teacher at Drake University, offers his rebuttal of Fenza's claims about poststructuralist theory in the provocatively titled "Emily Dickinson, Madonna, Boomers, Busters, the Old Criterion, and the Next Millennium—Deconstructing the Guardians of Nostalgia: A Defense of the 'Young Writer'" (1993). Schecter sees the dismissal of theory among certain creative writers as part of a conflict between generations. From his perspective—that of a 31-year-old member "of Generation X, a.k.a. 'Busters,' 'Post-Boomers,' and the '13th Generation'"—attacks on theory often betray "a virulent animosity, one directed at the whole of the youth culture, and especially at young writers themselves, those 'kids' brought up in these new theory-laden and media-laden environments" (14). Schecter speaks from the personal experience of a post-Fordist economy, a world of "increasing competition and diminishing prospects" (15). Against the admonition of their elders that they be prepared to sacrifice, younger writers respond that they see nothing but sacrifice in an economy that offers them dramatically fewer possibilities than it did their immediate predecessors. In addition, their personal experience of postmodern cultural conditions makes them more "attuned to cultural differences, identity-construction, and economic constraints on artistic form in a way that totally escapes their elders" (15). In other words, theory makes sense to them because it make sense out of the details of their daily lives.

Schecter's generation of writers can no longer embrace "the myth of a Romantically 'pure' literary 'artiste,' whose work, language, and narrative convention remain uncontaminated by concerns of economics, class, or cultural positioning" (15). For his generation, this positioning is unmistakably formative in the possibilities of one's art and life. Indeed, in the electronic age of space-time compression, creativity, art, and the artist have been redefined. With the old "idea of the 'writer' vanishing beneath the winking cursor of computer communication" (16), the conditions of creation and, significantly, teaching are transformed. It is virtually impossible to discover any creative activity either outside or within the university free of the economic and social networks of the electronic age. Even poetry, Schecter contends, "has its own mini-economy of teaching positions, conferences and AIDS benefits" (16). In a time of diminished expectations, the issue for the young writer outside the old established network of publishing and perquisites is not one of making a lot of money—it is a question of survival.

Faced with the new economic, social, and cultural conditions of creation, the work of the creative artist is to figure out what the future of art will be. The old language of the intuitive visionary—the "true self," the "quiet moment," the universal discovery—is gone, and it is the work of young writers to arrive at its replacement. This will mean that those studying writing in the academy will have to be liberally educated, "learning about philosophy, religion, sociology, history—aesthetic and literary as well as political—art, and most of all, science, that realm of activity that most controls our modern world" (17). This education will involve studying the intersections of high culture and low culture, so that joined to the list of academic subjects will be the study of "TV, movies, science fiction, computers, nuclear physics, shopping malls, rap music" (17). For Schecter, the area of academic study that has most conscientiously encompassed this wide range of concerns has been theory. In other words, it is theory that has attempted to comprehend this expanse of experience, insisting that "theory and practice are intertwined, and as one changes, so will the other" (18). It is the responsibility of writers, then, "to be up front about *theirs*" (16).

Schecter closes his essay with a long section on the consequences of his argument for the creative writing classroom. Rather than the "intuitive workshop mumbo-jumbo of 'learning to express yourself'" (18), the teacher must emulate those young people outside the academy who, "immersed in theory, technology, and art [are] creating a vibrant intellectual culture, a culture that has larger implications for society as a whole" (18). This will mean developing new standards for student writing, criteria that go beyond the unstated preferences of the instructor. Standards will be pluralistic, but they must nonetheless be consistently constructed. Schecter proposes to achieve this through a number of devices: "talk about aesthetics; talk about how to restructure the imaginative process; . . . a broad horizon of 'challenging' work from all sorts of writing communities" (19). The portfolio will be especially useful, since it enables the writer to measure the relation between intention and performance. Schecter explains, "If we agree there is no 'right form' of creative writing—that satire, parody, pastiche, and irresolution are just as interesting as unity, rising action and resolution—then it seems to me that the only criteria left for evaluating student work is its 'writerly stance'" (19). In the end, we have "a multitude of criteria; a multitude of 'literatures,' something that only a theoretical postmodernist . . . can fully appreciate" (19-20). Indeed, Schecter finally underscores the cultural diversity of the postmodern, arguing with Houston Baker that our students are more united by their differences than by any common heritage of great books and art.

I admit that in summarizing these responses I have tended to ignore differences among them and to emphasize arguments that support my own position. There is no denying, however, that these statements are an attempt to move creative writing in the direction of the postmodern in both intellectual and cultural terms. In other words, Forche, Andrews, and Schecter are all determined that creative writing courses take into account the intellectual currents of poststructuralism and the economic, political, and cultural conditions of the post-Fordist regime of flexible accumulation. Finally, in their strategic responses, they each work to contest the boundaries separating aesthetic texts, rhetoric, and theory, locating the site for working out these transgressions in the classroom.

New Directions in Research

I would now like to turn to the kinds of research projects that my proposal is designed to encourage. Here the intersections of a rhetorically conceived English studies and the cultural studies inspired by the Birmingham example will be immediately apparent. Indeed, I want to start with an analysis of the work of the Birmingham Center offered by Richard Johnson, one of its past heads. I will then move to a brief consideration of research projects in literary studies attempted by those presently working in a rhetorically constructed English studies. Finally, I want to examine examples of research among those who have considered the workings of textuality in its broadest formulation. These display striking parallels to those undertaken at Birmingham, even though there has been little or no communication between the two groups of workers. The efforts outlined, however, do not in any way exhaust the field. I simply offer some suggestive possibilities.

In "What Is Cultural Studies Anyway?" (1986-87), Johnson describes the Birmingham project in a manner familiar to workers in social-epistemic rhetoric. Cultural studies, he asserts, can best be considered in terms of its characteristic objects of study and its methods. Both objects and methods are organized around an examination of the formations of consciousness and subjectivity: "cultural studies is about the historical forms of consciousness or subjectivity, or the subjective forms we live by, or, in a rather perilous compression, perhaps a reduction, the subjective side of social relations" (43). For Johnson, cultural studies is related to the projects of structuralism and poststructuralism: "subjectivities are produced, not given, and are therefore the objects of inquiry, not the premises or starting-points" (44). Signifying practices thus become a crucial feature of investigation, constituting "the structured character of the forms we inhabit subjectively: language, signs, ideologies, discourses, myths" (45). In other words, cultural studies in this scheme is concerned with the ways social formations and practices are involved in the shaping of consciousness, a shaping mediated by language and situated in concrete historical conditions. The important consideration is that this relation between the social and the subjective is ideological, is imbricated in economic, social, and political considerations that are always historically specific. So cultural studies here is concerned with the ideological formation of subjects, of forms of consciousness, within historically specific signifying practices enmeshed in power. The objects of cultural studies for Johnson are thus the production, distribution, and reception of signifying practices within the myriad social formations that shape subjectivities. These range from the family, the school, the workplace, and the peer group to the more familiar activities associated with the cultural sphere, such as the arts (high and low) and the media and their modes of production and consumption. In other words, wherever signifying practices shape consciousness in daily life, cultural studies has work to do.

Johnson considers the methods of cultural studies as diversely varied and interdisciplinary. While his discussion of these methods is obscured by other considerations, Vincent Leitch has effectively summarized them in *Cultural Criticism, Literary Theory, Poststructuralism* (1992): "Among the predominant modes of inquiry are ethnographic descriptions, 'textual' explications, field interviews, group surveys, and ideological and institutional analyses" (147). The interdisciplinary nature of these methods is unmistakable. More important, in all cases, the data gathered by these diverse means is situated within the institution—family, work, art—that sponsored the examined activities and is related to the ideological—the arena of language, idea, and value. Johnson is especially concerned with elucidating the kinds of research cultural studies has encouraged, seeing these methods appearing across them. The research activities fall into three general categories: production-based studies, text-based studies, and culture-as-lived-activity studies. These categories are especially instructive in considering the work of a rhetorically constituted English studies.

Production-based studies deal with the "production and social organization of cultural forms" (54). This includes a broad range of objects of study, from the examination of the work of public relations, advertising, and the mass media to considerations of the production of race, class, and gender behavior within the schools. The methods here are diverse, calling on the procedures of the social sciences as well as textual analysis. This group of approaches focuses on the conditions of cultural production and distribution—of the media, a work of art, or the schools—without regard to the negotiation and resistance involved at the point of consumption. For Johnson, this is a serious flaw, especially in the tendency of certain mechanistic Marxisms to see the economic base as totally determinative of consciousness.

A second group of studies involves text-based efforts derived from work with literary productions and their reception and interpretation. In particular, Johnson has in mind the powerful methods of textual analysis developed by structuralist and poststructuralist literary theory and the ways these permit discussion of the relation of texts to subject formation. For example, one could study the relation of the kinds of literary texts read and the means of interpreting them in the schools to formations of class, race, and gender expectations among school children. Here the strategies discovered in textual interpretation are connected to students' lived experience. Johnson, however, is at pains to emphasize reading as itself an act of production, not simply a passive act of reception of a determinate text. Significantly, the negotiation and resistance of the various readers of texts must be considered.

A third cluster of approaches focuses on "lived cultures" and attempts "to grasp the more *concrete* and more *private* moments of cultural circulation" (69). Here the primary research method is ethnography, which works to document responses to cultural experience. Johnson points to studies of the ways adolescent girls and boys appropriate cultural forms for their own ends, ends often subversive of the producers' intentions—as found, for example in Dick Hebdige's study of adolescent culture in London. Since at this point interpretation strategies of negotiation and resistance are involved, textual strategies again become important. Johnson thus explains that the major flaw to which all three approaches fall prey is that each tends to focus on one moment of cultural performance—production itself or the cultural product itself or cultural negotiation itself—without regard for the entire process.

There are compelling reasons for finding in Johnson's scheme a counterpart to the concerns of rhetoric. His tripartite division of cultural studies into the categories of production-based, textual, and culture-as-lived studies corresponds generally with the rhetorical model of communication described in figures as diverse as Aristotle, Kenneth Burke, and Andrea Lunsford and Lisa Ede. In short, cultural artifacts are produced and circulated in some textual form (print, film, television, conversation), the text is consumed by an audience in the form of negotiated interpretations, and the interpretations are part of the lived cultures or social relations of the interpreters. As I have just indicated, Johnson's critique of the modes of cultural studies he presents is their tendency to focus on one moment of the process, rather than considering the various moments of the entire process. This has also long been a failing of literary and rhetorical studies that recent research projects have attempted to correct.

In chapters 6 and 7, I discussed at length the kind of research projects I am encouraging in efforts to examine literary texts. Here I will simply outline that argument. Examinations of literary texts should be situated within their conditions of production, distribution, exchange, and reception. This will involve considering the varieties of audiences for which they were produced during their own time as well as the diverse audiences they attracted over time. Varying reading practices must then be examined for their aesthetic interests as well as the imbricated economic, social, and political concerns. All texts occupy a space of intertextuality, a complex relation to other texts of their own time at their initial reception and to later texts for readers of later times. These ways of reading involve the investigation of contemporaneous rhetorical texts, particularly since these texts often explicitly foreground the ideological predispositions of their ways of reading. Aesthetic codes should be situated within the ideological and socioeconomic codes that lend them their significance. Furthermore, literary research will involve a consideration of both canonical and non-canonical texts. Indeed, examining the writing and reading practices that canonical debates forward will be central. Thus, literary texts are seen as products of a process of production, signification, and reception. This process in turn is situated within an examination of the range of subjects who produced the texts, the audiences that read them, the representations of experience they preferred, and the ways in which signifying practices operated in all of these.

The possibilities for this rhetorically constituted literary research can be seen in a large number of recently published studies. Here I want to name only a few of the best and most recent examples, some of which I already invoked in discussing "The Discourse of Revolution" course in the last chapter. Among these were Donna Landry's *The Muses of Resistance: Laboring-Class Women's Poetry in Britain, 1739-1796* (1990) and J. Paul Hunter's *Before Novels* (1990). The collection by Felicity Nussbaum and Laura Brown entitled *The New Eighteenth Century: Theory, Politics, English Literature* (1987) also contains rich examples of such efforts. Mary Poovey's *Uneven Developments: The Ideological Work of Gender in Mid-Victorian England* (1988) likewise pursues the methods I am encouraging. In addition, Poovey explicitly discusses the relation of this study to an English studies refigured along the lines of cultural studies, including its place in teaching and research, in her essay "Cultural Criticism: Past and Present." Critical responses to the "New Historicism" have also begun to provide the political perspective advocated here. Some of the essays in *Literary Practice and Social Change in Britain, 1380-1530* display what its editor refers to as "critical historicism," indicating by this many of the features of the rhetorical critique I have emphasized. Much useful work has also grown out of the efforts at Birmingham—for example, Alan Sinfield's *Literature, Politics, and Culture in Postwar Britain* (1989) and Michael Denning's *Mechanic Accents: Dime Novels and Working Class Culture in America* (1987). Henry Louis Gates, Jr.'s *The Signifying Monkey* (1988) is a rich rhetorical treatment of speech genres that effectively breaks down the divisions of rhetoric and poetic. Finally, Stephen Mailloux's *Rhetorical Power* (1989) attempts to offer a theoretical statement of the uses of rhetoric in reading literary texts closely related to my own. Our major differences have to do with the theoretical origins of our proposals, the scope of our disciplinary recommendations, and the role of politics in the reading practices described. Still, his study has proven useful to me, as it will to others. Of course, this listing only scratches the surface of a body of work that includes Gayatri Chakravorty Spivak, Fredric Jameson, Terry Eagleton, Janice Radway, Edward Said, Frank Lentricchia, and others.

I will now turn to studies in rhetoric and composition that attempt the kinds of research recommended here. This work is typically less well-known than its companion work in literary study. It also employs methods and materials that until just recently were considered outside the purview of English studies. I will accordingly offer slightly more detailed accounts of these efforts.

One conspicuous strength of recent work in rhetoric and composition studies is its attempt to focus on the process of text production. While the dominant paradigms in literary studies have restricted study to text interpretation—and then apart from any influencing context, labeling production an inaccessible function of genius—composition studies has attempted to study and describe the concrete activities of text construction. This is, of course, in keeping with the historical emphasis in rhetoric on teaching strategies for generating texts, primarily in the form of heuristical procedures for invention, patterns of arrangement, and principles of syntax and style.

More recently, this concern for production has manifested itself in empirical studies of the composing process, from the case studies of Janet Emig (1971) to the protocol analysis of Linda Flower and John Hayes (1981) and others. As a number of observers have pointed out, these studies often suffer from a conception of composing as an exclusively private, psychologically determined act, a stance that distorts because of its neglect of the larger social contexts of composing. This inadequacy in considering text production is being addressed by the turn in composition research to ethnographic study, or to use the term favored by Birmingham, the study of culture-as-lived activity. The pioneer in this effort in English studies in the United States has been Shirley Brice Heath (1983), who has related patterns of learning in language to subject formation within structures of class, race, and gender.

Two recent volumes have shown the effects of this work: *Reclaiming the Classroom: Teacher Research as an Agency for Change* (1987), edited by Dixie Goswami and Peter R. Stillman, and *The Writing Teacher as Researcher: Essays in the Theory and Practice of Class-based Research* (1990), edited by Donald A. Daiker and Max Morenberg. The teacher-as-researcher model attempts to make every teacher an ethnographic researcher of the concrete economic and social conditions of students, situating instruction in text production and interpretation within the lived cultures of the students, within class, race, gender, and ethnic determinations. Furthermore, both volumes have begun the work of considering the ideological as well as the narrowly institutional settings of learning, situating their examinations of student signifying practices within the conflicts of concrete economic, social, and political conditions. Although these studies have been somewhat tentative in foregrounding the political nature of their investigations so far, at their best they examine signifying practices within the context of production, texts, readings, and lived cultures.

Another group of studies dealing with text production has been organized around a consideration of collaborative learning and writing, a subject treated historically in Anne Ruggles Gere's engaging monograph *Writing Groups: History, Theory, and Implications* (1987). Since current work in this area is extensive, only a brief comment can be offered here. Although Kenneth Bruffee is the person whose name is most associated with this project, a number of critiques of his work—critiques not necessarily unfriendly—have recently attempted to figure collaboration in relation to the place of signifying practices in forming subjectivities within social and material conditions. Lisa Ede and Andrea Lunsford (1990), for example, have invoked the theory of Barthes and Foucault on the nature of authorship and the actual practices of writers outside the classroom to argue that collaborative writing constitutes the norm for composing, with writing as necessarily communal in nature. John Trimbur (1989) has also called upon ideological critique in treating the strengths and weaknesses of collaborative practices, attempting a refiguration of them in the light of a social conception of subject formation that allows for struggle and resistance at the site of group efforts. In short, discussions of text production within the context of collaborative learning have begun to interrogate the insistence on writing as the exclusively private and personal act of a docile and quiescent subject.

Methods of textual critique calling upon structuralist and post-structuralist language theory have been considerable. These have generally fallen into two groups. The first of these attempts to analyze the discourse of various disciplinary formations to locate their part in shaping subjectivities within historical conditions. Mina Shaughnessy (1977) undertook this form of analysis when she identified the use of medical language to discuss basic writers and the disadvantaged social groups from which they often emerge. As Trimbur (1988) has pointed out, for Shaughnessy, "cultural studies of writing might begin in at least one important respect as an effort of writing teachers to resist the dominant representations of subordinate groups and to contest the social construction of otherness as pathological problems for the professional intervention of educators, social workers, urban planners, and policy-makers" (15). Shaughnessy has in turn encouraged a host of resistant readings of institutional constructions of teachers and students, most notable in the work of Linda Brodkey, David Bartholomae, Patricia Bizzell, and Greg Myers. The uses of textual as well as ethnographic analysis along distinctly feminist lines in examining signifying practices and subject formation in writing is also seen in the recent work of Elizabeth Flynn.

Another group of workers fitting into this first textual category have attempted to locate the workings of discursive practices in the formation of scientific disciplines, exploring the structure of disciplinary formations and the subjectivities that inhabit them as a function of signifying practices. Carolyn Miller, Greg Myers, and Charles Bazerman have been especially prominent in this undertaking. Others have attempted the textual analysis of signifying practices in various nonacademic settings. For example, Barbara Hamilton's doctoral dissertation (1987) combined an ethnographic method with textual analysis in examining written presentence recommendations in criminal offenses in a Detroit court. Myrna Harrienger (1993) recently completed a dissertation considering the signifying practices of ill, elderly women in nursing homes, focusing on the ways in which medical discourse silences them. And Gary Heba (1991) has emulated Dick Hebdige's work on youth subcultures in a dissertation examining youth movies and their relation to the resistance of adolescents to hegemonic discourse practices.

The second group of textual studies focuses on developing lexicons for examining the relations of textual practices and power, considering the methods of textuality in forming subjectivity. Considerable work along these lines has been conducted in communication departments as a part of media studies—for example, in the work of Arthur Asa Berger, Stewart Ewen, and John Fiske. Much less has appeared in English departments, but the work has begun. George Dillon (1986), for example, has discussed the cultural codes inscribed within popular advice books, calling on the language of structuralist and poststructuralist categories. W. Ross Winterowd's *The Rhetoric of the "Other" Literature* (1990) provides a critical language for non-literary texts, invoking the work of Aristotle, Burke, and poststructuralism. Both regard reading and writing practices as interchangeable in that they are constructive rather than simply reflective of experience, although both also share a timidity about discussing the politics of signifying practices. Still, they make a start in the right direction. Workers in composition studies must devise lexicons to enable discussions of the structures and ideological strategies of written texts that take into account recent Marxist and postructuralist developments, presenting terminologies and methods that act as counterparts, for example, to the rich work of John Fiske in television studies. If students are to critique the role of signifying practices in forming consciousness through their own writing and reading practices, teachers must provide them with a language for identifying these practices and their operations.

I have already discussed the study of lived cultures through ethnographic means as recommended by the teacher-as-researcher development. As Janice Lauer and J. William Asher (1988) have indicated, ethnographic study of lived cultures has also been undertaken in settings outside the school, more specifically, in writing in the workplace. Until recently, however, these have not attempted to challenge the practices considered, taking them as objects of analysis, not of critique. In a recent dissertation, Jennie Dautermann (1991) has shown new possibilities as she examines the discourses of female nurses in a hospital setting as they collaboratively compose a manual for nursing procedures. Her study revealed the conflicts in power formations and the way subordinate groups have to negotiate them in a setting in which male doctors give orders and female nurses carry them out. In "Interpersonal Conflict in Collaborative Writing: What We Can Learn from Gender Studies" (1989), Mary Lay is similarly concerned with locating gender codes and their relation to power in collaborative writing in business settings. In "Ideology and Collaboration in the Classroom and in the Corporation" (1990), Jim Porter attempts to apply ideological critique to the teaching of collaborative writing in the business writing classroom as well as the business writing setting itself. All of these studies focus on the conflicts generated by signifying practices in their formation of discursive subject locations within an institutional setting, conflicts that reproduce the class, race, and gender struggles of the larger society.

All of these studies are representative of possibilities for rich, diverse, and open-ended research. Indeed, these possibilities will mushroom as our attention in English studies turns from canonical texts and their authoritative interpretations to signifying practices broadly conceived, the formation of the consciousness of subjects, and history and power. Instruction in reading and writing, literacy in its most expansive formulation, will be our central concern, and this will include attention to textuality in all its manifestations. Furthermore, the intersections of research projects with the classroom will keep the processes of theory and practice constantly in dialectic with each other. After all, a primary goal of our efforts as workers in English studies is to prepare young people to be better participants in democratic economic, political, and cultural arrangements. Our work is to fathom possibilities for language and living heretofore unimagined.

9
A Closing Word

During the last six years, I have had the good fortune to speak to a number of college English departments. In addition to receiving generous hospitality, I have usually been treated to candid criticisms of my presentations, criticisms that have helped me in writing this book. Of the many comments I received, the one that has most haunted me was offered by a literary theorist at a large Midwestern urban university. My error, he explained, was that I grossly overestimated the influence of the English department in the lives of our students and the workings of our society. English teachers, he insisted, are in the larger scheme of things just not all that important.

This casual encounter has since been an important influence in my professional experience, even though I finally decided that my colleague's assessment was wrong. Indeed, this book is a defense of my position. At the same time, I have found the experience a useful reminder of the constraints any effort at improving the quality of life in this country must face. English teachers are a small group with a limited purchase on the workings of power in our society. Still, while we are not as influential as I once, in my student days, thought, I do not believe we are as insignificant as my critic indicated.

At the minimum, English teachers are gatekeepers, influencing decisions about who will succeed to higher levels of education and greater degrees of prosperity. We do not, of course, do this by ourselves. Yet as Evan Watkins (1989) has so ably demonstrated, an important part—perhaps the most important part—of our jobs is passing on our evaluations of students to various bureaucratic structures. By assigning grades and writing letters, we contribute to decisions about who will be given a chance at the higher levels of the educational and employment ladders and who will be assigned a lower standing. I also think that Watkins is on target when he argues that our evaluations are often used as much to create and justify hierarchies in the workplace as they are to tell employers who is best suited for a particular position. In other words, employers use grades and other educational measures to justify assigning people to jobs that are really not that different in their intellectual demands. The credentials a worker brings to the job are thus used to validate differences in work assignments and, of equal importance, compensation, doing so for the simple reason that the nature of the work alone cannot justify such finely nuanced distinctions.

Watkins's analysis rings true to anyone who has spent much time teaching in an English department. The amount of energy spent in determining methods of evaluation and justifying them to students and administrators in most large first-year composition programs is staggering. In fact, in an age of diminished job opportunities, English teachers at all levels are forced to justify their evaluations to students, who have no illusions about the translation of grades, even in humanities courses, into economic benefits. English instructors are also important figures in the circulation of letters of recommendation for colleges, graduate schools, professional schools, and jobs.

In *Culture and Government: The Emergence of Literary Education* (1988), Ian Hunter discusses the uses of English courses in the construction of consciousness—the shaping of particular kinds of subject formations—in young people. Calling on Foucault, Hunter argues that literature courses employ technologies of self-formation. The most important feature of this activity is that it is largely concealed by the discipline's open commitment to freedom and self-expression. At the most obvious level, English teachers provide in their own practices a model for the ways a text ought to be read. They do so, however, without ever explicitly demanding that students follow their example. Quite the contrary, the purpose of encountering literature is to practice responding freely and openly to the aesthetic workings of the text, workings that by their nature demand this sort of unconstrained reading. While encouraging an environment of uninhibited interpretation, however, English teachers do not react in the same affirmative manner to all student responses. In other words, all readings are good, but some are more worthy of approval than others. Of course, teachers never—or very rarely—explicitly condemn any particular interpretation. Instead, students are continually invited to be independent and creative in their reading. Meanwhile, English teachers' subtle responses to these different expressions effectively reinforce the creation of a certain kind of reader.

Hunter argues that this pedagogy leads students to be self-correcting, arriving at decisions on their own that their teachers find worthy of endorsement and, indeed, praise for their originality and independence. Thus, both as a model and a respondent, English teachers encourage behavior that students take to be a personal choice. The institution's ethical and political construction of the student is obscured by claims for freedom and self-expression. As Hunter explains, these are "the means by which the 'self' that the individual brought in from a problematic social environment could be exposed to a normalising regimen embodied in the teacher's 'moral observation': an observation which the child learned to take over and internalise as conscience" (214).

I have described a strategy similar to this one in my analysis of the methods of expressive writing teachers (see Berlin 1988). In this classroom, the student is asked to locate and express his or her private voice, innermost being, or authentic self. Emphasis is preeminently on freedom and self-expression. Peers in the class and the teacher, however, finally decide which of the student's various expressions of self is the "true" one, usually by indicating what is not "authentic" or "genuine" in the student texts read. The result is that the student's "true" self is subtly constructed by the responses of others in the class. The subject formation the student "finds" in the act of self-investigation and freely chooses as his or her "best" self is finally a construction of the classroom experience. This subject position, of course, carries with it a great deal of ideological baggage. As I have argued here and elsewhere, no rhetoric is free of this effort to construct consciousness, although some are obviously more aware of the workings of the process than others.

Neither Watkins nor Hunter sees an escape from the responsibilities that have been given to English teachers. The important consideration for both, however, is that the method and content of the English classroom in carrying out its work of certification (Watkins) and subject formation (Hunter) is not determined by any innate feature of the poetic text. In the case of Watkins, the assigning of grades, not the content of the course, is what's important. For Hunter, it is the production of ethical subjects, not the inherent features of literary discourse, that matters. In short, the English course is simply a site in which particular kinds of work get done. It is in no way the case that literary texts dictate that some set of particular objectives be accomplished in a specific way. Indeed, to add to their argument, it is not even necessary that literary texts be the central concern of the course. The processes Watkins and Hunter describe are equally operative in writing courses that avoid literary texts.

Such arguments have been important background considerations in my discussion. I take them up here to underscore the assertion that English teachers are asked to perform important functions for our society, functions that operate in a manner not necessarily immediate and obvious. Regardless of our avowed intentions, by evaluating students and influencing them to be particular kinds of readers and writers, we finally perform the job of gatekeeping and consciousness formation. Of course, teachers have considerable latitude in how these functions are performed. While certainly not totally independent, teachers do make choices about the activities to be pursued in their classrooms. Of equal importance, as active participants in a democracy, they can engage in decision making about the uses to which their work will be put. Our grades may continue to be invoked to rank students outside the classroom, but we can encourage the critical examination of this arbitrary and frequently unjust method of deciding ability and merit. Our teaching strategies may unavoidably shape our students as ethical and social subjects, but this is all the more reason to discuss openly the best procedures for doing so. We cannot help influencing our students, but we can do all we can to be straightforward about our methods and motives. In short, we must take seriously our duty as public intellectuals inside and outside the classroom.

This sort of work has already begun in the admirable contributions of Susan Miller's *Textual Carnivals* and *Rescuing the Subject (1989)* and Lester Faigley's *Fragments of Rationality: Postmodernity and the Subject of Composition (1992).* My purpose in this book has been to join them in the critical examination of institutions and their methods and motives. I have accordingly offered an assessment of the past work of English studies and a proposal for future teaching and research. I thus want to make my last word a plea for collaborative effort. No group of English teachers ought to see themselves as operating in isolation from their fellows in working for change. Dialogue among college teachers and teachers in the high schools and elementary schools is crucial for any effort at seeking improvement to succeed. For too long, college English teachers have ignored their colleagues in the schools, assuming a hierarchical division of labor in which information and ideas flow exclusively from top to bottom. It is time all reading and writing teachers situate their activities within the contexts of the larger profession as well as the contexts of economic and political concerns. We have much to gain working together, much to lose working alone.

Jim Berlin's Last Work

Future Perfect, Tense

Remembering Writing Pedagogy

Linda Brodkey

Jim Berlin's posthumously published book, *Rhetorics, Poetics, and Cultures,* reminded me, among things, that pedagogy is what I have always liked most about composition. I think of pedagogy as the animation of a syllabus, those expected and unexpected human interactions it sets into play, some of which I know about, most of which I don't, some I deal with, some I don't, some augured by a syllabus, some not. A course description is only an approximation of a teacher's practical and theoretical commitments and concerns, but even so, Jim's description of the lower-division course called "Codes and Critiques" also reminded me that had we talked about pedagogy, we would have talked about ways differences in our theoretical understandings of discourse would amount to practical differences in how we respectively imagined composition and what each of us hoped to accomplish by asking students to write in our courses. I think the best way to lay out the practical consequences of our theoretical differences is to describe how I tried to animate a poststructural rather than structural understanding of discourse by asking students to write an autoethnography, a form that I had read but not written when I first assigned it and that I taught myself to write to better understand the intellectual work entailed.

Over the last decade I have regularly taught a seminar most recently called "Ethnographies of Literacy" that enrolls graduate students in composition and literary studies and, on occasion, education, communication, folklore, and anthropology. When I designed the course, I imagined introducing students to theoretical and methodological literature on ethnography and to such well known ethnographies of literacy as Shirley Heath's *Ways with Words* and Janice Radway's *Reading the Romance,* and I further imagined students writing critical essays on these readings. With the exception of students from anthropology, however, nearly everyone found it exceedingly difficult and, for all practical purposes, impossible to remember that ethnographers conduct field work and base their ethnographies, however loosely, on field notes. The difficulty was usually more apparent in discussions of

Ways with Words, which most students summarily dismissed as boring, than in discussions of *Reading the Romance*, which most students took seriously enough to read and discuss. But, in fact, all students were reading pretty much as they had been taught in their respective fields, and were evaluating ethnographic texts accordingly. Students from literature looked for literary things, and students from education, educational things, and so on. And those from anthropology looked for anthropological things, like field methods, field notes, and methodological procedures for turning data into information.

Since there isn't time in this course to conduct fieldwork, I tried to simulate the experience by having students collect data on their own writing and reading practices. They begin by observing and recording all that they read and write over a two or three day period. The recording of such quotidian data usually makes at least two things obvious. First, few graduate students spend more than 20% of their literate time writing, and, second, data must be interpreted to be recorded. In other words, decisions about how to record events are critical to observation, and thus the recording of any and all "literacy events," to use Shirley Brice Heath's useful definition, entails a fair amount of interpretation ("Protean Shapes"). In addition to deciding what to call such reading practices as the daily reading of cereal boxes, the circumstances of such reading are also likely to be important, since deciding whether such literacy events are habitual or strategic acts may ultimately depend on the presence or absence of others. Similarly, deciding what to call such common writing practices as filling out the plethora of forms by which students are expected to surveil themselves at every turn is complicated by the fact that the form they are signing is usually also committing the writer to some action, paying a bill, attending a seminar, advancing to candidacy. The individual labor of collecting and recording data taken in tandem with the collective labor of comparing and contrasting the recorded literate lives of students in the class go a long way toward explaining why field work is *work,* and in turn give students some basis for comparing the kind of intellectual work required in the field with that conducted in other places, such as libraries and laboratories.

Simulating the collection of ethnographic data works better for students already familiar with other forms of data collection in the social sciences than for those unaccustomed to treating things not already identified as texts as worth their attention. Since the second group consists primarily of students in composition and literary studies, the core group for the course, I decided to simulate another common intellectual labor of ethnographers, namely, the deliberate transformation of data into cultural information. The simulation begins with a kind of memory work, working back from the last to first thing students can recall writing, and then writing and presenting one of the "memories" as a literacy anecdote to the class, and ultimately extending that or another anecdote as a literacy narrative. While there's considerable variation in how far back people remember, what they remember, and what they have forgotten, over the years several things have held constant across groups, most notably that nearly everyone remembers liking the writing they did outside school and disliking the writing they did in school. This is invariably a surprise to students, and the subject of a great deal of speculation, since graduate students are, by definition, successful students, and most of them also are, by any measure but their own, successful writers as well as readers.

The constant that interests me as a teacher and scholar who has been offering variations of "Ethnographies of Literacy" for some years is that literacy anecdotes are almost invariably remembered and told as *psychological* anecdotes. They are so profoundly and persistently psychological that I think it's fair to say that the intellectual work of the course is in figuring out ways to interrupt the discursive history that makes it seem obvious and natural for most people to represent themselves to themselves as psychological cases. I am talking here not about *interiority* itself, but about the *valorization* of modern psychological discourses of interiority, about cultural discursive hegemony, about the triumph in the twentieth century of psychological discourses of interiority that prevents most students I have worked with from even imagining themselves as they have been learned to routinely imagine others—as culturally constituted subjects.

Modernist maps of the self are arguably constructed by superimposing the familiar and fascinating cartographies of human interiority charted by psychological theories onto the landscape of personal experience. By this end of the century, for instance, every reasonably well-educated, white adult professional I know seems to have amassed an extensive repertoire of therapeutic narratives. In addition to being able to represent ourselves to ourselves, and to anyone else who is willing to listen, as interestingly neurotic, many of us are also fluent in a rather remarkable variety of modern psychological "dialects." We know our undergraduate and graduate GPAs, our IQs (often on more than one test), and the precise percentile of our academic achievement scores on any number of the standardized tests administered over the course of schooling, not to mention secret knowledge of where we rank on self-assessment surveys published in popular magazines. Those of us who have children also track and teach them to track their scores with equal precision.

I doubt that I or anyone else could exaggerate the normative sway of psychological discourse over white professionals and, increasingly, professionals of color in the United States, a discourse so widely dispersed at this end of the twentieth century that an entire class of people has become so utterly fascinated with its mental health that psychological well being can be linked to physical appearance. Capitalizing on this fascination in *Make the Connection*, Bob Greene and Oprah Winfrey have recently gone so far as to "connect" professional fitness to physical fitness via "self-esteem," which, given the corporate drift of the academy, suggests that "buff" will soon be as necessary a credential for academics as it has long since become for most other professionals, with the possible exception of those in computers, who are reputed to be exercising their right to feed themselves from vending machines. I have taken license here with what I have been calling psychological discourse in order to draw attention to what I see as the most insidious discursive impediment facing anyone from the professional class who attempts to see themselves as social and cultural as well as psychological subjects. Even the most socially committed scholars I know, including myself, are implicated to the gills by psychological representations of the self and the normative effects of sorting and ranking not only themselves, but also the students whose writing they are hired to surveil.

While students in the graduate seminar reimagine themselves as cultural subjects by exploring in their autoethnographies some of the cultural possibilities attenuated in their anecdotes, the essays produced in the seminar are recognizably more in the tradition of psychology than cultural anthropology. Yet nearly everyone is at least intermittently able to make themselves strange to themselves, as it were, and culturally situate themselves *and* their writing (see "Writing on the Bias" and the student autoethnographies in *Writing Permitted in Designated Areas Only).* This postmodernist and poststructural practice of othering the self may superficially resemble the more familiar modernist and structural practice of self-alienation, but whereas self-othering explores multiple subjectivity (difference) as the effects of an indefinite number of interdependent and competing discourses of human subjectivity, self-alienation is an entirely predictable effect of dehumanizing ideologies. Put another way, self-othering is a strategy for writing and rewriting the self, but self-alienation is a strategy for reading and rereading the self.

Were I more a modernist than a postmodernist, that is, if I also saw discourses as cultural codes, as Jim viewed them on the strength of Pierre Bourdieu's structural analysis of cultural codes in *Distinction,* I would probably ask students to decode interiority, perhaps decode the scholarly and popular literature that is commonly invoked to warrant psychology as the exclusive discourse of the self: IQ, achievement, and placement tests, talk therapies, drug therapies, conduct manuals, domestic fiction, and so on. In other words, I would ask students to reread themselves by decoding such texts. Although the perverse hegemony of psychological discourses often makes me wish psychology *were a* cultural code, or even a set of cultural codes, rather than a vast and pervasive discourse, I try to resist my modernist impulses, resist assuming that discourses are literally encoded in texts that students need to learn to decode. In my own work, I have tried to distinguish between discourse as it is used in poststructuralism (ideology) and discourse as it is used in structuralism (text), but I know of no one who has more carefully explained the variation in what is meant by discourse across modern and postmodern theories than the applied linguist Alsatian Pennycook (1994). Jim's modernist conflation of discourse and cultural code in *Rhetorics, Poetics, and Cultures* reminded me that while his pedagogical assumption that texts can be ideologically encoded and decoded is warranted by the structuralist elision of discourse and text, my pedagogy rests on poststructural distinctions of texts from discourses.

If I do not imagine that texts are encoded, I can't very well ask students to decode them. Instead I assume that it's the discursive hegemony of psychology rather than psychological codes that disrupts the writing of autoethnography in the graduate seminar I've been discussing. The discourse is so widely dispersed that our psychological stories about ourselves seem uniquely our own. Yet internalized cultural discourses of the psychological self (as in self-esteem, or the lack thereof) are increasingly inflected across class, race, gender, sexuality, age, and nearly every other social or cultural grouping I can imagine, as can be documented by guests who routinely articulate themselves as psychological subjects on television talk shows, where it is patently obvious that only experts still labor under the illusion that psychology is a discipline rather than a discourse, a profession rather than a way of life in the U.S.

The intellectual labor of writing autoethnographic accounts of literacy entails locating and exploring the sites where people learn to think of themselves as readers and writers, and where even the most able among them rarely learn to see themselves as good writers. That so few people see themselves as good writers strikes me as a phenomenon best addressed not as a consequence of false consciousness, but as one of the consequences of modern schooling, as what happens to students in the classroom, the classroom that Keith Hoskin, the Foucauldian educational historian, argues originated in the early modern period and exists still as the site where writing, examining, and grading are inextricably linked via the conflation of disciplinarity and pedagogy. This is the site where each of us, good students and good teachers alike, learn to assume personal responsibility for our failure to learn or teach writing, and the classroom will remain the site of individual and collective failure of intelligence, will, application, so as long as we persist in reading ourselves and others at the expense of writing ourselves and others out of that place.

La Jolla, California

Note

This essay appeared originally in *JAC* 17 (1997): 489-93.

Works Cited

Berlin, James A. *Rhetorics, Poetics, and Cultures: Refiguring College English Studies.* Urbana, IL: NCTE, 1996.

Brodkey, Linda. *Writing Permitted in Designated Areas Only.* Minneapolis: U of Minnesota P, 1996.

Bourdieu, Pierre. *Distinction: A Social Critique of the Judgement of Taste.* Cambridge, MA: Harvard UP, 1984.

Green, Bob, and Oprah Winfrey. *Make the Connection.* New York: Hyperion, 1996.

Heath, Shirley Brice. *Ways with Words: Language, Life, and Work in Communities and Classrooms.* New York: Cambridge UP, 1983.

—. "Protean Shapes in Literacy Events: Ever-Shifting Oral and Literate Traditions." *Spoken and Written Language: Exploring Orality and Literacy.* Vol. 9. Ed. Deborah Tannen. Norwood, NJ: Alex, 1982.

Hoskin, Keith. "Education and the Genesis of Disciplinarity: The Unexpected Reversal." *Knowledges: Historical and Critical Studies in Disciplinarity.* Ed. Ellen Messer-Davidow, David Shumway, and David L. Sylvan. Charlottesville, VA: UP of Virginia, 1993.

Pennycook, Alastair. "Incommensurable Discourses?" *Applied Linguistics* 15 (1994): 115-38.

Radway, Janice A. *Reading the Romance: Women, Patriarchy, and Popular Culture.* Chapel Hill, NC: U of North Carolina P, 1984.

Rhetorics, Poetics and Cultures as an Articulation Project

Patricia Harkin

Rhetorics, Poetics and Cultures is for me most valuable as an account of the "whys" and "bows" of Jim Berlin's classroom practice: his last book describes his articulation of cultural studies and composition studies for graduate students at Purdue as they both study rhetorical history and teach introductory writing. It is that articulation that I'll examine in this essay—beginning with a brief and selective definition of the term. In Birmingham School cultural theory, "articulation" is construed as an active process through which meaning is expressed in local and contingent ways: in a specific context, at a specific historical moment, within a specific discourse. Thus articulation is both a saying and a connecting. It describes an enactment of meaning, while simultaneously connecting that meaning to multiple discursive systems. In recent discussions, the term has been used to point to acts of enunciating connections between and among gender, race, class and sexual orientation as well as to intersections between and among disciplinary inquiries.

But to call an "articulation" project merely an "inter-" or "multidisciplinary" inquiry would be to miss the point. Articulation becomes necessary precisely because disciplines—institutions that see only what they recognize no matter where they look—will necessarily repress or ignore some crucial aspect of the job that cultural studies is designed to do. A disciplinary study that focuses on class, for example, risks blurring race and gender; a writing program that construes writing only as communicative behavior risks occulting the ways in which "good" writing is an effect of class. Fredric Jameson describes articulation as "a punctual and sometimes even ephemeral totalization," in which several institutional formations come together, but only for a moment, to express a meaning for a specific set of circumstances ("Cultural Studies," 32). (Conceptions from film studies, anthropology, sociology, feminism, and queer studies, for example, articulate momentarily to describe the representation of "family" in the film

Father's Day; while nonetheless rejecting the universalizing gestures of disciplinarity that would turn them into a method.) In lieu of methodological instructions, Jameson offers a trope. "Articulation," he writes, "is like a turning molecular structure, an ion exchange between various entities, in which the ideological drives associated with one pass over and interfuse the other" a short-lived chemical compound that has to be aced before it disintegrates ("Cultural Studies," 32).

Beginning with "Rhetoric and Ideology in the Writing Class," Jim Berlin's work might be understood as a series of attempts to articulate a Birmingham School electron into the epistemic rhetoric molecule. His legacy has been to bring together the institutional formations of cultural studies and composition studies such that they could speak to each other (articulate in the sense of enunciating their disparate projects) and fit together (articulate in the sense of joining different parts). In a recent essay, I pointed out how formidable that project actually is, because both composition studies and cultural studies are multifarious institutional formations which are themselves comprised of many disciplinary constructions. Further, Jim's project was not only to imagine a linkup for composition studies and cultural studies but also to make this hybrid into a pedagogy—more precisely, to discern the pedagogy that his hybrid implies. Further, to the extent that his articulation orients itself toward agency, the project needs to be further informed by attention to race, gender, class and affectional preference. I list them separately (rather than as part of the disciplinary apparatus of Cultural Studies) because it seems to me that they are cultural facts as well as disciplinary terms, so they make as it were a fourth dimension of the problematic.

Given this complexity, it's not surprising that Jameson calls "articulation . . . the central theoretical problem or conceptual core of Cultural Studies" ("Cultural Studies," 32). Moreover, Jameson asserts that although articulation is "exemplified over and over again . . . (it is] less often foregrounded as such" ("Cultural Studies," 32). An exemplification *does* an articulation project—shows, for example, how subjectivities, values and knowledges are discursively constructed; a foregrounding *stipulates and explains* why and how disparate systems are connected so as to accomplish a given goal. Foregrounding emphasizes *praxis*—in this case, the generalized account of specific linkups that explains why Jim Berlin made the choices he did and how he fit together the theories of rhetoric, of culture, of reading, of semiotics, of ideology, of pedagogy, and of composing for students and teachers of Introductory Writing at Purdue. A foregrounded articulation shows how theories of writing and of culture are connected—what their connections can accomplish and how, and what they occult or slight, and how. One of the reasons why articulation is so rarely foregrounded, I think, is that its projects are both so complicated (a totalization) and so short-lived (punctual and ephemeral).

I'll try briefly to foreground the articulation that Jim's first year writing course "Codes and Critiques" exemplified. Jim wrote about the theory and the practice of his articulation process. Berlin's theory of rhetoric is his own—the social epistemic rhetoric that seeks to explain how cultural forces enact and even determine our perceptions of "what exists, what is good, what is possible." He acknowledges the sources of his cultural studies thought in the work of the Birmingham School. In the work of Raymond Williams, Richard Hoggart and Stuart Hall, among others, he found an emphasis on the lived experience of ordinary people as well as a profound suspicion of the traditional English department hierarchies that privilege reading over writing and reception over production just as capital is privileged over labor. For an account of ideology, he went to Goran Therborn, whose "method [Jim wrote] is at every turn rhetorical, by which I mean that he considers ideology in relation to communicators, audiences, formulations of reality, and the central place of language in all of these" (78; [84 in the present volume]). Fredric Jameson's *The Political Unconscious* provided a hermeneutic—"a method of reading" of multiple "interpretive horizons" whose "purpose is to discover the way in which a text . . . offers an imaginary resolution of a real contradiction" (107, 77). Like Jameson, Berlin went to Levi-Strauss for a way of describing cultural contradictions as part of a binary system that "govern[s] the behavior of a culture in its everyday operations" (59; [62 in the present volume]). These several formations gave him a way of accounting for the production of discourse, and a way of reading the discourses that shape our lives. What he did not yet have—or what he had not yet made explicit—was a theory of composing—a way of explaining to students how *they* should go about producing discourse.

Part of a theory of composing can be inferred, I think from the practice Jim describes in "Codes and Critiques." Jim gave students a heuristic that prompted them to find cultural contradictions that they would not otherwise perceive. When they followed it, they were expected to encounter what Janice Lauer calls "cognitive dissonance." Like Lauer, Jim saw invention as emerging from dissonance, and therefore he used cultural contradictions specifically to produce or engender that feeling. The teacher's role, for Jim, was that of problem poser, "providing methods for questioning that locate the points of conflict and contradiction" (102). Issues of class, race and gender would emerge, he said, as a part of class discussions. Students would record their differing descriptions, analyses, and explanations in their writing. These "responses [he writes] were at the center of classroom activity" (115). Issues of arrangement and genre would emerge from these varying responsive invention processes.

As Jim himself somewhat ruefully admitted, these procedures were not entirely successful. Often, he told us in person and in print, students construed Jim's carefully engendered "dissonance" merely as an obstacle to be overcome as they struggled to become a productive member of a capitalist economy. The students Jim dealt with are, by and large, products of a homogeneous, rural, politically and religiously conservative culture.

My mentees and I have named this typical student the "postmodern Hoosier rhetor." It is hard for her to see the racial and class based contradictions on which Jim's pedagogy was based, and even her perceptions of gender are likely to be very traditional. On the other hand, she is bombarded daily with the unresolved narratives of "Friends" and "Seinfeld," the constructed subjectivities of "Singled Out" and the talk shows, the fragmentation of MTV and the Soaps. Even though she might tell you that she was "raised" with master narratives about good and evil, conservatives and liberals, she is very much aware of and inured to the contradictions of postmodernity. When the postmodern Hoosier rhetor has a contradiction pointed out to her, then, she is less likely to contemplate the cognitive dissonance as a spur to invention and more likely simply to say "whatever." And since Jim's method calls for students to arrive at genre as a function of their invention processes, the pomo Hoosier rhetor reinvents the "whatever" genre—the essay that concludes by asserting that "everyone is entitled to their own opinion"—the very kind of writing that we hoped cultural studies would eliminate.

At Purdue we continue to work at developing ways of confronting the pomo "whatever" as a problem for invention. As we do, we are very much aware of the giant's shoulders on which we have stood to perceive it.

West Lafayette, Indiana

Note

This essay appeared originally in *JAC* 17 (1997): 494-97.

Works Cited

Berlin, James A. *Rhetorics, Poetics, and Cultures. Refiguring College English Studies.* Urbana: NCTE, 1996.

Harkin, Patricia. "In the Crossfire: (after) Jim Berlin." *Works and Days* 27/28 14 (1996): 291-98.

Jameson, Fredric. "On Cultural Studies." *Social Text* 34 (1993): 17-52.

—. *The Political Unconscious: Narrative as a Socially Symbolic Act.* Ithaca: Cornell UP, 1981.

Technologies of Self?-Formation

Susan Miller

I had a concern as I read Jim Berlin's "Closing Word" in *Rhetorics, Poetics, and Cultures.* I'm one of the few fans of Ian Hunter's *Culture and Government in English Studies,* so I was understandably thrilled that Jim relies on Hunter in this brief closing. Jim places his entire book's argument in the context of Hunter's case that English studies is powerfully and precisely devoted to installing in students a particular kind of self-monitorial, "schooled" subject position. English teaches its students to oppose their perceptions to a structure of self-correction and doubt, by means of its subtle approval and disapproval of their modes of interpretation. Jim says that Hunter's description of this practice fits his own critique of expressivist writing classes, where students' supposedly "real" personal voices appear after their teachers and better-schooled classmates name unacceptable responses as inauthentic, not "genuine." English teachers, Jim infers from Hunter's and his analyses, are thus responsible for, have power over, consciousness formation. Jim's closing then also calls for explicit classroom attention to exposing this powerful teaching practice in English, for telling students how English creates the internalized self-monitor, a schooled conscience, that separates their multiple, often split, immediate responses from the normalized thinking that wins them approval.

As I said, I was thrilled by this concluding revelation of how schooling in language produces normalized but always self-conflicted "real selves." Jim reasons here that when we teach differentially valued interpretations, we must focus both on letting students in on how institutions form subjects who always doubt themselves, and on choosing the content of courses in light of a tremendous social responsibility.

But I was, as I said, also concerned. It is not obvious to me that institutional claims to teach a universal moral sense should supplant families, regional customs, class, or ethnic politics, to normalize and covertly coerce conscience, nor that institutions can or should install a universal vision of "democratic" subjectivity. It is not necessarily positive that the teacherly subject position needed to accomplish this social work must simulate parents and thereby infantilize students, as I argue whenever I have a chance. When students must learn to frame every experience in dual perspectives—their own and the iconic English teacher's—the end result is a culture in which it is difficult to share an elevator with Native Americans without coding them as "Other," or to work for females without measuring them against "real" women, or to meet any student without immediately assuming that I have much to teach. Jim equates this habit of judgment, this internalized duality, with the "consciousness" that is the recurring theme in his positive programs for teaching, research, and a reformed English studies. While Hunter objects to the mass control of an educational technology that estranges students from unrefereed desires and from action, Jim urges that we tell students that we have this power. Yet his book's descriptions of actual teaching perpetuate this covert practice. Despite its closing use of Hunter and other emerging changes in his work, his class plans were chaperoned by doctrinaire leftism, which calls its political opposition victims of an "inauthentic" false consciousness—that is, of faulty interpretations.

In this book's descriptions of courses in cultural awareness, for instance, Jim rarely discusses acts of writing without using a fatherly imperative voice. He often says that students as *readers* discover, discuss, become aware, and reflect. But he says that students as *writers* "must" learn, "must" see, "must" identify and enact, and "must be made" aware. Student readers are teachable, that is, easily led into self- and cultural reflection, and into debates about the media's classed and sexed binaries. But as student writers, they only compose exercises in order to reflect on or display their grasp of democratic consciousness. In these model classes, their writing is not positioned to enact that consciousness because they, as *writers,* are not taught that they have the power to do so.

I think that Jim would have read by now John Guillory's *Cultural Capital,* which implies an alternative to fatherly pride in managing students' interiors, the work that I fear is still the central goal of composition teaching. Guillory's thesis is that it is not interpretation or ideology that determines students' politics or their political power. Instead, uneven access to means of literate/literary *production*—to *making* powerful language, not to reading it—now and always determines uneven class and social status, and thus also determines the possibility that specific student classes will actually intervene in uneven social arrangements. Guillory also argues that composition has replaced interpretative studies as the cultural site of discriminatory allotments of this access to political action. Composition now produces, he says, the distinction between basic and more elite language, produces the stratified ideological identity of the politically effective sociolect, and produces both its pretensions to universality and its power to make the medium of political discourse available. Guillory believes that students who can identify with those who make consequential language determine power relations, not those who interpret through an institutionally installed ideological consciousness.

My version of this claim is to argue for enabling students to act through language, first by placing its differential modes of making in the center of our teaching, as Jim suggested. By teaching texts rather than their making, by teaching awareness rather than rhetoric, and by teaching the power of meanings rather than the making of statements, we inadvertently reproduce a politics that is aware but passive. Rhetoric is not, that is, semiotics. And while it often suits us to equate the two (for reasons related more to professional politics than to democracy), writing is not reading.

I worry, consequently, about composition courses that frame student writing in imperatives to *reflect.* The content of such courses is not writing—is not persuasion to assume the positions of those whose acts of writing are interventions. Nor is it systematic demonstrations of *how* to write—not "well," but powerfully, to subvert more and less conventional subject positions. Writing taught as reading, that is, accomplishes political stasis. Courses in reading culture produce what conservatives call liberal armchair Marxism, a hermeneutics of suspicion. They appear to raise the prestige of their teachers, but they do not in fact accomplish that, nor create students who are entitled to write, as we see from their results.

I shared with Jim a pronounced tendency to avoid middle roads, the liberal positions that now determine the interest of English studies in newly diversified reading. Our shared goals are certainly why Jim's book wants to refigure English. But our mutual wish to learn how to use the active power of language also causes my concern. The students Jim portrays as needing consciousness are not directed toward practice in manipulating genres, but to a smart awareness of generic power; not toward guerrilla stylistics, but to savvy about stylishness; not toward strength to withstand forces that prevent their critiques from wide acknowledgment, but to interpretations of these forces. Yet culture as an object of study—no matter how it is studied—no more motivates active literate practices than does reading great literature.

I agree with Jim's closing: English studies remains the most powerful site of cultural reproduction, because it covertly installs a difference between schooled and unschooled perspectives in the name of a particular morality. But I want to add that if we teach the masses in the name of democratic virtue, we must actually privilege a dose of vulgar composition—how to find and fulfill a textual purpose for a specific readership, in full awareness that safe purposes and already socialized results are already waiting to choose us. If our courses are to undo, not perpetuate, the political silence of the individualistic "I am" that composition now supports, they should focus on what powerful writers know and do. They should not, that is, distance students from an ineffable "authorship," nor focus on what English teachers want students to "think" about the readings they now teach.

Younger scholars and graduate students in composition may think it exclusionary to urge more focused meetings of College Composition and Communication, more research reports that offer "news" about writing practices and processes, more empirical but not positivist studies of writing development, and more attempts to re-theorize the purposes and results of specific textual conventions in prose discourse. But Jim and I also shared a professional history in which we and many others were shunned, professionally insulted, denied tenure, and, like the suicidal dentist in the movie *M*A*S*H*, accused of having wasted our entire educations. We were subtly yet coercively begged to forego writing for reading. That history may explain why current composition has turned to cultural hermeneutics to give its work, and its workers, professional parity. But the field's troubles did not occur because people like us disliked literature or those who teach it. We do not. They resulted instead from an early insistence that our courses and our research are about *writing,* not interpretation, conscious or not.

Salt Lake City, Utah

Note

This essay appeared originally in *JAC* 17 (1997): 497-500.

Berlin's Citizen and First World Rhetoric

John Trimbur

The first sentence of Jim Berlin's last book *Rhetorics, Poetics, and Cultures* says that "English studies is in crisis." Berlin lists the predictable forces at work: the onset of "theory," postmodernism, "political correctness," the accumulative disequilibrium of an expanding canon, identity politics. Berlin invokes these forces, of course, to do more than account for the perceived crisis state. He believes the current crisis warrants a revived role for rhetoric in English studies, a restored and updated version of civic rhetoric. One of Berlin's key arguments throughout the book holds that rhetoric should take its place alongside poetics in the "business of the polis" and the "communal engagement" of reading, writing, and speaking he wants to see at the center of the English curriculum.

Berlin's case for rhetoric in *Rhetorics, Poetics, and Cultures* will be familiar to those who know his earlier work. What I find striking about his last book is that Berlin frames the "crisis in English studies" in terms of "major changes in the work activities and demographic makeup of the society for which college students are preparing," as well as in terms of current intellectual and political trends (xii). The cultural dislocations of the global economy and the post-Fordist restructuring of the workplace weigh as heavily on the perceived crisis as the usual academic suspects.

In "A Closing Word" at the book's end, Berlin returns to the mundane, workaday world and the role of English teachers in the subject formation and credentialing of undergraduates. Berlin wants to locate our work studying and teaching writing not only as academic specialists but also as factors in the school to job transition. From this perspective, the English curriculum and its pedagogy of evaluating and ranking students are meant to construct marketable, recommendable students—ethical subjects with particular skills and dispositions toward reading and writing that fit the prevailing economic relations and cultural realities.

There is an important tension at work in Berlin's treatment of the school to job transition that is worth exploring. On one hand, the notion that writing courses amount to "rhetoric for the meritocracy" has been a standard caveat at least since Richard Ohmann's *English in America* explained how composition prepares students for the corporate world. On the other hand, Berlin seems to insist that part of the role of writing instruction should be to prepare students for the world of work. Berlin is not proposing that the curriculum be given over to vocationalism, but at the same time he says, "I do not think we in the academy can simply ignore the advice of employers." In the next sentence, he comes close to sounding like such new age management gurus as Tom Peters and Peter M. Senge: "We must finally provide a college education that enables workers to be excellent communicators, quick and flexible learners, and cooperative collaborators" (50; [52 in the present volume]). None of the current sages of the postindustrial workplace could have put it any better.

What are we to make of Berlin's advice here? Has he been coopted by the allure of the post-Fordist workplace? Lost his Marxist bearings? Turned class collaborator? I don't think there's much danger. To my mind, what makes Berlin's advice so surprising is that writing teachers and theorists on the left have largely resisted the notion of work and the school to job transition altogether. Those are issues we have conveniently segregated in business, technical, and professional writing courses, keeping the first-year course "pure" and "critical."

My view is that in *Rhetorics, Poetics, and Cultures,* Berlin is challenging us to develop ways to think about how our activities as writing teachers are necessarily and unavoidably caught up in the school to job transition. And he offers some ways to do so. Preparing students for work, Berlin says, "can never be a simple accommodation to the marketplace." Instead, it should provide "an understanding of the operation of the workforce as a whole." In short, we need a "curriculum that places preparation for work within a comprehensive range of democratic educational concerns" (51; [54 in the present volume]).

Berlin evokes a social-democratic citizen-worker as the subject of rhetoric, a figure rooted in the earlier radical democratic traditions of John Dewey, Fred Newton Scott, and Gertrude Buck and distinct from the scientific meritocracy, on one hand, and the minority culture of liberal humanism, on the other. What Berlin seems to be getting at here is that citizenship and civic rhetoric depend in part on how work enables individuals to participate in the operations of society. Work provides a critical connection to others and to institutions. In the traditions of the labor movement, trade union militants are always the best workers, the leaders at the point of production where the class struggle takes place daily.

In many respects, we are suffering from a media blitz by baby boomers that has cast each successive generation as somehow lacking in relation to the movement of the 1960s. Since the mid-1970s, young people have been routinely characterized as careerist, vocational, obsessed with jobs, apolitical. We have grown accustomed to representing work and careers as private and individual matters, counterposed to the public and the interests of the larger community. One of the great strengths of *Rhetorics, Poetics, and Cultures* is that Berlin wants to resist this privatization of work, to merge labor and citizenship in the notion of economic democracy, where production is geared to social needs instead of private profit and workers control democratically organized workplaces.

To my mind, this vision of citizen-workers in an economic democracy provides an important corrective to current emphases in cultural studies approaches to teaching writing that tend to see students above all as consumers—of styles, images, narratives, media messages, cultural products. But the merging of citizen and worker also produces some difficulties that are worth mentioning. The term "citizen" combines uneasily with the term "worker" because the identity of the former is based on geography while the identity of the latter is based on a relation to the means of production.

The notion of the citizen emerges in the French Revolution as the mutual recognition of individuals and groups who understand themselves to be independent from church and court, a "people" with their own separate interests, identities, and institutions. Citizenship was not conferred but claimed by the masses who took over the streets and defended the revolution against the nobility and the properties classes.

As the radical force of the citizenship is institutionalized, however, it calls up its opposite—the alien, women, children, the criminal, the unpropertied, the illiterate, the insane, the lumpen, the undocumented. Since the allegiance of the citizen is to the people and the nation, loyalty begins and ends with the geography of national borders, enforcing the difference between naturalized citizens and illegal immigrants. Citizenship, in other words, is perpetually in danger of a

First Worldist orientation, where the key question is territorial and the defense of national integrity. This contrasts sharply with an internationalist perspective concerned with the common interests of working people caught up in a global division of labor that cuts across national boundaries.

When the term "citizen" and "worker" come up, it is good to remember what Karl Marx said: "Working people have no country." The proletariat is an international class whose interests cross national lines.

Worcester, Massachusetts

Note

This essay appeared originally in *JAC* 17 (1997): 500-2.

Work Cited

Berlin, James A. *Rhetorics, Poetics, and Cultures: Refiguring College English Studies.* Urbana, IL: NCTE, 1996.

Aesthetics, Party Lines

Victor J. Vitanza

What I will have said, I address to "Jim" and to any of you in as much as "Jim" might be in your thoughts.

Jim and I used to talk on the phone. It was a kind of party-line conversation. I don't know if you know what a party line used to signify. When I was a kid, between 5 and 8 years old, my parents and I lived way outside the city limits of Houston, TX. We had a party line; that is, we shared a telephone line with another family in our area. Often my parents would pick up the receiver to make a call and the other party was on it. Actually, more often than not. Trying to get a call out to another was like trying to reach the proverbial excluded third party. I remember overhearing more conversations between my folks and the other party on line than a conversation with a third party (the normally intended audience for telephones).

The conversations I had with Jim on the phone, which were like none others that I have ever had in my life with another, were comparable, party-line telephone calls. We talked about You. The always intended, yet uncanny Audience, the ones we wanted to reach. We talked about what your expectations might be, and of course we talked about our differences concerning what and how we wanted to communicate to you. To be sure, we talked about much that we agreed about, and we talked about our careers and we talked about domestic things such as our families, our kids playing soccer and basketball.

A call would usually begin with hellos but *without* additional niceties, for there was always a cut to the chase. There is one particular call that I especially remember. I had just walked into the house with the last bag of groceries that I had purchased and a satchel of books that I had earlier checked out of the university library. The phone rang. (Rinnggggg, Rinnggggg.) I picked it up and Jim said, "Hello, Vitanza." From his salutation, I knew what kind of conversation it was going to be. When he said, "Hello, Victor," it meant a domestic, local call; when he said, "Hello, Vitanza," it meant a long distance, business call. I said hello and immediately preempted him by saying that I just got back from the library with a load of books on aesthetics. At the time, Jim was writing *Rhetorics, Poetics, and Cultures* and I was writing *Negation, Subjectivity, and the History of Rhetoric.* We both knew that we were writing sections on Aesthetics and politics and we both knew how difficult such a combination of loci were. I mentioned to Jim that I had just checked out Josef Chytry's *The Aesthetic State* and several other books; and he mentioned to me that he was reading Martin Jay's article "'The Aesthetic Ideology' as Idology." We continued the conversation on this theme for another 10 or so minutes, exchanging bibliographical references, all related to the problem of what Paul de Man labelled "the aesthetic ideology."

Much time has passed, though there were intervening party-line conversations. Both books are in print now. I see what Jim had to say; he has not, as far as I can reasonably assume, seen what I have had to say. I can only imagine. Aesthetically and politically. Politically and aesthetically.

As I was telling another audience a few weeks ago, most, if not all of our arguments, are with the dead, yet very much alive. Often, I feel like Bellow's Augie March, writing letters of disagreement, or on occasion agreement, to the dead, yet alive. Virtually, I feel like an Augie on a party line. Dialing the numbers, waiting while it rings (Ringgggggg, Ringggggggg). And then someone picks up the phone, saying hurriedly, "Hello!"

And cutting to the chase *I would have said:* "Hello, Jim, I just got your book and though I have yet to read it, the cover looks like road kill on a rural Texas highway and the book smells like a sun-baked turd from an armadillo." There would be sardonic laughter and he would say, "Just a second Vitanza, I'm finishing up mentoring a student." And I would hear Jim say a few words to one of his graduate students at Purdue and then say, "Now, I have to take care of Vitanza." And he would continue, without transition, saying, "And I have your book . . . it was sent to me today. .. you understand, I would never buy such a satanic book, nor leave it lying around for young ones to read. . . . Let me tell you that your book cover with a background of aqua satin sheets looks as if it were done for a David Lynch film—which is a perfect match up, given your film noir approach to a history of this profession." And the repartee would continue, back and forth, punctuated with much good humored laughter. Later the snippets of biting critique would have been heard and counter-responded to in passing. But always eventually with so much laughter! It was always a virtual roasting!

Jim, as he often claimed, was a "laughing Marxist." The only one that I ever met. (Rinnggggg, Rinnggggg).

"Hello."

"Hello, Jim, it's me."

"Oh, Hi, Victor. Glad you called. I've got a seminar tonight and I plan to tell my students about you. I mentioned your name last week and the class paused and asked, 'Victor? Who's Victor?' And then one of them said, 'Oh, yes, you mean Victor Villanueva!'"

After his laughter would have subsided.

I would have replied, "Jim, I just finished your book and I see that you mention my name on page 69 [73]and direct your comments on postmodernism to me. I have to tell you, by the way, your response is a straw-man argument. Who in the hell is David Harvey to speak for you as a worthy critic of PostModernism with all of its perverse complexities? And then you turn to Martin Jay and his saying that Lyotard does not 'afford much in the way of positive help with the choices that have to be made.' You merely suggest in passing that you readjust *Gamino*. Jim, return to the repressed and this time give us evidence that you actually read Lyotard and that you yourself understand his notion of justice. And Jim, What about Kant himself? Did you read Kant? The modernist father of aesthetics? Did you read what Lyotard has said in the *Differend* and in *Lessons on the Analytic of the Sublime* and elsewhere about Kant's third critique? and its givenness to radical heterogeneities. And Kant's fear of what he saw in his thinking of the sublime. His attraction to and repulsion by the Ugly, the Monstrous! And Lyotard's own incipient fear of the sublime? in relation to justice. And yet, what Lyotard says about the sign of history? Jim, why do you rely so heavily on Harvey and Jay's readings? On secondary material? to be dismissive? Where are your own readings of Kant and Lyotard's texts? Why support your important position with their shakey testimonials!? Are you preaching only to the already converted? If either Harvey or Jay can be found lacking, the house that Jim built falls . . . and like a house of cards."

Jim would have said to me, in a counter-wicked way, "well, I *think* I read your book, too; but it's really hard to say or know. You see, I think that your book does not really exist because the audience here cannot understand the book or follow its overly detailed and serpentine-byzantine lines of thinking; and if they could understand the book or broken lines of thinking, they could not communicate the intuitiveness of the book because your position is too evangelical; and if some of them could communicate it to others in the audience here, what you have to say in the book would just scare the holy shit out of everyone! Victor, it's such a melay-knee-al thing you wrote!" And so on. And soon. And so on . . . the discussion would . . . will have gone. The unending life-in-death death-in-life, conversation.

I know, I know: though there is a "so on," it's rife with the conditional mode. I would like to think, however, that the conditional is the mode of hope. The conditions for the possibilities of hope for a revolution of justice, the most difficult of key, everyday words and concepts. Justice. Our task with Jim is to rethink justice.

Jim had party-line conversations with all of us. Some gentle. Some caustic. Many in laughter. In the healing balm of laughter. He best knew how to balance work with laughter, laughter with work. Jim had conversations with all of us. And had conversations with many of you . . . no, with all of us . . . and especially the multitudes who have yet to enter our field's or discipline's conversations. Conversations about composing justice. Collaboratively! Composing justice for Jim was not a division of labor but a co-labor of work and laughter.

Earlier, I said that *our* conversations, our arguments, are with the dead, the past. Our arguments are not only with the past but with the future. With a co-labor of past and future. With *What will have been.* And so much has been and will have been because of JB's exuberant laughter. His making party-line conversations possible. Lest we forget, Jim's praxis of laughter was never laughing at, but was—and must continue to have been—laughing *with.* And therein lies the condition for his, no, *our* perpetual rebeginnings on our own, more global, party-line.

Arlington, Texas

Note

This essay appeared originally in *JAC* 17 (1997): 503-5.

Afterword

Janice M. Lauer

According to his computer record, on the morning of February 2, 1994, Jim was working on the final revision of this manuscript. That evening, after attempting his usual five-mile run, he returned home and suffered a heart attack from which he did not recover. His loss to us in the field of composition is irreparable.

But as an important part of his legacy to the profession, Jim left us this book, which was near completion. During the spring semester of 1993, a research grant from Purdue's School of Liberal Arts enabled Jim to complete a draft of the book, to submit it to a number of us at Purdue and colleagues elsewhere for comments, and to revise the work based on the advice he received. In the fall semester on sabbatical, he made final revisions based on extensive reader reviews from NCTE and eighteenth-century scholars at Purdue. In a meeting about the manuscript at the CCCC after Jim's death, Steve North, Pat Bizzell (one of the final reviewers), and I decided not to attempt any further revisions.

This book, a revisioning of the field of English, was dear to Jim. He had. a passion for the profession, seeing its potential for empowering students to critique and revise the cultural conditions shaping their lives. A fighter for social justice, he considered the current material and political arrangements in the Western world as marginalizing and disempowering many. Opposing these conditions, he maintained, was an important mission of the field of English, with composition in the forefront. Yet in his view, the profession largely held an Arnoldian vision of literary studies and relegated composition to a lower echelon of power and status. Despite his two earlier books on the history of composition instruction in changing economic and political conditions, histories of the field of English were still overlooking composition and its central role. This book strives to retell the history of English studies in the United States, analyzing the complex relationship between rhetoric and poetic, between composition and literature.

In studying the problem of inequality within English studies, Jim followed the advice he always gave to graduate students: historicize the problem. In this book, he probes shifting power relations in the field of English, exposing the hierarchies that emerged as literature became a scholarly field and the tensions that arose as composition claimed a place in the academy for its theory and research on writing. On the advice of a final reviewer of the manuscript, Jim was in the process of toning down his anger and blame. Yet the manuscript survives as a crusade for a change in our understanding and practice of the teaching of reading and writing. I am glad that at the time of his death he had not muted the urgency of his message.

As Jim argues in the book, cultural studies provides a way to redress the problems afflicting the profession. As a basis for composition courses, he maintains that it equips students to expose the ideological forces and codes that shape their subjectivities. In a number of conversations that Jim and I had about the criticisms leveled against cultural studies for leaving students discouraged and negative, Jim strongly insisted that the act of critique was so powerful that students would never again view themselves as coherent autonomous subjects nor their culture as entirely benign and therefore they would inevitably resist and work for change. Jim was impatient, however, with cultural studies theorists outside the field of composition whom he met at conferences, because he found them ironically trapped in theorizing, without attention or dedication to praxis, particularly ignoring the role that composition instruction could play in both critique and the construction of counter-discursive practices.

As a final tribute, this Afterword provides the opportunity to say that as a scholar, teacher, and citizen, Jim practiced what he preaches in this book. He was active in CCCC and NCTE and was interested in all levels of teaching English. He took on many causes, fighting for the rights of students, for rhetoric and composition faculty up for promotion and tenure, and for colleagues at Purdue and elsewhere whom he felt were being treated unjustly. He participated in local politics, especially on issues of the environment and in the Gulf War demonstrations. And as so many memorial tributes to Jim at the CCCC, at Purdue, and in the journals have attested, he stood as a strong intellectual and moral leader in the profession.

West Lafayette, Indiana

Works Cited

Alison, Archibald. *Essays on the Nature and Principles of Taste.* 1790. London: G. Olms, 1968.

Althusser, Louis. *Lenin and Philosophy and Other Essays.* Translated by Ben Brewster. New York: Monthly Review Press, 1971.

Andrews, Tom. "Writing after Theory." *AWP Chronicle* 25.2 (October/November 1992): 13-15.

Applebee, Arthur N. *Tradition and Reform in the Teaching of English: A History.* Urbana, IL: NCTE, 1974,

Aronowitz, Stanley, and Henry A. Giroux. *Education under Siege: The Conservative, Liberal, and Radical Debate over Schooling.* South Hadley, MA: Bergin and Garvey, 1985.

Atwill, Janet Marie. "Refiguring Rhetoric as Art: The Concept of Techne and the Humanist Paradigm." Dissertation, Purdue University, 1990.

Bakhtin, M. M. *The Dialogic Imagination: Four Essays.* Translated by Caryl Emerson and Michael Holquist. Edited by Michael Holquist. Austin: University of Texas Press, 1981.

Bakhtin, M. M., and P N. Medvedev. *The Formal Method in Literary Scholarship: A Critical Introduction to Sociological Poetics.* Translated by Albert J. Wehrle. Cambridge: Harvard University Press, 1985.

Baldwin, Charles Sears. *Ancient Rhetoric and Poetic: Interpreted from Representative Works.* New York: Macmillan, 1924.

Barilli, Renato. *Rhetoric.* Translated by Giuliana Menozzi. Minneapolis: University of Minnesota Press, 1989.

Barthes, Roland. *Mythologies.* Translated by Annette Lavers. New York: Hill and Wang, 1972.

Bartholomae, David. "Inventing the University." *When a Writer Can't Write: Studies in Writer's Block and Other Composing-Process Problems.* Edited by Mike Rose. New York: Guilford, 1985. 134-65.

Baudrillard, Jean. *Selected Writings.* Edited by Mark Poster. Stanford, CA: Stanford University Press, 1988.

Bauer, Dale M. "The Other 'F' Word: The Feminist in the Classroom." *College English* 52 (1990): 385-96.

Bazerman, Charles. *Shaping Written Knowledge: The Genre and Activity of the Experimental Article in Science.* Madison: University of Wisconsin Press, 1988.

Beaud, Michel. *A History of Capitalism, 1500-1980.* Translated by Tom Dickman and Anny Lefebvre. New York: Monthly Review Press, 1983.

Bellah, Robert N., Richard Madsen, William M. Sullivan, Ann Swidler, and Steven M. Tipton. *The Good Society.* New York: Knopf, 1991.

Bennett, Tony. *Outside Literature.* London: Routledge, 1990.

Bennett, Tony, and Janet Woollacott. *Bond and Beyond: The Political Career of a Popular Hero.* New York: Methuen, 1987.

Benveniste, Emil. *Problems in General Linguistics.* Translated by Mary Elizabeth Meek. Coral Gables, FL: University of Miami Press, 1971.

Berger, Arthur Asa. *Signs in Contemporary Culture: An Introduction to Semiotics.* New York: Longman, 1984.

Berlin, James A. *Writing Instruction in Nineteenth-Century American Colleges.* Carbondale: Southern Illinois University Press, 1984.

—. *Rhetoric and Reality: Writing Instruction in American Colleges, 1900-1985.* Carbondale: Southern Illinois University Press, 1987.

—. "Rhetoric and Ideology in the Writing Class." *College English* 50 (1988): 477-94.

—. "Rhetoric Programs after World War II: Ideology, Power, and Conflict." *Rhetoric and Ideology: Compositions and Criticisms of Power.* Edited by Charles W. Kneupper. Arlington, VA: Rhetoric Society of America, 1989. 6-20.

—. "Postmodernism, Politics, and Histories of Rhetoric." *PRE/TEXT* 11.3-4 (1990): 169-87.

—. "Composition and Cultural Studies." *Composition and Resistance.* Edited by C. Mark Hurlbert and Michael Blitz. Portsmouth, NH: Boynton/Cook-Heinemann, 1991. 47-55.

—. "Freirean Pedagogy in the U.S.: A Response." *(Inter)views: Cross-Disciplinary Perspectives on Rhetoric and Literacy.* Edited by Gary A. Olson and Irene Gale. Carbondale: Southern Illinois University Press, 1991. 169-76.

—. "Rhetoric, Poetic, and Culture: Contested Boundaries in English Studies. *The Politics of Writing Instruction: Postsecondary.* Edited by Richard H. Bullock, John Trimbur, and Charles I. Schuster. Portsmouth, NH: Boynton/ Cook-Heinemann, 1991. 23-28.

—. "Composition Studies and Cultural Studies: Collapsing the Boundaries." *Into the Field: Sites of Composition Studies.* Edited by

Anne Ruggles Gere. New York: Modern Language Association, 1993. 99-116.

Berman, Paul, ed. *Debating P.C.: The Controversy over Political Correctness on College Campuses.* New York: Dell, 1992.

Bizzell, Patricia. "The Ethos of Academic Discourse." *College Composition and Communication* 29 (1978): 351-55.

—. "College Composition: Initiation into the Academic Discourse Community." *Curriculum Inquiry* 12 (1982): 191-207.

—. "On the Possibility of a Unified Theory of Composition and Literature." *Rhetoric Review 4.2* (1986): 174-80.

Blair, Hugh. *Lectures on Rhetoric and Belles Lettres.* 1783. Edited by Harold F. Harding. Carbondale: Southern Illinois University Press, 1965.

Bledstein, Burton J. *The Culture of Professionalism: The Middle Class and the Development of Higher Education in America.* New York: Norton, 1976.

Bleich, David. *The Double Perspective: Language, Literacy, and Social Relations.* New York: Oxford University Press, 1988.

Blitz, Michael, and C. Mark Hurlbert. "Cults of Culture." *Cultural Studies in the English Classroom.* Edited by James A. Berlin and Michael J. Vivion. Portsmouth, NH: Boynton/Cook-Heinemann, 1992. 5-23.

Bloomfield, Robert. *The Poems of Robert Bloomfield.* London: Longman, 1821.

Bourdieu, Pierre. *Distinction: A Social Critique of the Judgement of Taste.* Translated by Richard Nice. Cambridge: Harvard University Press, 1984.

Bowles, Samuel, and Herbert Gintis. *Schooling in Capitalist America.* New York: Basic Books, 1976.

Brantlinger, Patrick. *Crusoe's Footprints: Cultural Studies in Britain and America.* New York: Routledge, 1990.

Brodkey, Linda. "On the Subject of Class and Gender in 'The Literacy Letters.'" *College English* 51 (1989): 125-41.

Brown, James A. *Television "Critical Viewing Skills" Education: Major Media Literacy Projects in the United States and Selected Countries.* New York: Lawrence Erlbaum, 1991.

Bruffee, Kenneth A. "Collaborative Learning: Some Practical Models." *College English* 34 (1973): 634-43.

—. "Collaborative Learning and the 'Conversation of Mankind.'" *College English* 46 (1984): 635-52.

Burke, Edmund. *Philosophical Enquiry into the Origins of our Ideas of the Sublime and the Beautiful.* 1757. New York: Columbia University Press, 1958.

—. *A Letter to the Sheriffs of Bristol. 1777. The Writing and Speeches of Edmund Burke.* 12 vols. Boston: Little, Brown, 1901. 2: 187-245.

—. *Reflections on the Revolution in France.* London: J. Dodsley, 1790.

Burke, Kenneth. *Language as Symbolic Action.* Berkeley: University of California Press, 1966.

—. "Rhetoric, Poetics, and Philosophy." *Rhetoric, Philosophy, and Literature: An Exploration.* Edited by Don M. Burks. West Lafayette, IN: Purdue University Press, 1978.

Cairns, William B. *A History of American Literature.* New York: Oxford University Press, 1912.

Campbell, George. *The Philosophy of Rhetoric.* 1776. Edited by Lloyd F. Bitzer. Carbondale: Southern Illinois University Press, 1963.

—. *The Duty of Allegiance.* London: Aberdeen, 1777.

Carlton, Susan Brown. "Poetic, Rhetoric, and Disciplinary Discourse." Dissertation, Purdue University, 1991.

Carroll, Peter N., and David W. Noble. *The Restless Centuries: A History of the American People.* 2d ed. Minneapolis: Burgess, 1979.

Colley, Linda. *Britons: Forging the Nation, 1707-1837.* New Haven, CT: Yale University Press, 1992.

Connors, Robert J. "The Rise and Fall of the Modes of Discourse." *College Composition and Communication* 32 (1981): 444-55.

—. "Mechanical Correctness as a Focus in Composition Instruction." *College Composition and Communication* 36 (1985): *61-72.*

—. "Personal Writing Assignments." *College Composition and Communication* 38 (1987): 166-83.

—. "Rhetoric in the Modern University: The Creation of an Underclass." *The Politics of Writing Instruction: Postsecondary.* Edited by Richard H. Bullock, John Trimbur, and Charles I. Schuster. Portsmouth, NH: Boynton/Cook-Heinemann, 1991. 55-84.

Cooper, Marilyn M., and Michael Holzman. *Writing as Social Action.* Portsmouth, NH: Boynton/Cook-Heinemann, 1989.

Corbett, Edward P J. *Classical Rhetoric for the Modern Student.* 2d ed. New York: Oxford University Press, 1971.

Cowper, William. *The Task.* 1785. Menston: Scolar Press, 1973.

Crabbe, George. *The Poetical Works of George Crabbe.* Edited by A. J. Carlyle and R. M. Carlyle. London: Oxford University Press, 1932.

Daiker, Donald A., and Max Morenberg. *The Writing Teacher as Researcher: Essays in the Theory and Practice of Class-based Research.* Portsmouth, NH: Boynton/ Cook-Heinemann, 1990.

Dautermann, Jennie Parsons. "Writing at Good Hope Hospital: A Study of Negotiated Discourse in the Workplace." Dissertation, Purdue University, 1991.

Denning, Michael. *Mechanic Accents: Dime Novels and Working-Class Culture in America.* New York: Verso, 1987.

Derrida, Jacques. *Of Grammatology.* Translated by Gayatri Chakravorty Spivak. Baltimore: Johns Hopkins University Press, 1976.

Dillon, George L. *Rhetoric as Social Imagination: Explorations in the Interpersonal Function of Language.* Bloomington: Indiana University Press, 1986.

Doody, Margaret Anne. *The Daring Muse: Augustan Poetry Reconsidered.* New York: Cambridge University Press, 1985.

Douglas, Wallace. "Rhetoric for the Meritocracy." *English in America: A Radical View of the Profession.* Edited by Richard Ohmann. New York: Oxford University Press, 1976. 97-132.

Dowst, Kenneth. "The Epistemic Approach: Writing, Knowing, and Learning." *Eight Approaches to Teaching Composition.* Edited by Timothy Donovan and Ben W. McClelland. Urbana, IL: NCTE, 1980.65-85.

DuPlessis, Rachel Blau. *The Pink Guitar: Writing as Feminist Practice.* New York: Routledge, 1990.

Eagleton, Terry. *Walter Benjamin; or, Towards a Revolutionary Criticism.* London: Verso, 1981.

—. *Literary Theory: An Introduction.* Minneapolis: University of Minnesota Press, 1983.

—. *The Ideology of the Aesthetic.* Oxford: Basil Blackwell, 1990.

Ebert, Teresa L. "The 'Difference' of Postmodern Feminism." *College English 53* (1991): 886-904.

Eco, Umberto. *A Theory of Semiotics.* Bloomington: Indiana University Press, 1976.

Ede, Lisa, and Andrea Lunsford. *Singular Texts/Plural Authors: Perspectives on Collaborative Writing.* Carbondale: Southern Illinois University Press, 1990.

Edgeworth, Maria. *Letters for Literary Ladies.* 1795. Edited by Gina Luria. New York: Garland, 1974.

Elbow, Peter. *What Is English?* New York: Modern Language Association, 1990.

—. "Reflections on Academic Discourse: How It Relates to Freshmen and Colleagues." *College English* 53 (1991):135-55.

Ellsworth, Elizabeth. "Why Doesn't This Feel Empowering? Working through the Repressive Myths of Critical Pedagogy." *Feminisms and Critical Pedagogy.* Edited by Carmen Luke and Jennifer Gore. New York: Routledge, 1992. 90-119.

Emig, Janet. *The Composing Processes of Twelfth Graders.* NCTE Research Report No. 13. Urbana, IL: NCTE, 1971.

Equiano, Olaudah. *The Interesting Narrative of the Life of Olaudah Equiano or Gustavus Vassa, the African.* 1789. New York: Negro Universities Press, 1969.

Ewen, Stuart. *All Consuming Images: The Politics of Style in Contemporary Culture.* New York: Basic Books, 1988.

Faigley, Lester. "Judging Writing, Judging Selves." *College Composition and Communication* 40 (1989): 395-413.

—. *Fragments of Rationality: Postmodernity and the Subject of Composition.* Pittsburgh: University of Pittsburgh Press, 1992.

Fenza, D. W. "Tradition and the Institutionalized Talent." *AWP Chronicle* 24.4 (February 1992): 11, 14-20.

Feyerabend, Paul *K. Against Method: Outline of an Anarchistic Theory of Knowledge.* London: Humanities Press, *1975.*

Fiske, John. *Television Culture.* London: Methuen, 1987.

—. *Introduction to Communication Studies.* 2d ed. London: Routledge, 1990.

Flower, Linda, and John R. Hayes. "A Cognitive Process Theory of Writing." *College Composition and Communication* 32 (1981): 365-87.

Flynn, Elizabeth A. "Composing as a Woman." *College Composition and Communication* 39 (1988): 423-35.

Forche, Carolyn. "Literary Acts of Resistance." *AWP Chronicle* 25.1 (September 1992): 1-6, 8.

Foucault, Michel. *Power/Knowledge: Selected Interviews and Other Writings, 1972-1977.* Edited by Colin Gordon. Translated by Colin Gordon et al. New York: Pantheon, 1980.

Freire, Paulo. *Pedagogy of the Oppressed.* Translated by Myra Bergman Ramos. New York: Continuum, 1970.

Gates, Henry Louis, Jr. *The Signifying Monkey: A Theory of Afro-American Literary Criticism.* New York: Oxford University Press, 1988.

Gellis, Mark. "Burke, Campbell, Johnson, and Priestley: A Rhetorical Analysis of Four British Pamphlets of the American Revolution." Dissertation, Purdue University, 1993.

Genung, John Franklin. *The Practical Elements of Rhetoric.* Boston: Ginn, 1886.

—. *A Study of Rhetoric in the College Course.* Boston: Heath, 1887.

—. *Outlines of Rhetoric.* Boston: Ginn, 1893.

George, Diana, and John Trimbur. *Reading Culture: Contexts for Critical Reading and Writing.* New York: HarperCollins, 1992.

Gere, Anne Ruggles. *Writing Groups: History, Theory, and Implications.* Carbondale: Southern Illinois University Press, 1987.

Ginsberg, Warren. "Institutionalizing Identity at the State University of New York at Albany: The New Ph.D. in English." *English Studies/Culture Studies: Institutionalizing Dissent.* Edited by Isaiah Smithson and Nancy Ruff. Urbana: University of Illinois Press, 1994. 157-66.

Giroux, Henry. *Schooling and the Struggle for Public Life: Critical Pedagogy in the Modern Age.* Minneapolis: University of Minnesota Press, 1988.

—. "Schooling as a Form of Cultural Politics: Toward a Pedagogy of and for Difference." *Critical Pedagogy, the State, and Cultural Struggle.* Edited by Henry A. Giroux and Peter L. McLaren. Albany: State University of New York Press, 1989. 125-51.

Giroux, Henry A., and Peter McLaren. "Language, Schooling, and Subjectivity: Beyond a Pedagogy of Reproduction and Resistance." *Contemporary Issues in U.S. Education.* Edited by Kathryn M. Borman, Piyush Swami, and Lonnie D. Wagstaff. Norwood, NJ: Ablex, 1991. 61-83.

Goswami, Dixie, and Peter R. Stillman. *Reclaiming the Classroom Teacher: Research as an Agency for Change.* Upper Montclair, NJ: Boynton/Cook, 1987.

Graff, Gerald. *Literature against Itself: Literary Ideas in Modern Society.* Chicago: University of Chicago Press, 1979.

—. *Professing Literature: An Institutional History.* Chicago: University of Chicago Press, 1987.

Gramsci, Antonio. *Selections from the Prison Notebooks of Antonio Gramsci.* Translated by Quintin Hoare and Geoffrey Nowell Smith. New York: International, 1971.

—. *Letters from Prison.* Translated by Lynne Lawner. New York: Harper and Row, 1975.

Greenwald, John. "Bellboys with B.A.s." *Time,* 22 November 1993, 36-37.

Grossberg, Lawrence, and Cary Nelson, eds. *Marxism and the Interpretation of Culture.* Urbana: University of Illinois Press, 1988.

Grossberg, Lawrence, Cary Nelson, and Paula A. Treichler, eds. *Cultural Studies.* New York: Routledge, 1992.

Guthrie, Warren. "The Development of Rhetoric Theory in America, 1636-1850." *Speech Monographs* 13 (1946): 14-22; 14 (1947): 38-54; 15 (1948): 61-71; 16 (1949): 98-113; 18 (1951): 17-30.

Habermas, Jurgen. "Modernity versus Postmodernity." *New German Critique* 22 (1981): 3-14.

Hairston, Maxine. "Comment and Response." *College English* 52 (1990): 694-96.

Hall, Stuart. "Cultural Studies and the Center: Some Problematics and Problems." *Culture, Media, Language: Working Papers in Cultural Studies,* 1972-79. Edited by Stuart Hall et al. London: Unwin Hyman, 1980.

—. "Encoding/Decoding." *Culture, Media, Language: Working Papers in Cultural Studies,* 1972-79. Edited by Stuart Hall et al. London: Unwin Hyman, 1980. 128-38.

—. "The Rediscovery of 'Ideology': Return of the Repressed in Media Studies." *Culture, Society, and the Media.* Edited by Michael Gurevitch et al. London: Routledge, 1982-56-90.

—. "Cultural Studies and Its Theoretical Legacies." *Cultural Studies.* Edited by Lawrence Grossberg, Cary Nelson, and Paula A. Treichler. New York: Routledge, 1992. 277-94.

Hall, Stuart, and Martin Jacques. *New Times: The Changing Face of Politics in the 1990s.* London: Verso, 1990.

Halloran, S. Michael. "Rhetoric in the American College Curriculum: The Decline of Public Discourse." *PRE/TEXT* 3 (1982): 245-69.

Hamilton, Barbara Bova. "The Rhetoric of a Judicial Document: The Presentence Investigation, Document Design, and Social Context." Dissertation, University of Southern California, 1987.

Hands, Elizabeth. *The Death of Amnon. A Poem. With an Appendix: Containing Pastorals, and other Poetical Pieces.* Coventry: N. Rolleson, 1789.

Haraway, Donna J. *Primate Visions: Gender, Race, and Nature in the World of Modern Science.* New York: Routledge, 1989.

Harkin, Patricia, and John Schilb, eds. *Contending with Words: Composition and Rhetoric in a Postmodern Age.* New York: Modern Language Association, 1991.

Harrienger, Myrna. "Medicine as Dialogic Rhetoric and the Elderly Ill Woman." Dissertation, Purdue University, 1993.

Harvey, David. *The Condition of Postmodernity: An Enquiry into the Origins of Cultural Change.* Oxford: Basil Blackwell, 1989.

Havelock, Eric Alfred. *The Liberal Temper in Greek Politics.* New Haven, CT: Yale University Press, 1964.

Heath, Shirley Brice. *Ways with Words: Language, Life, and Work in Communities and Classrooms.* Cambridge: Cambridge University Press, 1983.

Heba, Gary M. "Inventing Culture: A Rhetoric of Social Codes." Dissertation, Purdue University, 1993.

Higham, John. *Strangers in the Land: Patterns of American Nativism, 1860-1925.* 2d ed. New Brunswick, NJ: Rutgers University Press, 1988.

Hill, Adams Sherman. *The Principles of Rhetoric and their Application.* New York: Harper and Brothers, 1878.

—. *The Foundations of Rhetoric.* New York: Harper and Brothers, 1892.

Hill, Bridget. *Women, Work, and Sexual Politics in Eighteenth Century England.* Oxford: Basil Blackwell, 1989.

Hirsch, E. D., Jr. *Cultural Literacy: What Every American Needs to Know.* Boston: Houghton Mifflin, 1987.

Hodge, Robert, and Gunther Kress. *Social Semiotics.* Ithaca, NY: Cornell University Press, 1988.

Holbrook, Sue Ellen. "Women's Work: The Feminizing of Composition." *Rhetoric Review* 9.2 (Spring 1991): 201-29.

Huber, Bettina J. "Women in the Modern Languages, 1970-90." *Profession* 90 (1990): 58-73.

Hunter, Ian. *Culture and Government: The Emergence of Literary Education.* London: Macmillan, 1988.

Hunter, J. Paul. *Before Novels: The Cultural Contexts of Eighteenth Century English Fiction.* New York: Norton, 1990.

Hurlbert, C. Mark, and Michael Blitz. *Composition and Resistance.* Portsmouth, NH: Boynton/Cook-Heinemann, 1991.

"Resisting Composure." *Composition and Resistance.* Edited by C. Mark Hurlbert and Michael Blitz. Portsmouth, NH: Boynton/Cook-Heinemann, 1991.1-8.

Ide, Richard S. "Issues of Authority and Responsibility: Freshman Writing and English at USC—An Amicable Separation." *ADE Bulletin 101* (1992): 23-25.

Jameson, Fredric. *The Political Unconscious: Narrative as a Socially Symbolic Act.* Ithaca, NY: Cornell University Press, 1981.

—. "Postmodernism; or, the Cultural Logic of Late Capitalism." *New Left Review* 146 (1984): 53-93.

—. *Postmodernism; or, The Cultural Logic of Late Capitalism.* Durham, NC: Duke University Press, 1991.

Jarratt, Susan Carol. *Rereading the Sophists: Classical Rhetoric Refigured.* Carbondale: Southern Illinois University Press, 1991.

Jay, Martin. "'The Aesthetic Ideology' as Ideology; or, What Does It Mean to Aestheticize Politics?" *Cultural Critique* 21 (1992): 41-61.

Johnson, Richard. "What Is Cultural Studies Anyway?" *Social Text* 16 (1986-87): 38-80.

Johnson, Samuel. *The History of Rasselas, Prince of Abyssinia.* 1759. Edited by G. B. Hill. Revised by J. P. Hardy. Oxford: Clarendon Press, 1927, 1968.

—. *Johnson on Shakespeare.* Edited by Arthur Sherbo. The Yale Edition of the Works of Samuel Johnson. Vol. VII. New Haven, CT: Yale University Press, 1968.

—. *The Vanity of Human Wishes.* 1749. Menston: Scolar Press, 1970. Kennedy, Alan. "Committing the Curriculum and Other Misdemeanors." *Cultural Studies in the English Classroom.* Edited by James A. Berlin and Michael J. Vivion. Portsmouth, NH: Boynton/Cook-Heinemann, 1993. 24-45.

Kennedy, George A. *Classical Rhetoric and Its Christian and Secular Tradition from Ancient to Modern Times.* Chapel Hill: University of North Carolina Press, 1980.

Klaus, Gustav. *The Literature of Labour: Two Hundred Years of Working-Class Writing.* New York: St. Martin's Press, 1985.

Knoblauch, C. H. "The Albany Graduate English Curriculum." *ADE Bulletin* 98 (1991): 19-21.

—. "Critical Teaching and Dominant Culture." *Composition and Resistance.* Edited by C. Mark Hurlbert and Michael Blitz. Portsmouth, NH: Boynton/ Cook-Heinemann, 1991. 12-21.

Knoblauch, C. H., and Lil Brannon. *Rhetorical Traditions and the Teaching of Writing.* Upper Montclair, NJ: Boynton/Cook, 1984.

Kuhn, Thomas S. *The Structure of Scientific Revolutions.* 2d ed. Chicago: University of Chicago Press, 1970.

Landry, Donna. *The Muses of Resistance: Laboring-Class Women's Poetry in Britain,* 1739-1796. New York: Cambridge University Press, 1990.

Lauer, Janice, and Andrea Lunsford. "The Place of Rhetoric and Composition in Doctoral Studies." *The Future of Doctoral Studies in English.* Edited by Andrea Lunsford, Helene Moglen, and James F. Slevin. New York: Modern Language Association, 1989. 106-10.

Lauer, Janice, and William J. Asher. *Composition Research: Empirical Designs.* New York: Oxford University Press, 1988.

Lay, Mary M. "Interpersonal Conflict in Collaborative Writing: What We Can Learn from Gender Studies." *Journal of Business and Technical Communication* 3.2 (1989): 5-28.

Leitch, Vincent B. *Deconstructive Criticism: An Advanced Introduction.* New York: Columbia University Press, 1983.

—. *American Literary Criticism from the Thirties to the Eighties.* New York: Columbia University Press, 1988.

—. *Cultural Criticism, Literary Theory, Poststructuralism.* New York: Columbia University Press, 1992.

Lentricchia, Frank. *After the New Criticism.* Chicago: University of Chicago Press, 1980.

Levi-Strauss, Claude. *Structural Anthropology.* Translated by Claire Jacobsen and Brooke Grundfest Schoepf. New York: Basic Books, 1963.

Lloyd-Jones, Richard, and Andrea Lunsford. *The English Coalition Conference: Democracy through Language.* Urbana, IL: NCTE/MLA, 1989.

Lonsdale, Roger, ed. *Eighteenth-Century Women Poets: An Oxford Anthology.* New York: Oxford University Press, 1989.

Luke, Carmen, and Jennifer Gore, eds. *Feminisms and Critical Pedagogy.* New York: Routledge, 1992.

Lyotard, Jean-François. *The Postmodern Condition: A Report on Knowledge.* Translated by Geoff Bennington and Brian Massumi. Minneapolis: University of Minnesota Press, 1984.

Lyotard, Jean-François, and Jean-Loup Thebaud. *Just Gaming.* Translated by Wlad Godzich. Minneapolis: University of Minnesota Press, 1985.

Macaulay, Catharine. *Letters on Education.* 1790. New York: Garland, 1974.

Mailloux, Steven. *Rhetorical Power.* Ithaca, NY: Cornell University Press, 1989.

McCloskey, Donald N. *If You're So Smart: The Narrative of Economic Expertise.* Chicago: University of Chicago Press, 1990.

McCormick, Kathleen, and Gary Waller, with Linda Flower. *Reading Texts.* Lexington, MA: Heath, 1987.

McRobbie, Angela. "Dance and Social Fantasy." *Gender and Generation.* Edited by Angela McRobbie and Mica Nava. London: Macmillan, 1984.

Miller, Carolyn. "A Humanistic Rationale for Technical Writing." *College English* 40 (1979): 610-17.

Miller, Nancy K. *Getting Personal: Feminist Occasions and Other Autobiographical Acts.* New York: Routledge, 1991.

Miller, Susan. *Rescuing the Subject: A Critical Introduction to Rhetoric and the Writer.* Carbondale: Southern Illinois University Press, 1989.

"The Feminization of Composition." *The Politics of Writing Instruction: Postsecondary.* Edited by Richard H. Bullock, John Trimbur, and Charles I. Schuster. Portsmouth, NH: Boynton/Cook-Heinemann, 1991. 39-54.

More, Hannah. *Strictures on the Modern System of Female Education.* 1799. New York: Garland, 1974.

Morton, Donald, and Mas'ud Zavarzadeh, eds. *Theory/Pedagogy/Politics: Texts for Change.* Urbana: University of Illinois Press, 1991.

Murray, Robin. "Fordism and Post-Fordism." *New Times: The Changing Face of Politics in the 1990s.* Edited by Stuart Hall and Martin Jacques. London: Verso, 1990. 38-53.

Myers, Greg. "The Social Construction of Two Biologists' Proposals." *Written Communication* 2 (1985): 219-45.

—. "Reality, Consensus, and Reform in the Rhetoric of Composition Teaching." *College English 48* (1986): 154-74.

—. *Writing Biology: Texts in the Social Construction of Scientific Knowledge.* Madison: University of Wisconsin Press, 1990.

Nelson, Cary, ed. *Theory in the Classroom.* Urbana: University of Illinois Press, 1986.

—. "Always Already Cultural Studies: Two Conferences and a Manifesto." *MMLA* 24.1 (Spring 1991): 24-38.

Noble, David F. *Forces of Production: A Social History of Industrial Automation.* New York: Knopf, 1984.

Nussbaum, Felicity, and Laura Brown. *The New Eighteenth Century: Theory, Politics, English Literature.* New York: Methuen, 1987.

Nussbaum, Martha Craven. *The Fragility of Goodness: Luck and Ethics in Greek Tragedy and Philosophy.* Cambridge: Cambridge University Press, 1986.

Ohmann, Richard M. *Politics of Letters.* Middletown, CT: Wesleyan University Press, 1987.

Ouchi, William. *Theory Z: How American Business Can Meet the Japanese Challenge.* Reading, MA: Addison-Wesley, 1981.

Pace Nilsen, Alleen. "Sexism in English: A Feminist View." *Perspectives: Turning Reading into Writing.* Edited by Joseph J. Comprone. Boston: Houghton Mifflin, 1987. 446-53.

Paine, Thomas. *Rights of Man.* London: J. S. Jordan, 1791.

Parker, William Riley. "Where Do English Departments Come From?" *College English* 28 (1967): 339-51. Reprinted in *The Writing Teacher's Sourcebook.* Edited by Gary Tate and Edward P. J. Corbett. New York: Oxford University Press, 1981. 3-19.

Pattee, Fred Lewis. *The First Century of American Literature, 1770-1870.* New York: Appleton, 1935.

Payne, William Morton. *English in American Universities.* Boston: Heath, 1895.

Poovey, Mary. *Uneven Developments: The Ideological Work of Gender in Mid-Victorian England.* Chicago: University of Chicago Press, 1988.

Porter, James E. "Ideology and Collaboration in the Classroom and in the Corporation." *The Bulletin of The Association for Business Communication* 5.32 (January 1990): 18-22.

Rathbun, John W., and Harry H. Clark. *American Literary Criticism.* Vol. 2. Boston: Twayne, 1979.

Rivers, Isabel, ed. *Books and their Readers in Eighteenth-Century England.* New York: St. Martin's Press, 1982.

Rodriguez Milanes, Cecilia. "Risks, Resistance, and Rewards: One Teacher's Story." *Composition and Resistance.* Edited by C. Mark Hurlbert and Michael Blitz. Portsmouth, NH: Boynton/Cook-Heinemann, 1991.115-24.

Rudolph, Frederick. *The American College and University: A History.* New York: Vintage, 1962.

—. *Curriculum: A History of the American Undergraduate Course of Study since 1636.* San Francisco: Jossey-Bass, 1977.

Russell, David R. "Romantics on Writing: Liberal Culture and the Abolition of Composition Courses." *Rhetoric Review* 6 (1988): 132-48.

Therborn, Goran. *The Ideology of Power and the Power of Ideology.* London: Verso, 1980.

Todorov, Tzvetan. *Symbolism and Interpretation.* Translated by Catherine Porter. Ithaca, NY: Cornell University Press, 1982.

Trimbur, John. "Beyond Cognition: The Voices in Inner Speech." *Rhetoric Review* 5 (1987): 211-21.

—. "Cultural Studies and Teaching Writing." *Focuses* 1.2 (1988): 5-18.

—. "Consensus and Difference in Collaborative Learning." *College English* 51 (1989): 602-16.

Turner, Graeme. *British Cultural Studies: An Introduction.* Boston: Unwin Hyman, 1990.

—. *Film as Social Practice.* New York: Routledge, 1993.

Turner, Sharon. *History of the Anglo-Saxons, Comprising the History of England from the Earliest Period to the Norman Conquest.* 1799-1805. London: Longman et al., 1823.

Tyler, Moses Coit. *A History of American Literature during the Colonial Period, 1607-1765.* New York: G. P. Putnam's Sons, 1897.

—. *The Literary History of the American Revolution, 1763-1783.* New York: G. P. Putnam's Sons, 1897.

Veysey, Laurence R. *The Emergence of the American University.* Chicago: University of Chicago Press, 1965.

Vickers, Brian. *In Defence of Rhetoric.* Oxford: Clarendon Press, 1988.

Vitanza, Victor. "Three Countertheses; Or, A Critical In(ter)vention into Composition Theories and Pedagogies. *Contending with Words: Composition and Rhetoric in a Postmodern Age.* Edited by Patricia Harkin and John Schilb. New York: Modern Language Association, 1991. 139-72.

Wallerstein, Immanuel. "The Bourgeoise(ie) as Concept and Reality." *New Left Review* 167 (1988): 91-106.

Ward, John. *A System of Oratory.* 1759. London: G. Olms, 1969.

Watkins, Evan. *Work Time: English Departments and the Circulation of Cultural Value.* Stanford, CA: Stanford University Press, 1989.

Watt, Ian. *The Rise of the Novel.* Berkeley: University of California Press, 1957.

West, Cornel. "Interview with Cornet West." *Universal Abandon? The Politics of Postmodernism.* Edited by Andrew Ross. Minneapolis: University of Minnesota Press, 1988. 269-86.

Wheatley, Phyllis. *Poems on Various Subjects, Religious and Moral.* 1773. New York: AMS Press, 1976.

Williams, Raymond. *Marxism and Literature.* Oxford: Oxford University Press, 1977.

Winterowd, W. Ross. *The Rhetoric of the "Other" Literature,* Carbondale: Southern Illinois University Press, 1990.

Wollstonecraft, Mary. *A Vindication of the Rights of Men.* 1790. Gainesville, FL: Scholars' Facsimiles and Reprints, 1960.

—. *A Vindication of the Rights of Woman.* 1792. New York: Penguin, 1982.

Woods, Marjorie Curry. "The Teaching of Writing in Medieval Europe." *A Short History of Writing Instruction.* Edited by James J. Murphy. Davis: Hermagoras Press, 1990. 77-94.

Wordsworth, William. *Lyrical Ballads.* 1800. London: Oxford University Press, 1969.

Wozniak, John Michael. *English Composition in Eastern Colleges, 1850-1940.* Washington, D.C.: University Press of America, 1978.

Young, Iris Marion. *Justice and the Politics of Difference.* Princeton: Princeton University Press, 1990.

Zavarzadeh, Mas'ud, and Donald Morton. "Theory Pedagogy Politics: The Crisis of 'The Subject' in the Humanities." *Boundary 2* 15.1-2 (Fall 1986/Winter 1987): 1-22.

—. *Theory, (Post)Modernity, Opposition: An "Other" Introduction to Literary and Cultural Theory.* Washington, D.C.: Maisonneuve Press, 1991.

—. "A Very Good Idea Indeed: The (Post)Modern Labor Force and Curricular Reform." *Cultural Studies in the English Classroom.* Edited by James A. Berlin and Michael J. Vivion. Portsmouth, NH: Boynton/Cook-Heinemann, 1992. 66-86.

Index

Author

James A. Berlin began his teaching career in elementary schools in Flint and Detroit, Michigan. After earning a Ph.D. in Victorian literature at the University of Michigan, he became assistant professor of composition at Wichita State University. While there, he served as first director of the Kansas Writing Project, an affiliate of the National Writing Project. He next taught at the University of Cincinnati, where he was director of freshman English. From 1987 until his death in 1994, he was professor of English at Purdue University.

Professor Berlin was author of *Writing Instruction in Nineteenth-Century American Colleges* (1984) and *Rhetoric and Reality: Writing Instruction in American Colleges, 1900-1985* (1987). His subsequent publications included *Cultural Studies in the English Classroom* (edited with Michael J. Vivion, 1992) as well as a number of essays on the relations of rhetoric, postmodernism, and cultural studies.

Printed in the United States
49991LVS00003B/101